3/3/23

D1596313

WITHDRAWN

HOCKEY'S HIDDEN GODS

Hockey's Hidden Gods

The Untold Story of a Paralympic Miracle on Ice

S. C. Megale

ROWMAN & LITTLEFIELD
Lanham • Boulder • New York • London

Published by Rowman & Littlefield
An imprint of The Rowman & Littlefield Publishing Group, Inc.
4501 Forbes Boulevard, Suite 200, Lanham, Maryland 20706
www.rowman.com

86-90 Paul Street, London EC2A 4NE, United Kingdom

British Library Cataloguing in Publication Information Available

Library of Congress Cataloging-in-Publication Data Available

ISBN 9781538166642 (cloth) | ISBN 9781538166659 (epub)

For Edward J. O'Shea: rear admiral, doctor, and philanthropist, but most importantly, Grandpa. Of all the books I will ever write, this one—combining American patriotism, true stories, and the unbreakable will of people with disabilities—is the one I knew was yours.

I will love you and strive to make you proud, Grandpa, for not only the rest of your days, but for all the rest of mine.

—BIRDIE

Contents

Foreword

I'd like to thank you for your interest in our book, *Hockey's Hidden Gods*. I'm pretty sure you're going to discover that it is the best untold sports story of this century.

As soon as the final buzzer had sounded and it was definite that the U.S. national sled hockey team had just won gold in the 2002 Paralympics, everyone began comparing our incredible triumph to the 1980 "Miracle on Ice." There were many similarities to both our stories, but we came up with our own slogan that we thought was an even better fit when describing our journey to the gold medal: "The Impossible Dream."

When you look back to the start of sled hockey in the United States less than ten years prior, combined with the fact that Team USA had won only *one* international game after competing in the 1998 Paralympics *and* the 2000 World Championships, you might say that any hope of winning any medal, let alone a gold medal, was truly an *impossible dream*.

We had no idea at the time, but the word going around was that if we didn't at least win bronze, funding for sled hockey was likely to dry up for good.

I think the fact that we won gold when we weren't expected to win anything opened eyes to the astonishing raw talent of our team and the truth that, with the right funding and management, Team USA could be a powerhouse for years to come. That's just what happened. The U.S. national sled hockey team has gone on to win a medal in every Paralympics since Salt Lake City! They won bronze in Torino, Italy (2006), then three gold medals in a row in Vancouver (2010), Sochi (2014), and Pyeongchang (2018), to make them the number-one sled hockey team in the world twenty years later.

Today, the U.S. national sled hockey team has more than a half-dozen military veterans playing, most introduced to the sport when they were in rehab after suffering horrific wounds in the wars that followed 9/11. They fell in love with the sport.

I'd like to thank my old friend Paul Edwards for making the phone call that eventually would have such a huge impact on the rest of my life—the call that introduced me to this momentous opportunity. I say this with a lot of pride: Even though I played almost fifteen years of professional hockey and was lucky enough to play in a Calder Cup Final (AHL), three Stanley Cup Finals (NHL), and two Canada Cup Finals (International), coaching the U.S. national sled hockey team in the gold medal game and winning it all in the 2002 Paralympics in Salt Lake City is what I consider the highlight of my hockey career, which has spanned more than sixty years.

As they say, it's more about the journey than the destination, and this book, as written by S. C. Megale, will explain what an extraordinary journey it was to the gold medal. I knew Megale was the perfect author for this work. We needed a writer who was not only talented and had respect for the game of hockey, but also who we could trust to handle the important subjects of struggle, disability, and humanity with grace. One meeting with Megale and I knew we found the right match. The reader is in good hands.

Enjoy the book!

Rick "Nifty" Middleton
#16, Boston Bruins
#9, New York Rangers
National Hockey League

PREFACE

ON A COLD DECEMBER EVENING IN 2019, THE ELEVATOR SHUDDERED and opened to a kitchen storage area. Metal shelves and cardboard boxes surrounded me. Sinks, counters—tape on the floor. It starkly contrasted with the armchairs and towering oil paintings of the Harvard Club's main level above. This was the handicap-accessible entrance to the conference room.

I weaved through the underground of this elite New York City dinery. Busboys clad in white stepped aside to allow my passing, and up a ramp and into a narrow hall led me to a door. Four men sat at the table awaiting me.

One was Rick Middleton, an NHL veteran. His back was to me, and he stood with haste. Beside him was Tom Moulton, Middleton's former assistant coach, and the third man was Gary Brandt, their project manager. I smelled Los Angeles on Yaron Kaplan, the fourth, who wore a blue blazer with no tie and sported long, curly hair. We shook hands hard, all of us.

Then I parked, twisted open a water bottle, and said "So what are we doing tonight?"

They pitched me, for the first time, the story of *Hockey's Hidden Gods*.

I wrote this book because I love hockey. That I have a disability myself is a coincidence. Replace "I wrote this book" with "I won gold," and those two sentences likely could be taglines for every player featured in these pages.

In fact, as much as I fell in love with the team—both the actual players and their team of professionals seeking to capture this story—I hesitated to accept this project. I feared circulating what many in the disabled community call "inspiration porn": using handicapped triumph as a cheap fix of emotion for able-bodied people, an example they can look at and say, "Doesn't that put our problems in perspective?"

Let me be clear: If the story told here uplifts you, we are glad for it. Really, we're laying the table for it. There is no lack of material herein that impresses and inspires. But writing a feel-good tale was never my priority.

My priorities can be organized into three.

Hockey, history, heart.

Ice hockey is my favorite competitive sport. Alone in my office, I can be found unfolding a dinner tray and stabbing a fork at my meal with reduced accuracy as I watch my favorite teams, the Hershey Bears and the Washington Capitals, soar back and forth on my computer screen. I played a little (more on that later) and hope to coach one day. It is my aspiration to capture enough action and exhilaration in this book to appeal to fans of the sport in general.

I also, as stated above, aim to chronicle and present the history of this early twenty-first century event and the unique sport of sled hockey itself. Having graduated in 2021, I am a beginner historian with a degree in history from the University of Virginia and a passion for discovering and recording what textbooks have overlooked. I believe in exciting research that breaks down ambiguity and produces direct data for the reader to interpret. I believe history writing that—if nothing more—reveals untold aspects of the complex, mysterious, and absolutely profound human experience matters.

Finally, the heart. Although my fear of oversimplifying these players as mascots of perseverance remains, they—and I—pursued this project with the hope that these pages would shed light on the human spirit and provide encouragement for readers who might be struggling with physical or mental challenges themselves.

To hockey fans, historians, and seekers of heart, I hope you feel you are in the right place.

I know I am.

S. C. Megale

Introduction

THIS BOOK WAS DUE FEBRUARY 1, 2022, AND I MISSED THE DEADLINE.
Science fiction author Douglas Adams famously said he cherished
the *whooshing* sound deadlines make when they pass by, but this time,
I'd had every intention of submitting the book on schedule. The chapters
had been organized and my finger was poised over the send button. But
something stopped me that day.

I received an email from a subject of this hockey team who had previously declined an interview with me. He'd changed his mind—less than
ten hours before the manuscript was due. I accepted the interview, figuring I could buy myself some time and write in his piece quickly. When
I answered the phone at 11:41 p.m. (he worked nights), I introduced
myself and said I wanted to hear his story.

"I think you really don't want to hear my story," he said.

Taken aback, I blinked and assured him that his voice matters. That
he matters. He alluded to the tension, the strife, the sometimes squalor
that went on in the journey to gold, and he said, "Can we just say there
are a crazy group of guys that won?"

In one sense, he wasn't wrong. This is a story about a bunch of guys who
won. But it is much more than that, and what they won, much more
than gold.

This is the story of the 2002 Paralympic United States sled hockey
team. It is the unknown, untold "Miracle on Ice." Odds of winning were
dismal and the road to victory, unfathomable. Its cast includes a decorated NHL star as coach; fifteen athletes with disabilities who wrestled
their way back to life from hospital beds; and a legacy of pioneers with

no money, no national governing body's support, varying handicaps, and a clean, passionate adoration for the game we all love: ice hockey.

This book begins with an introduction to the sport of sled hockey: how the game began on a frozen lake in Sweden by a group of rehab patients. The ways its rules and equipment relate to and differ from standard ice hockey provide context for the rest of the story.

From there, the book alternates between the main story and player profiles. The main narrative is affixed to a timeline and chronicles how the United States sled hockey team, on home soil, battled its way to gold in the shadow of September 11, 2001, and after a history of crushing defeat. Relational friction and relentless politics drove a wedge through the team that threatened to capsize it. This is what my last-minute caller wasn't sure I wanted to hear. Rick Middleton was also faced with a ticking clock—just five months to pull off a worst-to-first turnaround. Action-packed game chapters will demonstrate how his hockey strategy, the talents of the players, and the contributions of the volunteers surrounding them paid off. Interspersed throughout are the biographic profiles of the players—almost like long trading cards—that invite the reader deeper into the origins, accidents, and fight-back-from-hell stories these exceptional men lived. They will help frame the world of sled hockey at large and the everyday Americans who became titans in it. Combined, both chapter types create a three-dimensional view of individual grit meeting national desperation and the choices that led to walking away triumphant.

The methodology of my research relied heavily on live interviews. Via Zoom, I conducted interviews with thirteen of the fifteen players, several of the staff and administrators, former players, and some of the non-American figures involved in the 2002 gold medal victory. Interviewees were asked to place accuracy above drama, and all were given opportunities to review the final section on themselves. All consented to being recorded.

Attempts to contact every player, regardless of interpersonal conflicts, for their voices to be included were also made. I continue to welcome input from figures who declined or missed the opportunity to be interviewed, should they change their minds or become available and if it is within my means. It is impossible to please everyone when presenting these events, but my goal was to never villainize, and to attempt to see all sides of the conflicts. This is harder without talking to everyone in question, but I did what I could. I personally judge no one, as my own imperfections make this book look like a pamphlet for Disneyland.

Accompanying the live interviews was primary source archival work. This included studying the manuals and newsletters distributed to U.S. representatives at the Paralympic Games as well as some correspondences and game summary statistics. Secondary sources such as newspaper and magazine articles were also referenced. Many of these items were given to me in boxes of paraphernalia collected by the subjects and were clippings from their original sources, or printouts of website articles which no longer exist. Because of this, details like dates, page numbers, and links are sometimes lost and unfortunately may not appear in my citations. Finally, photographs and film served to color the verbal accounts—including 133 raw videos from Never Dull Productions, many of them running an hour or more, in which I inhabited for weeks. I was also excited to, with the help of Rolf Johansson and Peter Noonan, finance and facilitate the conversion of probably the earliest sled hockey footage still in existence (a Super 8mm film about thirteen minutes long from 1971) into digital format to preserve it for generations to come.

Although this is proudly an American story, I gave my best effort not to write this book only from the perspective of the United States. Canadians and Swedes contributed their voices to this work, and Japanese and Swedish sources were consulted.

When available, in historical fashion, I provide birth and death dates for the figures I introduce. However, I've elected to forgo this practice during the game chapters when mentioning international players, unless I profile them beyond the action. This was so as not to disrupt the infamous pace of play—and therefore add to the authenticity of the scene. Those who were otherwise left without dates are for lack of available information.

In their own introductions, other historians I have read acknowledge their biases and blind spots pertaining to the subject. This honesty helps the reader understand the limitations of the book and therein welcomes more discussion once the book closes. I acknowledge the obvious blind spot in that I have never formally played ice hockey. (In street hockey, I filled an unreasonable amount of net as the goalie, and I once risked cruising my 300-pound motorized wheelchair onto a frozen pond during an episode of daring.) I lack the upper body capacity for sled hockey but hope to try it with assistance after this book releases. Secondly, my disability, while an asset to my empathy, is also not a catch-all for perfectly understanding the various physical handicaps experienced by the players. Thirdly, much of the meat of this narrative, as previously mentioned, relied on interviews, which have historical limitations. No one's memory is perfect, and the testimony I received was not always verifiable or complete. I aimed to be as inviting as possible, but our nature as human beings is such that we do not always say exactly what we mean, or feel we can. History writing is therefore restricted when events are digested only from today's perspective and not in combination with the materials created at the time. I made use of materials from the event as much as possible and united them with the people who gave them new life. In many ways, their retelling of the story is a story in itself.

Three hours and forty-five minutes later, at 3:26 a.m., I hung up the phone with my last-minute interviewee. His name was Jeff Uyeno, the equipment manager who served the team in 2002 and continues to serve the NHL Blackhawks. I heard his story—his accomplishments and some of the pain that came with them—and promised him I'd not submit the book until his voice had been added to this mosaic, which would take more than just that evening. I gambled my contract on it.

I did that because this story is not just the celebration. It's the conflict and conquest, too. It's about letting heroes both sung and unsung be heard by the nation at a time when the nation needs as many heroes as it can get.

"Isn't there a bigger picture?" Uyeno said. "Isn't there more than this gold medal?"

There is.

It's all here.

Key for Player Stats

No.	Number
Pos.	Position
GP	Games Played
G	Goals Scored
A	Assists
PTS	Total Points (G+A)
PIM	Penalty Infraction Minutes
"+/-"	Plus/Minus Record (players receive a plus-one to their record for each goal scored by their team while they were on the ice [at even strength or on the power play] and a minus-one for each goal scored against their team while they were on the ice [at even strength or shorthanded])
PPG	Power Play Goals
S	Shots
SG%	Goals Scored as a Percentage of Shots
GPT	Number of Games Played by Team
GKD	Goalkeeper Dressed
GTG	Game-Tying Goals
GWG	Game-Winning Goals
MIP	Minutes in between the Pipes
MIP%	Percentage of Minutes in between the Pipes (calculated by dividing MIP by 280, the total minutes of gameplay for USA sled hockey in the 2002 Paralympics)
GA	Goals Against
SHG	Shorthanded Goals (the number of goals the player scored while the player's team was shorthanded)
SVS	Saves

SOG   Shots on Goal

SVS%   Save Percentage (calculated by dividing SVS by SOG)

GAA   Goals Against Average (calculated by dividing GA by MIP, then multiplying by 45 [the minute length of a sled hockey regulation game in 2002])

SO   Shutouts

CHAPTER ONE

Lake of Legend

Sled Hockey's History, Rules, and Equipment

When hell freezes over, I'll play hockey there too.
—UNKNOWN[1]

THE BASICS

SLED HOCKEY, ALSO CALLED *SLEDGE* HOCKEY IN THE INTERNATIONAL community, and even more recently *para* ice hockey, is a way of playing standard ice hockey. In theory, the two are not considered separate sports. Rather, many consider them the same sport distinguished only by whether adaptations to address a physical disability are used. Those physical limitations merited slight changes to rules and equipment, which are examined further in this chapter. Sled hockey therefore derives from the same ancestral tree of stick-and-ball games as does standard ice hockey. Tombs in ancient Egypt depicted men playing a crude form of hockey with a semicircle made of papyrus fiber and leather as early as four thousand years ago. The Dutch refer to a greyish, misty seventeenth-century painting by Hendrick Avercamp (1585–1634) showing people playing a sport called IJscolf to stake their claim on early ice hockey development. Those in the painting wear wide brim hats and ruffs around their necks, but they use sticks and a mixture of skates and regular shoes to play with one another on a frozen pond. Probably the closest relative to the ice hockey known

I

today was bandy, developed in the Fens of East Anglia as early as 1813.[2] Records of the sport developing in the Americas follow close behind.

I state this to make my point clear: Sled hockey is ice hockey.

The names *sled hockey* and *sledge hockey* are interchangeable. The United States favors *sled hockey*, as did the subjects of this book, so that is the term that will be used except in connection with distinctly international players, such as the founder, who will be discussed in this chapter. Much like how the etymology of *hockey* is uncertain (it could have come from the French word *hoquet*, meaning "shepherd's crook," or perhaps from a fabled Colonel Hockey who used the game as we know it to keep his soldiers conditioned in Windsor, Nova Scotia), *sledge* eludes conviction.[3] It seems to come from the Middle Dutch word *sleedse*, which is related to the word "sled." Possibly it combines "sled" and "edge," but as the sport did not arise in an English-speaking country, this seems unlikely. To make matters moot, in 2016 the International Paralympic Committee (IPC) rechristened the sport "para ice hockey," which it is formally called today. Either way, the name was not philosophized on much while men (and, later, women) whacked each other for the puck.

THE BEGINNING

Like many origin stories, the birth of sledge hockey is steeped in mythology. Echoed from article to article is only the vague assertion that the sport was founded at a rehab center in Stockholm by a handful of unnamed men with disabilities in the 1960s. The more those sparse facts are repeated, the more the hockey community seems to accept that much as sufficient. They are not wholly accurate, however. With a considerable amount of digging, translating, and interviewing, specific details emerged, directly from the founder himself. So scarce and well-hidden is this information that it is reasonable to say this book may be the only American publication to record it.[4]

The exact location of sledge hockey's founding was atop a frozen Lake Drevviken.[5] The rehab center that articles ambiguously refer to is Handikappbadet located in Stora Sköndal, south of Stockholm. Rolf Johansson (b. July 21, 1944), a polio survivor, was the primary founder of sledge hockey (or *kälkhocky*, in his language). He was accompanied by a few of his friends who the rehab also treated. In his own words, translated from Swedish,

> In the winter of 1963–1964, the ice was in full swing with activities such as curling, ice fishing, skiing. . . . I went to go there [to the lake] sledging [sledding, as in down a hill], which had been my favourite pastime from my time at Lindingöhemmet. Karl-Gunnar "Kalle" Karlsson [(1935–?)] had made the sledges in his own mechanical workshop and they had long medians [likely to support extended paralyzed legs]. . . . So one day, it's hard to say exactly when, someone threw a puck onto the ice, and of course I and everyone else [still seated in the sleds] started to chase the puck, and thus the sport of sledge hockey was born.[6]

From this account, it seems that the popular activity of sledding— using what roughly translates to "toboggans," which look more like

The very first sledge hockey players on Lake Drevviken. In the foreground are members of Johansson's team (called Norrbacka), Klas-Göran and Brendt. Johansson is probably just out of frame and may have been responsible for the pass we are observing. Note the drive on the players' faces. "Sledge hockey is a combat sport," wrote Johansson, "it is a sport for tough guys. . . ." COURTESY OF ROLF JOHANSSON miniature sleighs—evolved into sledge hockey when those seated in the toboggans began chasing a puck on ice. Karlsson was then responsible for the first ever alterations to a sled with the objective of customizing it for the sport of hockey. He shortened the sled to improve maneuverability on the ice and crafted goal cages to play the game with. Johansson and Karlsson, along with a few guinea pig players, returned to that same lake every weekend until their creation had matured enough to get ice time at Nackas outdoor rink in 1968.[7]

Johansson, Karlsson, and Bengt-Gösta "Gösen" Johansson (b. 1944; unrelated to Rolf, who will continue to be referred to as Johansson here) formed a committee of three to represent sledge hockey and spread it across Sweden and northern Europe. By 1969, five teams competed at the Nackas rink, and a team from Norway had formed to play against Rolf Johansson.[8] They played on one Saturday a year, alternating meeting locations between Oslo and Stockholm; the first matchup took place in 1968 at the Jordal Amfi arena, which had opened to host the 1952 Winter Olympics.[9] Johansson claims the Swedes always won.

Originally, able-bodied players tiptoed into the sport as well, but Johansson attests that they withdrew early in the game's development. He attributes this to how exhausted they were from rowing with the sticks and moving around in the sleds, or how frequently players came away with "black nails and broken knuckles."[10]

Years went by with sledge hockey still localized to northern Europe. There were no more micro-tournaments to bring attention to the new sport, only trainings on Nackas rink in brutal conditions, and with players who didn't wear any protection. "Sometimes it was 20 degrees cold and you almost lost the feeling in both hands and feet," wrote Johansson, "or else the next training would have us playing hockey with 1 dm [about four inches] of snow on the ice, or it was pouring rain and you were totally soaked when you went home. No weather prevented the three of us from being there and practicing."[11]

He believes this is what kept sledge hockey from dying out.

The first ever Winter Paralympics, then called the Winter Olympics for the Disabled, took place in Örnsköldsvik, Sweden, from February 21–28, 1976.[12] This came sixteen years after the development of the

Handicappede kniver i ishockey på kjelker

Turneringen som lørdag ble arrangert av Oslo Helsesportslags ispiggerutvalg i Norges Handikapidrettsforbunds regi på Jordal Amfi og Bingen, viste at kjelke-hockey er en fin form for handicapidrett. De svenske lag som deltok — IFAH og IF Nacak, begge Stockholm — har begge spilt ishockey på kjelker i mere enn to år, og funnet frem til en kjelketype som egner seg godt. Man bruker håndtaket på stavene til å slå med, og har efterhvert oppnådd meget god ferdigret. Et norsk lag, Pionér fra Oslo Helsesportslag, har to ganger besøkt Stockholm og lært seg spillemetoden, men tapt med sifrene 0—15 og 0—12.

Oslo Helsesportslag har efter iherdige anstrengelser, og med velvillig bistand fra mange hold, selv produsert 15 kjelker, som viser seg å holde mål med svenskenes.

De aktive utøvere er svært begeistret, og det er grunn til å tro at ishockey på kjelker vil bli meget utbredt. De største vanskelighetene ligger i anskaffelse av tildels dyre kjelker og passende baner for trening og konkurranser. Ved lørdagens turnering var IF Nackas Rolf Johanson desidert beste spiller, takket være sin hurtighet og sitt fine pasningsspill.

Resultater:
Oslo — Pionér 0—4, Oslo — Nacka 0—3, Svelvik — IFAH 0—9, Oslo — IFAH 0—2, Pionér — Svelvik 7—0, Svelvik — Nacka 0—14, Pionér — Nacka 0—0, Oslo — Svelvik 0—0, Nacka — Pionér 2—0, Nacka — IFAH 0—0.

Nacka	4	3 1 0	19— 0	7p.
IFAH	4	2 2 0	11— 0	6p.
Pionér Oslo	4	2 1 1	11— 2	5p.
Oslo H.sp.lag	4	0 1 3	0— 9	1p.
Svelvik Hspl.	4	0 1 3	0—30	1p.

The first-ever publication about sledge hockey, 1968.

very first Summer Paralympics, which was the very first Paralympics. Although organized adaptive/disabled sport on the club level had occurred since the nineteenth century, no international governing body for handicapped athletics existed before the opening of the first Summer Paralympics in 1960.[13]

In response to World War II, neurologist Sir Ludwig Guttmann, MD (1899–1980), opened a spinal injury center at the Stoke Mandeville Hospital in Great Britain in 1944 at the request of the British government. He developed rehabilitation activities for the many veterans with disabilities under his care, which evolved into recreational sport and eventually competitive sport.[14] Best said by the International Paralympic Committee,

> On 29 July 1948, the day of the Opening Ceremony of the London 1948 Olympic Games, Dr. Guttmann organized the first competition for wheelchair athletes which he named the Stoke Mandeville Games, a milestone in Paralympic history. They involved 16 injured servicemen and women who took part in archery. In 1952, Dutch ex-servicemen joined the movement and the International Stoke Mandeville Games were founded.[15]

In 1960, the Stoke Mandeville Games became the Paralympic Games and found its first official stage in Rome, Italy, attracting nearly four hundred athletes from twenty-four countries. Black-and-white photos depict athletes with disabilities parading around Acqua Acetosa Ground on the 18th of September, on what appears to be a simple outdoor track field no bigger than most found at modern high schools.[16] The quadrennial tradition to hold the Summer Paralympic Games immediately after the Summer Olympics has continued ever since.

Now, the 1976 inaugural Winter Paralympics hoped to follow in those footprints: sledge hockey was to be included in the program for the games in Örnsköldsvik. The only two teams expected to compete were Sweden and Norway, but when Norway pulled out, Sweden split its team in two and played itself anyway as an exhibition. This event cannot be called the official debut of Paralympic sledge hockey, as no opposing country was present. However, Johansson is certain that Sweden's decision to go forth rather than cancel in Norway's absence was the turning point of sledge hockey as an international sport. Several countries were watching with interest as the Swedes played, and Swedish TV broadcasted the game to intrigued audiences at home.

As a competitor in the Summer Paralympics in Toronto that same year, Rolf Johansson earned gold in the men's 100m wheelchair race. There he met Dick Loiselle, the executive director of the Games, whose interest in sledge hockey was piqued. That winter, Loiselle traveled to Johansson's hometown to see the sport firsthand. At the end of the visit, Johansson sent Loiselle away with a sledge hockey stick (the Canadians remember it as being an entire sled) to take to Canada, the way settlers took potatoes back to the Old World, and by 1980, the first Canadian sledge hockey organization, the Alberta Sledge Hockey and Ice Picking Association, was born.

From there, Johansson became quite a busy ambassador. He contacted famous Swedish hockey player Sven Tumba (1931–2011) and invited him to get down on his level, into a sledge, and play the game. The support of a celebrated national player would be priceless. Tumba

Sven Tumba (left) and Rolf Johansson (right) at "Handikappidrotten's Day" in Täby, 1977. COURTESY OF ROLF JOHANSSON

agreed, and, in 1977, the two posed for a photo in sledges on the ice.[17] The decorated and powerful presence of Tumba furthered Sweden's engagement with Johansson's creation.

In 1985, in Switzerland, Johansson demonstrated sledge hockey at the Workshop for Wheelchair Athletics. The very first world championship of sledge hockey (not the first under the IPC, which would come later) was held in Oslo the following year in 1986. Then, in August of that same year, Enid Bekkar, chairman of the British Paraplegic Winter Sports Association, invited Johansson to train their national team that coming November 28–30.

Anatoli Firsov (1941–2000), a decorated national hockey player from the USSR, expressed interest in Johansson's program in 1990. A reporter had connected the two of them, and Firsov promised Johansson he'd arrange for Johansson to visit Moscow and help create the first Russian sledge hockey team. Unfortunately, Firsov fell ill days after his visit, and ultimately would pass away before this could be done.

PARALYMPIC PREMIERE OF SLEDGE HOCKEY

With the 1976 Winter Games incurring disqualifying circumstances after the Norwegians pulled out, the 1994 Winter Paralympics in Lillehammer, Norway, is considered sledge hockey's official Paralympic debut.

In total, thirty-one nations comprising 471 total athletes participated across five sports. Including the formal debut of ice sledge hockey, para alpine skiing, para biathlon, para cross country, and ice sledge racing were the other sports contested. Competition ran from March 10 to March 19. Helge Bjørnstad (b. 1971), a sledge hockey player from Norway, lit the opening flame.[18] The countries competing in sledge hockey for the first time ever on a Paralympic stage were Sweden, Norway, Canada, Great Britain, and Estonia. The United States, with its players and programs still in their infancy, engaged in talks about competing but ultimately did not secure a place.

Johansson recalled the first Paralympic sledge hockey game in history. Sweden contested with Canada. "The match was incredibly even; the game was undulating back and forth," wrote Johansson, "but we scored the first goal through Sven-Eric 'Solla' Carlsson, who thus became the first man to score a sledge hockey goal at a Paralympic games."[19] Johansson, #11, took a massive blow to the ribs, cracking several. Although the Swedes won that game, 2–1, Johansson tried and failed to play through the pain without painkillers at the next game facing Norway. The Swedes lost, 1–2, and Johansson planned to sit out the rest of the tournament.

As the de facto "Father of Sledge Hockey," however, Johansson felt the pressure of his teammates' hopeful questions. They asked if he would be able to play in the first-ever gold medal game, in which Sweden would soon compete. Johansson, sensing something greater—something that would be worth the pain—was about to happen, transferred into his sled and agreed to play.

Norway proved to be the most formidable challenger in the world. After three periods, the score was 0–0. The game went to overtime. Sudden death would decide the winner. At 3:13 in the extra period, Sweden's Jan Edbom (b. 1957) finally scored, and the cheers resounded. The Norwegian goalie slammed the ice with his stick.

This first gold medal game in the history of the sport would look eerily similar to the one Norway waged at the climax of the Games in 2002. It is also interesting to note that almost exactly one hundred years before, on March 22, 1894, the city of Montréal hosted the first ever Stanley Cup. It was played on natural ice, with upright pegs instead of goal nets, and referees wearing street clothes and Derby hats.[20] The first recorded ice hockey game ever was held also in Montréal only nineteen years before that, on March 3, 1875, and the first Canadian–U.S. league, the International Hockey League (IHL), was founded in only 1904.[21] The modern version of ice hockey is a young sport even for able-bodied players. Sledge hockey's development, in comparison, really was not all that late. One could even say the rate of advances for sledge hockey since its genesis moved faster.

Rolf Johansson was recognized in 1995 by King Carl XVI Gustaf (b. 1946), who invited him to Stockholm Castle to receive His Majesty the King's Medal in the eighth size for excellence in sports achievement. The royal cabinet arranged all his travels, and so, "early in the morning of 28 January," wrote Johansson, "in pitch darkness and a blizzard, on narrow, winding, serpentine roads through the Alps," he was driven to the railway station.[22] Planes and taxis eventually brought him before the king, who bowed to his level to shake his hand.

CATCHING ON IN THE UNITED STATES

If Rolf Johansson is the "Father of Sledge Hockey," another man is the "Father of *Sled* Hockey in the United States." His name was John Schatzlein (1949–2019), and in White Bear Lake, Minnesota, at the age of fourteen, he fell from a cottonwood tree. Disability stole athletic dreams from him. Years later, Schatzlein became a pioneer for handicapped sports. He helped establish a wheelchair basketball team at Southwest State University (now called Southwest Minnesota State University), where he served as student body president and advised university officials on making the campus more accessible.

In December of 1989, Schatzlein received an inquiry from the Canadian Sledge Hockey Organization. They'd identified him from his job at the Sister Kenny Rehabilitation Institute (est. 1942 in Minneapolis and later called the Courage Kenny Rehabilitation Institute at Abbott Northwestern Hospital) as a patient advocate, and they wanted him to form a U.S. club team the Canadians could play against. They sent Schatzlein a VHS tape of the sport and an outline of the requirements. Canada wanted to contest the U.S. team in Ottawa as soon as that February.

"I called them back and said we would have a team there," wrote Schatzlein. "With no money, no rules, no equipment, and little time (5 weeks), we set about the task."[23]

Schatzlein had many connections in the disabled community and a talent for talking. Sitting in a wheelchair himself, he was burly, with salt-and-pepper hair and beard and a spark in his eyes. He smiled in such a way that, even if you'd never met him, you could hear his laughter through a photograph.

Using these talents to recruit members, Schatzlein developed the very first sled hockey team in the United States. He named his organization the American Sled Hockey Association (ASHA) after consulting the ideas and voices of those involved. Robert "Bob" Facente served as the first head coach, with his son, Robert Facente Jr., as assistant coach.[24] Schatzlein himself both managed and played as a goalie. The team met Canada's challenge and played in Ottawa in February of 1990.[25] The event was called the Canadian Winter Games, hosted by the Canadian Federation of Sports for the Disabled.

It was the first formal sled hockey game the United States ever played.

Schatzlein followed it up soon after with a World Cup Tournament in Oslo, Norway, that same year. The team returned to Ottawa for the Canadian Winter Games not long after in 1992, and this time was pleased to earn a bronze placement.[26]

Of course, travel expenses often came right out of Schatzlein's pocket. While Schatzlein convinced USA Hockey to donate equipment, he and his wife, Helen, took out a second mortgage to fund the aspirations—and airline fees—of the team. By 1992, Schatzlein had drafted bylaws for ASHA and begun the process of seeking recognition from a national governing body. His goal was to put his U.S. team in the rink at the 1994 Lillehammer Paralympics.

Schatzlein corresponded via letter with National Handicapped Sports (NHS), headquartered in Rockville, Maryland, and later with the United States Olympic Committee (USOC) out of Colorado Springs, Colorado. His first response came from NHS on October 7, 1993. The board of directors voted against sanctioning his team, citing four reasons.

First, NHS felt that Schatzlein's team offered no indication that it was indeed *national* as opposed to locally based in Minnesota. In other words, being the *only* team in the United States was not enough, in their view, to call them the "United States team." Second, NHS criticized Schatzlein's selection process as lacking a clear methodology. Third, the board had voted a day prior to suspend further funding of new programs in order to conserve their budget. Finally, NHS, seeing that the Lillehammer games were only about five months away, stated that they did not want to "rush" into something as large as governance of a new sport.

The author, NHS competition services manager Brian J. Williams, closed by offering his suggestions for Schatzlein's recourse, which included contacting the USOC and continuing to grow and legitimize the Minnesota team.

"I do feel that the future of the American Sled Hockey Association is a great one," Williams wrote, "and the ball has just begun to role [*sic*]."[27]

The letter, overall, seems reasoned.[28] However, its use of quotation marks around "national" (i.e., "It was evident there was no 'clear' selection process for this 'national' program"),[29] and the fact that Schatzlein had offered to fully fund the expenses required to compete in Lillehammer, surely riled Schatzlein's frustration.

He took Williams's suggestion and wrote next to Jan Wilson, coordinator for Disabled Sports Services at the USOC. Wilson, too, denied the request to sanction Schatzlein's team in time for the Lillehammer games. The USOC's logic was simple: ASHA was not a member of the USOC, and time was too short to begin that process.

"Sledge hockey could be a very important aspect of future United States Paralympics Teams," wrote Wilson, "and I encourage your organization to continue efforts to recruit new players and develop the sport nationwide."[30]

Schatzlein pressed on, and, as late as January 1994, two months before the Lillehammer Paralympics, the USOC considered a second recommendation to accept ASHA's sled hockey team. Dave Ogrean, executive director of USA Hockey (who retired from his second term in 2017), supported the proposal.[31] Ultimately, however, a committee vote rendered the final rejection, again citing concerns over the selection process and lateness of the request.

And so, while both governing bodies expressed interest in the future of the sport, Schatzlein's team did not attend the Lillehammer Paralympics.

That is not to say this fresh-faced team saw no action after Ottawa. In December of 1993, ASHA hosted the Friendship Cup. Several of the players who would eventually play for the 2002 Paralympic team attended this preliminary tournament—showing up, competing, and bunking in Schatzlein's basement. The family dog barked madly at the confusing sight of young men seemingly removing their legs straight from their sockets before going to sleep.

By 1994, awareness of the sport had spread. Clinics throughout the Northeast Passage in New Hampshire attracted 90 interested participants, and across the country 159 prospective players showed up to try the sport.[32] Four teams existed now: Team Boston, the Chicago Blizzard (which sired the players who would be the founding members of the sled hockey program at the Rehabilitation Institute of Chicago—the RIC

Blackhawks), All Island (AI) Sports, and the Northern Blades, all of which competed in the Thornhill Sledge Hockey Tournament in March of 1994 in Toronto (in lieu, it seems, of Lillehammer).

Schatzlein's team also competed in Nynäshamn, Sweden, for the first IPC World Championship in 1996—the event would go on to take place every four years, midway between Winter Paralympics. In 1997, Schatzlein's team contested as well at the IPC Swedish Winter Games in Sollefteå, Sweden. There, Queen Silvia of Sweden (b. 1943) opened the games and met with participants from around the world.[33] At both events, Facente continued to coach, but his reputation as something of a partier preceded that of a serious athletic visionary. The team suffered double-digit losses.[34] At the 1996 championship, Sweden emerged in first place, Norway in second, and Canada in third, and the U.S. team traveled across Europe, getting their wheelchairs stuck on escalators, hoisting a drink or two with Facente, and, now and then, dabbling in a little sled hockey.

It was not the driven athletic force Schatzlein needed.

When Schatzlein met Richard Allen DeGlopper (b. 1948) in 1997, everything began to move forth.

Put simply, DeGlopper, a native New Yorker, became involved in adaptive athletics because he loved his daughter. She, Teri, was born in 1977 with mild cerebral palsy. Wanting to endow her with every positive experience possible, DeGlopper and his wife, Cheryl, introduced Teri to the New York State Games for the Physically Challenged (now called the Empire State Games for the Physically Challenged). Governor Mario Cuomo (1932–2015) had funded these games through the state parks budget, but when his term ended, lovers of the games feared his successor would not carry on the program. DeGlopper, who had become quite a familiar face, was approached by the games' director, Pam Maryjanowski, and asked to form a new nonprofit that could continue the events.

DeGlopper's nonprofit was called Western New York Physically Challenged Youth, Inc. However, Cuomo's successor, Republican George Pataki (b. 1945), did not discontinue the games, and DeGlopper found himself with a 501(c)(3) without a purpose.

DeGlopper had encountered this growing sport called sled hockey at a clinic in Brockport, New York, facilitated through pioneers from St. Catharines, Ontario. Seeing an opportunity to develop the new sport for the kids he currently worked with at the games, DeGlopper adopted sled hockey as the official initiative for his until-then directionless non-profit. His first team was called the Niagara Challengers. Later, a second team—the Buffalo Freeze—developed in order to accommodate the first cohort of players, older and more skillful now, as new players came in. Eventually DeGlopper would even convince the NHL Buffalo Sabres to sponsor them. "When you volunteer," he said, "you never know where that road will take you and how many lives you might impact."

This is how, at a tournament across the Canadian border, Schatzlein and DeGlopper crossed paths—Schatzlein handling mostly adult players and DeGlopper, youth. DeGlopper was coaching the Buffalo Freeze at the time, and it did not take long for Schatzlein to notice DeGlopper's passion and organizational talents. He asked DeGlopper to host tryouts at Buffalo State College—a good midpoint for athletes from the Midwest and the Northeast—for the 1998 Paralympics in Nagano. While still no backing from a larger national organization had been procured, the IPC had accepted ASHA to represent the United States in the 1998 Paralympics. The United States would at last be sending a team.

Schatzlein, who had finally realized his dream of getting a United States sled hockey team to the Paralympics, fell ill at the Nagano games, in life's cruel way. He had an unknown allergy to MSG, which does not harmonize well with Asian cuisine. Upon returning home, DeGlopper absorbed ASHA, freeing the organization from its reputation of debt, and formed the United States Sled Hockey Association (USSHA) in 1999.

USSHA's short life of three years is all thanks to the groundbreaking 2002 gold medal victory ahead—the event that finally convinced USA Hockey to take a greater role in the sport, formally sanctioning it in 2006.

TIMELINE

- **1948**—Stoke Mandeville Games, precursor to the Paralympics
- **1960**—First Paralympic Games (summer) in Rome, Italy

- **1963/1964**—Sledge hockey invented on Lake Drevviken, Sweden
- **1976**—First Winter Paralympics in Örnsköldsvik, Sweden; sledge hockey exhibited
- **1980**—First Canadian sledge hockey team founded
- **1989**—Canada solicits John Schatzlein to organize the first American team
- **1990**—United States team competes in its first international game, located in Ottawa
- **1994**—Sledge hockey officially premieres as a sport at the Paralympics in Lillehammer
- **1996**—First IPC World Championships held in Nynäshamn, Sweden
- **1997**—IPC Swedish Winter Games in Sollefteå, Sweden
- **1998**—Nagano Paralympics; the United States competes in Paralympic sledge hockey for the first time
- **2000**—Second IPC World Championships held in Salt Lake City
- **2002**—Malmö Open in Sweden (RIC Blackhawks competed)
- **2002**—Winter Paralympics in Salt Lake City
- **2006**—USA Hockey officially sponsors sled hockey

RULES

Sled hockey rules have evolved over time. Today, it uses the Official Playing Rules of USA Hockey (standard hockey) as its default. A supplemental document called the Official Rules of Sled Hockey, updated seasonally, serves to declare differences in game play. As already emphasized, many sled hockey athletes would argue that the phrase "standard hockey" ought apply to both games, as most do not draw a firm distinction between sled hockey and what their able-bodied colleagues play. (If someone with a disability is driving a car with hand controls, for example, do we say the person is driving or disabled driving? Even if the driving was competitive, in a race, the distinction is superfluous. They are driving). I agree with this, but for the purpose of clarity in the upcoming sections, I will refer to able-bodied hockey—the tradition that came first and is most common today—as "standard hockey."

The composition of teams in both sports are the same. Rinks are the same as well, except some adaptations for sled hockey might be made to remove the lip between the box and ice or to replace the boards at the bench with glass so seated players can see through. As of 2021, the breakdown of periods is the same, but in 2002, when the subjects of this book played in the Paralympics, sled hockey games were divided into three fifteen-minute stop-time periods as opposed to the standard three twenty-minute periods of today.

There are some penalties unique to sled hockey. The most infamous of these is T-boning, or teeing, which consists of ramming the sled into another player at a 90-degree angle, resulting in either a minor, major, or misconduct penalty, at the discretion of the referee. Suspension times for penalties are two minutes for minor, five for major, or ten for misconduct, and the most severe penalty, a match penalty, results in expulsion from the game. "The signal for Teeing," states the Official Rules of Sled Hockey, "is using a clinched fist of the non whistle hand and moving into the middle of the forearm of the whistle hand."[35] As will be discussed later in the book, T-boning is not always accidental, and intimidation is sometimes the name of the game. Intentional T-boning is a choice a player makes, like when the hit is necessary to prevent a shot and the penalty worth it.

Charging, another penalty, looks similar to T-boning, but is distinguished by being otherwise legal bodychecking were it not for unreasonable speed and force as a result of the distance traveled on the ice.[36] Holding and hooking, wherein a player holds another player's sled with his or her hand or uses a stick to hook the sled in place, respectively, are also penalties unique to sled hockey, although they are similar, in effect, to those penalties called in standard hockey.

Although not penalties, two goal-related faux pas are also only found in sled hockey. First, a player may not use the sled to propel the puck into the goal (similar to the prohibition against kicking the puck into the net in standard hockey). Second, a goal is disallowed if the player makes it while any part of his or her sled is inside the crease of the goal, unless a defending player forced the sled into this position (similar to the rule in standard hockey which disallowed any goal made while a player's skate was in the crease. This rule was changed in 1999 to allow goals like these so long as the player was in control, and was the topic of controversy during the 1999 Stanley Cup, where Dallas Star Brett Hull (b. 1964) won the game with just such a goal).

The concept of "offsides" is the same as in standard hockey: No offensive player may pass the blue line ahead of the puck. However, in sled hockey, the blades located directly beneath the seat of the sled, rather than any part of the body (such as feet, which are usually the most extended body part), determine whether or not a player is offsides. This rule was likely established in order to not discriminate between double amputees and players with longer sled frames used to accommodate their legs.

Although sled hockey players use two shorter sticks instead of one, sticks cannot be raised to shoulder-height when near a player, nor can they be thrown, checked with (called a "buttend" when done using the shaft above the upper head), or used to hold down the puck, just as in standard hockey. Head, face, and neck interference with stick or body also results in a penalty. The sharp picks on the end of the sticks, used to propel the players down the ice, can cause significant pain and fear when used to buttend an opposing player, and this is viewed as a serious infraction.

Referees usually come from standard hockey careers and usually are able-bodied. USA Hockey publishes handbooks and videos for officials to learn the nuances of sled hockey in order to become literate in both.[37] Because players are low to the ground and much action is done with their hands, it is imperative that the referee be closer to the players than is usual in standard hockey.[38] And, of course, the referees must have their heads on a swivel to avoid the embarrassment of being clipped from behind by a fast moving sled.

During face-off, the referee drops the puck from a crouching position as opposed to from the hip. Players facing off align themselves with either their back or their feet towards the referee, but their sides must be facing the net ends of the rink.

The mission of sled hockey is access to hockey for everyone. Thus, primarily in youth sled hockey, "pushers" are permitted; these individuals, often volunteers, propel the sled by pushing a handle behind the seat for players who lack the physical capacity to move their sleds. Pushers may not push faster than the average speed of surrounding players and may not interfere with the puck. Because sled hockey players ergonomically cannot skate backwards, pushers also may not pull their assigned player backwards unless to remove the player from harm's way. Naturally, pushers cannot offer coaching advice on the ice.

For youth and some club players with specific medical conditions, there exists the option to wear a red pinny, signifying this player as ineligible to be bodychecked, but likewise that player is then forbidden from bodychecking someone else.

The pusher and pinny sled hockey rules are excellent ways to make the sport even more inclusive, but they have never applied to competition at the Paralympic level. At this level, the game embodies unchaperoned ferocity.

EQUIPMENT

According to the Official Rules of Sled Hockey, the basic pieces of equipment unique to sled hockey are (a) the sled (or the "sledge"), made up of the frame, skag, bucket, skate holder, and skate blade; and (b) sticks and picks. The "frame" refers to the elongated metal base beginning at the bucket (or seat) and ending at the skag. Frames are made of either steel, aluminum, titanium, or magnesium and may include up to four bars crossing the main side rails horizontally, called cross members. The space between frame and ice—where the blades under the seat on one end and the skag under the footrest on the other support the sled—must be between 8.5 and 9.5 centimeters, leaving enough space for the puck to travel underneath the player. The width between the two blades, used for balance, was originally 4 inches apart, which limited maneuverability. These standards were updated prior to the 2002 Paralympics, allowing for much narrower positioning of the two blades and facilitating greater speed and dexterity.

Sled hockey players use two sticks instead of one. The sticks are curved at the end, which serves to whack the puck—one-handed—and most professional players can shoot effectively with either hand. However, as some of the shots in this book will reveal, there's still nothing like a natural leftie. On the opposite end are picks used to grip the ice and propel the sled

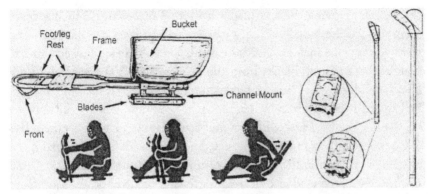

This infographic from USA Hockey shows basic sled structure, stick anatomy, and movement technique. The skag, not labeled, is the piece dipping down to touch the ice where the "Front" arrow is pointing. USA HOCKEY

forward. Players twirl the sticks 180 degrees as needed to use either end. Wood, carbon, aluminum, fiberglass, or plastic may be used to construct the stick. Today, the maximum length of a stick is 100 centimeters, an increase from the 75-centimeter maximum imposed on the players during the 2002 Paralympic games. It is permissible for players to attach their sticks to their gloves. For some, due to various disabilities, this is crucial.

Hockey pants are not required of the players, but all other standard hockey equipment is either mandatory (like helmets) or strongly encouraged (like mouth and neck guards).

Because sled hockey deals with a demographic sensitive to physical impairment, the game guidelines allow for some customization upon approval—and several on the 2002 U.S. team sought or created customized equipment. Their ideas were effective enough that they often were adopted as mainstream by other sled hockey players in later years.

For example, the United States goalie, Manny Guerra Jr. is credited for innovating the goalie glove and replacing the blades of the goalie's sled with plastic, aligning them in a new orientation so he could easily rock side to side in the net. Sylvester Flis, a Polish immigrant who was a star forward on the 2002 team, joined forces with his brother to change the game entirely when he transferred the sled's center of gravity from widely dispersed across the sled to right under his seat. He did this by removing the skag (the piece under the feet that juts down and touches the ice) and moving the seat blades in from 4 inches to 1⅝ inches apart. Then, before the Salt Lake City games, he narrowed the distance even more to only one inch apart. Many of Flis's teammates followed suit and bought these custom blades from the Flis brothers. Whereas before, the puck would get stuck in the blades under players' buckets and referees had to tilt everyone over in search of it, now the puck would ricochet off the blades and Flis could turn and accelerate without resistance. This is what lent him his unbeatable speed, and even his international rivals credit his innovation for completely transforming the sport.

We have seen evidence of the progression of sled hockey equipment beginning with the early sleds of Rolf Johansson. In the United States, Rich DeGlopper worked to advance equipment as well. At first, he constructed sleds for his youth program with donated and scavenged materials, utilizing labor networks in the New York state prison system.

Albion Correctional Facility inmates welded sled frames out of chromate steel, the same material used to build racecars.[39] The sleds were heavy and durable. Foam-padded plywood sheets donated by a medical table supply company were used to construct the seats. Even the seatbelts were scavenged from junkyards. The blades were old skate blades with the rivets drilled out. DeGlopper bolted them to the new sled frame. "It would be common that the refs would be picking up nuts and bolts on the ice during a game," noted DeGlopper, adding that this was quite dangerous for anyone to skate into. A group of local high school woodshop teachers carved the sticks out of hickory. DeGlopper and Schatzlein both encountered not only the challenge of funding but the difficulty in enticing a manufacturer to produce equipment when demand was still so low.

Then DeGlopper met Laurie Howlett (b. 1951), who was tabling with his merchandise at a tournament. Like DeGlopper, Howlett was the loving parent of a child with a mild disability (a cleft lip). In the late 1970s and early 1980s, he'd engaged with the disabled community while seeking treatment for his son. After observing how handicapped children exhibited just the same eagerness to play and discover, Howlett felt moved to create specialized toys for them. He designed wheeled seats for the kids to be pulled in, parents responded enthusiastically, and his garage workshop soon garnered a reputation.

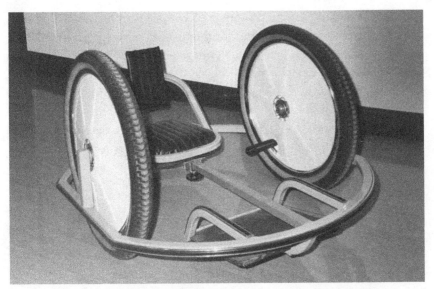

An early adaptive bicycle created by Laurie Howlett. Note the low-to-the-ground seat and the extending metal frame similar to later ice hockey sleds. COURTESY OF LAURIE HOWLETT

In 1992, Jennifer Kodis at Five Counties Children's Centre in Peterborough, Ontario, contacted Howlett.[40] Kodis was interested in establishing a sled hockey program, and Howlett, she felt, would be perfect for the job of producing their first sleds. He accepted, and slowly improved his craft over time.

DeGlopper and Howlett pushed off each other to advance sled hockey equipment. Howlett, branded as Unique Inventions, Inc., is now one of the leading manufacturers in the field. However, as evidenced above, it took direct adaptations from players themselves to churn out the finest equipment for today's usage.

The history of sled hockey and the development of its rules and equipment occurred in stages. The contributing ideas and individuals overlapped in time, hundreds of miles apart. While Rolf Johansson was marketing his newly invented sport to Canada and Switzerland, Laurie Howlett was making wheeled, seated bicycles and tricycles he had no idea would one day be the prototype of U.S. sled hockey sleds. The realization of this sport around the world is a series of staggered discoveries, meetings, tragedies, and choices, all interlapping to carry the baton from one decade to the next.

It would take the 2002 gold medal victory to blast the sport beyond its tightly knit disabled community and into the visibility of the entire nation. However, the less decorated pioneers before that event committed exhaustive years and resources into paving the way to such a moment.

CHAPTER TWO

Manny Guerra Jr., #67

"Junior"

Pos.	GPT	GKD	GP	MIP	MIP%	GA	SVS	SOG	SVS%	GAA	SO	W	T	L
G	6	6	5	235:00:00	83.93	5	56	61	91.8	0.96	2	5	0	0

IN THE 1920S, MANNY GUERRA SR. LOOPED HIS ARM THROUGH HIS mother's and walked across the U.S.–Mexico border. They stepped carefully through the sandy brush and looked ahead at the horizon. Somewhere beyond, Guerra Sr.'s late father had reached a city called Chicago and found work in the heat and roar of enormous steel mills. The promise of opportunity, although hard, lay ahead.

The Mexican national holding his mother was a young man at the time, and resembled a darker, mustachioed Dean Martin—smooth skin, handsome black eyes, and almost always in a work suit with a thick tie. He smoked cigarettes between his fingers and turned heads. The Guerras continued migrating north by train, foot, and vehicle until at last arriving at the windy city, where Guerra Sr. married Francisca Hernandez, an American born in Dallas. She was a fellow Roman Catholic and commanded an elegant beauty, her black hair pulled into a bun and her eyes bright. The couple had eight children, including Manuel Guerra Jr., born on July 7, 1967.

Manny Guerra Jr., also nicknamed "Junior," was their last child and only son. According to medical advice, he was one too many. Guerra's mother had suffered a miscarriage before him, damaging her internal organs, and tragically succumbed a week after delivering him.

Grief dimmed the Guerra residence. Guerra's father, consumed by work at Valley Mould Steel, struggled to keep eight children and a roof in one piece. At just the age of one, Guerra went to live with his grandmother in Guadalajara, Mexico, to relieve his father from the responsibility. It was here, in July of 1968, that Guerra contracted polio. He had never been vaccinated.

When the news reached Guerra Sr. via a handwritten letter, he called his son home. The elder Guerra dialed health professionals everywhere seeking help. Medical memories dominate Guerra Jr.'s childhood.

Finally, the family found Dr. Spyros Dallas at the Chicago Children's Hospital. An orthopedic surgeon, Dr. Dallas spoke through a thick Greek accent and practiced with a degree from Athens. He earned a reputation for combining medicine with madness, in only the best ways one can. At the Lincoln Park Zoo in Chicago, Dr. Dallas had performed surgery on injured gorillas, and he looked at Guerra's impairments with a similar touch of insanity. He studied how Guerra was able to move his leg, feel it, but how it buckled under the slightest weight. The doctor was determined to find a solution.

Dr. Dallas performed on Guerra the first surgery in the country that sought to lengthen the bone by increasing blood flow to the marrow. It was a success. The surgeon replaced Guerra's hip and fused his ankle. On Guerra's broken femur he repeated the novel bone-lengthening process, attached screws, and watched the femur grow back. Altogether, Guerra endured twenty-one surgeries at the creative hands of Spyros Dallas, who later died in a car accident in 1994.

Every time Guerra returned to school after recovering from an operation, his teachers at John L. Marsh Elementary threw welcome back parties in the classroom. It seemed to be an annual tradition. Despite this kindness, so much time spent in the hospital and so many differences in appearance and ability made it difficult for Guerra to make friends. A clunky brace anchored his left leg to the ground and wrapped around his entire waist for support. He sat on the sidelines at gym, watching the other kids play and run.

In seventh grade, Guerra asked his teacher what he had to do to become a crossing guard. This raised some eyebrows, but soon Guerra found himself in a reflective vest waving his classmates to and from the building. In this way, he met and got to know almost everyone at school. Hesitant nods from fellow students turned to smiles and waves. It was also around this time that Guerra requested permission from his father to remove the hot, cumbersome leg brace, which had created sores and skin marks. He agreed, and loss of weight literally and figuratively buoyed young Guerra. Confidence grew inside him, and that year he asked to be allowed to play dodgeball in gym as well.

That crossing guard whistle opened doors for Guerra. Kids invited him to play boot hockey, a blend of hockey and soccer, where the rules of hockey stand but feet are used to pass a ball on solid ground. Not able to move his body with speed, Guerra claimed the net as a goalie. He used two layers of hoodies as padding and tied seat cushions with shoelaces to his legs. He used a baseball glove instead of a hockey mitt. Cut foam served as a blocker. Whatever it took to play.

The Guerra family moved to Minneapolis, and Guerra's father remarried a Jehovah's Witness named Bertha Casas Sola, who gave birth to Guerra's two half-sisters a few years later. The three young children practiced the religion with Casas Sola. In school, Guerra's classmates would scrape back their chairs, stand, place their hands on their hearts, and recite the Pledge of Allegiance to the American flag. Guerra stood but looked around uncomfortably as they chanted the words. He was taught to boycott this tradition. On weekends, he knocked door-to-door sharing the good news of the Gospel. Guerra Jr. continued in the religion until adulthood, and Guerra Sr., while never converting, set up chairs in his living room for his wife's Bible study and hosted church meetings on Tuesdays. As the religion forbids the celebration of birthdays, Guerra's older sisters took to sneaking him out of the house once a year to treat him on his birthday. He'd asked them to buy gifts for his half-siblings, too, who faced the same restriction.

After graduating as a systems analyst from ASPE Institute of Technology and beginning a career in IT, Guerra Jr. established his own family. He married his first wife, Debra, and became stepfather to Debra's baby girl. The couple had met at church, as she too was a Jehovah's Witness, but their devotion to the religion soon cooled. A son arrived nine months after their marriage, and two more sons four years after that. It was around this time that tragedy would strike again.

On his way home from working a job at the University of Minnesota, a vehicle slammed into Guerra's car. The other driver had just run a stop light and broadsided Guerra with a loud crunch of metal. At first, after both vehicles jerked to a halt, Guerra opened the car door and spilled out, walking away from the accident. The sun kissed his skin and no pain touched his body. With each step, however, he noticed a piercing feeling in his back, and he stumbled. It was as if his back could no longer support his weight. Only days later, he could barely hold himself up at the sink to brush his teeth. Guerra lost the ability to play ball, which he had worked so hard since childhood to make possible.

Guerra sought treatment for his injuries at the Sister Kenny Rehabilitation Institute, and it was there that he met Dr. Richard Owen. Dr. Owen, a victim of polio himself, walked into the exam room with two leg braces and two crutches. He sported big, bushy eyebrows and Coke-bottle glasses. *Aw, man . . .* , Guerra remembered thinking. It was not the picture of health he wanted to see.

Dr. Owen pulled all of Guerra's medical records, reviewing all twenty-one surgeries. He looked up at Guerra sharply. This was not a patient looking to be healed, he realized. This was a patient looking to be just comfortable enough to move the hell on with life. Dr. Owen ordered relief for Guerra's calloused hands, which he'd used daily to lock his knee in place. He recommended a manual wheelchair. Instead of talking to Guerra about treatment, he talked to Guerra about time.

One has to use it to live—not wait until the crossing guard lets you.

Dr. Owen suggested adaptive sports for Guerra. At first, the stubborn patient refused, just as he had refused to hang the handicapped placard in his car until his wife snapped it onto his rear-view mirror herself in a huff. After a bout of depression, doing nothing for almost a year and resorting to the use of the wheelchair, Guerra gave in to Dr. Owen's invitation.

He attended the Sister Kenny Institute one Thursday night to find a room full of single and double amputees arming themselves with equipment and preparing to wheel onto the basketball court in their chairs. Guerra looked around at groups of people talking and thumping shoulders as able-bodied athletes would. He choked out a few hellos and then found himself pumping his wheels towards one side of the court. The game began.

Guerra's tall rubber wheels squeaked on the court. Players soared by him. The smell of sweat and freshly shined wooden floors mixed in the air. He learned how to pivot in the chair, how to shoot from a sitting position, how to move. He learned how to make that seat a part of his body. Halfway through the game, someone passed to Guerra, and he whammed his palms against his wheels to close in on the net. An opposing player crashed into him and whacked both of Guerra's arms away from the ball. Heart pounding, Guerra looked over.

It was Dr. Owen. He looked like an angry owl.

That was when Guerra realized adaptive sports were not some token, some charity. They were authentically competitive.

Guerra kept going every Thursday, and soon his teammates introduced him to the Courage Center, another institute offering different adaptive athletics. There he played wheelchair softball, built muscle, and built a name—eventually including a third nickname, "Big Juicy." He laughed telling me that one.

In 1991, Guerra finished a physical therapy session at the Sister Kenny Institute and pumped his wheels down the long white hall towards the basketball gym. The sound of a cheering crowd and a buzzer reached his ears and he stopped. Slowly, he approached the doorway of an open office and watched over a man's shoulder a small TV playing a VHS recording of a sled hockey game. Instantly his time in the crease on the streets of Chicago flashed in his mind.

Guerra and the stranger in the office watched for several minutes, mesmerized, as the camera swerved left and right following the puck on that white-and-red rink. Neither said a word to each other. Then the man clicked a remote and the television cut to black. He turned to Guerra.

"What was that?" asked Guerra.

"Sled hockey," said the man. "1990. Ottawa tournament."

Infatuation stole Guerra's expression, and the man smiled.

"You want in?"

The man's name was John Schatzlein. At the time the two met, Schatzlein was the current sled hockey manager and had been goalie for the team the year before. He had adapted the Wilmington Ice Garden in Minnesota to be fully accessible to athletes with disabilities, removing the 4-inch lip encircling the rink and modifying the benches to be removable. Guerra gave him his name and number, not knowing at the time that he'd soon be taking Schatzlein's old position in the net.

Schatzlein introduced Guerra to the other players, and to his own garage. Buckets, screws, and blades to build sleds lay on his workbench. They both paused and eyed the materials. Guerra was told he had to build his own equipment. That worked for him, at least, because he found he didn't like the way sleds usually sat. At four to five feet long, in a regular sled, Guerra's legs would be outstretched with his shoes facing the incoming puck. Instead, Guerra sawed his sled down to approximately two and a half feet and, rather than stretching his legs forward, crossed them in the sled bucket like a sitting Buddha. This improved his speed and allowed the cold, white ice to spread right in front of him, ready for smacking with his glove.

This, itself, was another problem. The goalie glove Schatzlein provided sported a spiked, heavy metal plate on the palm side. The spikes were used for gripping the ice, but snow packed between them by the third period, making Guerra's hand thrice as hard to maneuver. To address this, Guerra studied the ridges on the sole of an old pair of track shoes in his house. He noticed the ridges were spaced farther apart. Guerra cut the sole from the shoe and bent it into a U-shape, sewing it onto his glove with furniture thread. The innovation worked perfectly—grasping the ice, but shedding excess buildup. Guerra's design would be used by Paralympic goalies worldwide only a few years later.

His final contribution to goalie equipment for sled hockey, addressing the problem of his sled blades, came later in his career. Oriented north-to-south, his blades made it impossible for him to lunge left to right, post-to-post, with ease. He devised a plan to replace the metal blades with plastic ones and readjust the metal blades to face outward instead, providing a safety for him to fall down on and slide horizontally with. He could then use his elbows to pop himself back up and swerve to the other direction when needed. Going into that fateful 2002 Paralympics following a brutal embarrassment in the previous games, Guerra hoped to master this new move and prove his design.

Let's return, however, to the beginning of Guerra's sled hockey career. He was assigned to the Minnesota North Stars club team and began to practice. The NHL team of the same name provided Guerra and his comrades with jerseys and allowed them to wear their brand. Those days of boot hockey in Chicago paid off and wore a slick groove for Guerra's skills to sharpen through. At this time, Guerra was employed by Dain Rauscher, a financial services firm; its CEO, Irving Weiser, heard of Guerra's efforts and was moved enough to buy the ice time Guerra required to practice. Guerra traveled from rink to rink, wherever ice time was available, and there, saving pucks and shivering between the freezing posts of the net, he reflected on the mentors and friends who'd gotten him here—his father's sweat at the steel mills, Dr. Owen's hard whack on the basketball court, and now Weiser's generosity. Like a watered plant, Manny Guerra Jr. grew into a champion. By the time he played his first tournament game in Ottawa, Guerra endured 50 shots and saved 43 of them. He came home with more awards than he could fit into his suitcase.

Guerra and Schatzlein formed a strong friendship, sharing the dream that USA Hockey would become the national governing body for sled hockey and form a U.S. team. He lobbied with Schatzlein at meetings with Winter Paralympics organizers and various executives, including a breakfast-for-dinner meeting at Perkins Restaurant & Bakery with Walter Bush Jr., the president of USA Hockey. Their handshakes and efforts greased the tracks of a hesitant USA association to eventually agree to send jerseys and equipment, and, after medaling performances in 2006, formally sponsor a United States sled hockey team.

That would not have happened, of course, without Manny Guerra Jr. making the final three saves in the 2002 Salt Lake City shootout that won the gold. In the four games leading up to that moment, Guerra had allowed only three goals. The puck, he said, was "as big as a watermelon."

As soon as he repelled that last shot on the ice, you could say he sealed the deal.

Guerra is now a father of four and grandfather of just as many. He earned a bronze medal in the 2006 Torino Paralympics and retired from the sport that same year. His gold medal, which he once brandished in one hand with a beer in the other in the faces of the opposing athletes in Salt Lake City (all of whom had said his team would never amount to anything), now stays hidden in a sock drawer. It comes out only occasionally, usually to show a young kid much like the Manny Guerra Jr. on crutches or in a wheelchair that he once was.

Guerra has stayed involved in sled hockey by coaching (both able-bodied and disabled teams), advocating—and, of course, blocking the hits that come his way.

CHAPTER THREE

Nagano

Hockey is a tough, physical game, and it always should be.
— MARIO LEMIEUX, NHL

ON THURSDAY, MARCH 12, 1998, A WHISTLE SHRIEKED. THE TIMER stopped. Sled hockey players shuddered to a halt on the ice. No foul had been called, no time out declared. It was not the end of a period.

Akihito (b. 1933), the 125th and then-current emperor of Japan, and his wife, Empress Michiko (b. 1934), had walked into the stands. The Japanese sled hockey players pivoted to face him. Others in the crowd did as well. Although short in stature, the poised, square face of the emperor, with neatly combed hair and bushy brows, held gravity. Japanese emperors no longer identified as gods in post–World War II Japan, but many countrymen still revered them as such.

The fifteen United States sled hockey players, however, while respectfully silent, likely felt a mixture of confusion and annoyance. The fanfare of the emperor's unexpected arrival ushered in a roughly forty-five-minute break in the game and dissipated any momentum Team USA and captain Joe Howard, #23, had attempted to muster.

It was the team's third game at the 1998 Winter Paralympics in Nagano, Japan. Large, V-shaped columns supported the roof of the spacious Aqua Wing Arena, where the puck had dropped at 1:30 p.m.[1] Since then, the United States had managed to net only one goal at the stick of Howard. Japanese defenseman Tadashi Kato, who had only one

31

Paralympic Winter Games Nagano 1998, Sled Hockey – Men's. U.S. Team, back row, left to right: unidentified, equipment manager Kay Robertson, unidentified, assistant coach Rich DeGlopper, Richard "Tiny" Simpson, Dan Henderson, Mike Doyle, Manny Guerra and Joseph Howard; middle row, left to right: head coach Angelo Bianco, George Kiefner, Ed Clark, Dave Conklin, Tony Fitzgerald and Carlo Casarano; front row, left to right: team leader John Schatzlein, Corbin Beau, Victor Calise, Francis "Kip" St. Germaine and Mike Kult.

Paralympic Winter Games, Nagano, 1998, U.S. men's sled hockey team.
COURTESY OF THE CRAWFORD FAMILY U.S. OLYMPIC AND PARALYMPIC ARCHIVES, 2002

Aqua Wing interior. COURTESY OF KAY ROBERTSON

leg and who days before had borne the flag of Japan in one arm and held a crutch in the other at the opening ceremonies, decided the game. He scored once in the first period and again in the third, rendering the final score 2–1, Japan.

"The most difficult thing," then–head coach Angelo Bianco told reporters after the loss, "about playing Japan is that we're probably their biggest fans. We have a lot of respect for them. To lose to them is not any dishonor, it's just a disappointment for our team."[2]

Disappointment was probably an understatement. The United States' first game, against Canada on March 5, 1998, the same day as the opening ceremonies, resulted in a frustrating 1–1. Team USA had almost gotten away with shutting out the Canadians until U.S. #19, Corbin Beu, incurred a penalty while wrestling in the corner of the rink. Canada scored on the power play.[3] Four days later, Norway crushed the United States, 2–0, despite an astonishing 28 saves from goalie Manny Guerra, #67 (sometimes pictured as #26). Howard's closest shot had ricocheted off the post six minutes into the game, and he fumbled a feed from teammate Kip St. Germaine, #12. Norwegian goalie Arne Birger refused all attempts, and the team controlled passing with ease in the U.S. defensive zone.[4] Tensions were high.

With no victories, this game against Japan needed to be high-scoring—beating Japan by at least three goals, scoring at least four—to even qualify for the medal games.[5] This prompted the United States to take more risks . . . and more harried passes and sloppy shots. In fact, USA outshot Japan, 14–8, but the hits just weren't clean enough. The defeat somehow stung more than the ones before it.

This was for perhaps two reasons. First, as Coach Bianco would later comment, everything hurts more when preceded by the word *almost*. The United States *almost* tied Japan, the host team, at least when compared to their unequivocal 2–0 loss at their last scrimmage. Secondly, as Bianco stated to reporters, Team USA had formed a rivalry of both admiration and familiarity with Japan. Months before, in December of 1997, Japan had formally invited the U.S. team to Nagano to contest one another in anticipation of the Paralympics. The plane tickets to Tokyo were complimentary of Japan, as were the van shuttles to Nagano and the hotel

A packed audience backdrops the Team USA players' bench.
COURTESY OF KAY ROBERTSON

rooms. Doorways were narrower at the Hotel Mielparque Nagano than those of hotels in the United States—and the players made their marks by accidentally denting and scraping paint off the entranceways with their wheelchairs. The Japanese hosts did not mind. In fact, in a gesture of affection, Team Japan had arranged for a taste of home to be delivered to the locker room of Team USA after a game: carts of McDonald's fast food, wrapped up in yellow and white.

On the ice, the teams sought to both best each other and learn from each other. They spared no force. Dave Conklin, #20, in fact, collided with a Japanese player at their final scrimmage, breaking his leg. He waited through the entire plane ride home to set it at an American hospital.

Overall, the Japanese people took hosting the Paralympics seriously and treated it as an honor of national interest. By the time Naoyu Maruyama, an amputee Alpine skier, lit the opening torch at M-Wave Stadium, as many as thirty-one countries and 561 athletes gathered to compete. Nagano schoolchildren attended the games as an educational outing and were assigned to cheering sections for each and every team, creating an atmosphere of welcome and support. They mobbed Team USA off the ice with requests for autographs. The organizers put considerable thought into the event's "snowlets" mascots—four colorful owls—which represented the four major islands of Japan and the four years between Olympics. Snowlet merchandise sold out for the able-bodied Games but were restocked in time for the Paralympics.[6] Nearly 7.5 million handmade origami cranes, representing literal embodiments of prayers, donated by the people, hung from the ceiling at the closing ceremonies.[7] A giant eastern dragon—deep forest green—paraded down the center of the stadium as Team USA watched, wearing matching black ranch hats.

As for the sled hockey rink itself, "The ice was like glass," said left winger Victor "Vic" Calise (b. 1972), #9. The Nagano logo embedded in the center may as well have been a mirror. Everything smelled crisp and clean.

Calise, of Queens, New York, injured himself in a mountain biking accident in 1994. As a boy, he and his friends would steal shopping carts, collect traffic cones, and go from neighborhood to neighborhood setting up goals with the cones and playing street hockey. He would be one of the star players on the 1998 Paralympic team, and later in life serve as commissioner of New York City Mayor's Office for People with Disabilities. His manner is direct yet warm, a combination that makes it hard not to trust him. In conversation, Calise purses his lips and nods or shakes his head in a way that makes one feel he's listening, even if he has a few choice thoughts in response. Those traits would come in handy as the fresh U.S. team attempted to synchronize in Nagano.

Indeed, between games, Team USA strived to find congeniality with each other in a way that might convert to victory on the ice. Certainly almost no one on the team had known anyone else long. ASHA, still headed by John Schatzlein, had collected the players from all over the country to form a presentable roster. Tryout camps were held in May, September, and October of 1997, and after final selections were made, monthly practices were required even though most players lived hundreds of miles away. In only April of 1997, ASHA named Angelo Bianco, a paraplegic from New Egypt, New Jersey, to replace Bob Facente as head coach.[8] It seemed no one else wanted the job or could afford to take it. National funding was nonexistent for sled hockey athletes and staff. Everyone interested in participating had to pay their own way.

Bianco shattered his vertebrae in the Gulf War while serving in the United States Air Force. He'd played ice hockey as a boy and learned sled hockey following his injury and discharge. An Italian-American, Bianco sported an olive complexion and a sizeable poof of dark hair. Although he was an improvement over his predecessor—mainly because he knew enough about hockey to mobilize the team—Bianco resonated giddy, somewhat disorganized energy. His criticism could be offensive. But he reveled in the different personalities and nicknames of the players. He affectionately called the amputee players "amps," for instance, and nicknamed the team's backup goalie in Nagano, a full-blooded Cherokee who stood 6-foot-4, "Tiny."[9] Tiny's older brother, you see, was 6-foot-9.

Thus, Bianco in some ways resembled more of a fan—an easily riled one—than a serious coach: "One reason I get along so well with these guys is because, after we leave the ice—the hockey stuff—I roll away with them."[10] He meant this to emphasize that he, too, had a disability and could understand their challenges. This is true. But the quote can also be taken literally, as he was known to join the team partying or sharing beers after the games.

It was not hard to fraternize in an exciting new continent, after all. Kay Christie Robertson (b. 1949), the team's equipment manager and daughter of a Christian evangelist missionary in the Philippines, remembers rubbing away frustration and self-doubt as she massaged the players' shoulders, legs, and arms one by one in her hotel room. Team nurse Karen Clark attended to their physical ailments as well.

Robertson accompanied the team to the seventh-century Buddhist temple Zenkō-ji, lamenting that none of the prideful players allowed her to push their wheelchairs over the rough cobblestone or through flocks of apathetic pigeons. They insisted on struggling over the terrain themselves. Beneath the temple was a pitch-dark passage said to represent mortality, and there pilgrims could seek the "Key to Paradise," a large (at least twelve inches long) key attached to the wall of the tunnel. It is

The pigeons attack. COURTESY OF KAY ROBERTSON

allegedly placed opposite a sacred statue of the Buddha, unviewable to the public on the other side of the wall, and touching the key is said to bring enlightenment and salvation.

The voices of the American players echoed through the tunnel as they cursed and laughed, unable to find it.

Perhaps the mythology holds truth. Team USA failed to secure a single victory in Nagano and scored only twice during the entire Paralympic event. They finagled one win against Great Britain at an unscheduled match, but hesitated to take credit for the triumph, as Great Britain had played Japan earlier that day, and their athletes were overworked and tired. American Dan Henderson, #22, called it a "battle for last place," where the United States played with a certain abandon. He was awarded a rather lackluster "Man of the Match" title.

The real titles were around the necks of their rivals. Norway reigned with the gold, trailed by Canada with silver and Sweden with bronze.

What the 1998 team did not deliver in game play in Nagano it made up for at home. "We spread sled hockey like it was the gospel," said Calise. Staff and players from 1998 traveled the country introducing exhibitions and bringing new blood into the program. They made by with dinners served in crockpots by the grateful parents of players with disabilities. Bianco and DeGlopper dreamed of making the team a national force. "We invested in the future," said Calise, implying that the learning curves of 1998 were essential to the soon-to-be victories of 2002.

Those outcomes were far away, however, from that somber journey home from Japan. With the defeats so fresh, it was hard for the United States team to look at the 1998 Paralympics as anything but a failure. The plane ride was quiet. Unbeknownst to Bianco, who sat wearing a deep frown, whispers of replacing him had already begun.

CHAPTER FOUR

Joe Howard, #23

"Momo"

Pos.	GP	G	A	PTS	PIM	"+/–"	GWG	GTG	PPG	SHG	S	SG%
F	6	5	8	13	6	9	0	0	1	0	17	29.41

IN SOLLEFTEÅ, SWEDEN, IN 1997, JOE HOWARD HURLED A SLEDGEHAMmer onto his sled. He pummeled through the nuts and bolts and broke it in half. This wasn't out of anger—which was new for Howard. He was used to converting frustration to ferocity and had earned a reputation as something of a hothead. Today, though, he broke his sled to be the best.

Howard was at the IPC Swedish Winter Games. He had just faced off against Jan Edbom, who at the time was ranked the top player in the world. Edbom, Swedish, wore a yellow jersey that stretched over wide shoulders and an enormous frame.[1] He resembled an NFL linebacker and, true to his heritage, boasted Nordic alpha-wolf energy. In later years, Edbom's Twitter profile picture would show him looking into the camera, holding a glass of liquor in one hand with a cigar in his mouth. The photograph displays a harsh flash and seems to have caught Edbom by surprise, as if this is what he's always up to and the camera just happened to interrupt. Edbom enjoyed front man status on his team and would go on to become a sports commentator. When the two of them played together, he outpaced Howard decisively. Edbom's sled did not have the long railings extending forward to support prosthetics, as Howard's did.

And so Howard kept banging.

Until this point, Howard had refused to part with his prosthetics. He didn't want the outside world to see him with only his stump—but a desire to win finally outweighed that.

Joseph Edward Howard was born in Boston, Massachusetts, to Carol Anne Howard and stepfather James Carmine Violante on May 22, 1966. Carol possessed the darker skin of her Italian and Indian blood. James was only 5-foot-2, but compensated with a bushy beard. The family—with three sisters born before Howard and three brothers after—lived in the D Street projects of South Boston. Racial tension suffocated the projects, and Howard remembers his neighbors discussing the new bussing policies that transported his sisters to a primarily black school each morning. Even at his young age, he was disturbed to see black people chased out of the streets and fights break out. That's what he meant when he would tell others he grew up in a "tough area."

Howard played hockey starting at the age of four and dabbled in football and boxing. His parents woke him between 3:00 and 4:00 in the morning to get dressed and ready for practice and school, where he was a good student and a Catholic altar boy. In 1978, his brother was tragically killed in a construction site accident, and the family moved to Weymouth, Massachusetts—hoping to escape the projects environment and the reminders of their loss.

The February 22, 1980, "Miracle on Ice" Olympic victory for the United States inspired Howard. He watched in awe as Mike Eruzione (b. 1954) lifted the U.S. flag and draped it over his shoulders. Bobby Orr (b. 1948), Terry O'Reilly (b. 1951), and Rick Middleton rounded out his list of hockey heroes. But he didn't want to be them. "No hockey player wants to go out there and be someone else," he said. He wanted to be the first Joe Howard.

James told his stepson he could be just like that one day, and he invited Howard to play hockey with him and some of his friends in their thirties—who, of course, seemed like giants to young Howard. The seriousness of those older players trusting Howard on the ice planted a seed of determination in him. They taught him how to get out of corners, how to maneuver past them with skill and youthful dexterity, and how to skate backwards (a talent that, ironically, would become moot by the time Howard became a gold medalist, as sleds do not reverse). Howard was feeling confident.

Off the ice, James worked two jobs to support six children who weren't his. He labored in a warehouse for Tech HiFi, a stereo and audio equipment company still in business as of 2022. Meanwhile, Carol tended to the home with love and told Howard he could do anything—words that would be challenged only months later.

On March 20, 1982, at the age of fifteen, Howard played pinball in a bowling alley. He and his friends usually hopped a train—clinging to the rails on the side of a train car—to get home, as the tracks lay only a block behind the bowling alley. The train moved faster today, around noon. It thundered by, car after car, and flashed shadows onto Howard as he ran alongside it. He jumped, grabbed the rail, and only felt grease. He slipped off one rung, then the next, and next, until he went under the giant metal beast.

He felt nothing at first except wetness all over. He lay there until the red and blue lights of emergency vehicles swung over him. A man was holding a tourniquet to his leg—his name was John, and he owned B & D, the sandwich shop. The tourniquet likely saved Howard from bleeding to death before the EMTs arrived. John's voice faded in and out, encouraging him to stay awake. Howard blacked out for two weeks.

He died twice.

Once, he was conscious above his body, watching nurses and doctors operate over the stretcher below. Everyone was in white, save for one man in a formal grey suit.

When he woke in Massachusetts General Hospital, having been transferred from South Shore Hospital, his first thought was that his mom was going to kill him all over again. She never knew he jumped train cars like that. But she came beside him, her expression a mixture of horror and love. Then he asked who the man in the grey suit was.

Chills must have engulfed Carol's body as the room went silent. She explained that the emergency specialist had arrived at the operating room still dressed for a wedding in his formal grey suit. Howard had been deeply unconscious the entire time the man was in the room. He would have had no way of knowing.

Howard's final move was to Shriner's Burn Institute, where specialists worked to repair what they could. Doctors relocated skin from his back to his torn-up legs. All in all, Howard was under hospital care for two months.

Well-hidden amid the pain were two memorable bright spots of his stay, however: At Massachusetts General, right winger Terry O'Reilly of the NHL Boston Bruins visited Howard's bedside. O'Reilly and Howard had an affinity for the penalty box in common. Called "Bloody O'Reilly" by the press and "Taz" (for Tasmanian devil) by teammate Phil Esposito (b. 1942), O'Reilly was famous for merciless play and earned as many as 265 penalty minutes in a single season in 1979–1980.[2] Then, at Shriner's, Bobby Orr visited Howard as well. Little did they know what Howard would go on to do in the world of hockey.

Even with a loving family's support, relearning life was hard. Howard was given prosthetic equipment, and his dreams of a career in the NHL had shattered. That said, he channeled his emotions not into *Why me?* but rather *What next?* Modifications were made to the family's house to accommodate his wheelchair. He graduated from Tad Technical Institute and worked as an auto mechanic. His life carried on vestiges of normalcy, but his connection to the ice capsized.

By the time sled hockey came to his attention in 1997, fifteen years after the accident, hockey seemed to be from another lifetime. Howard was testing the ropes of adaptive skiing on Loon Mountain in New Hampshire and crossed paths with another athlete with ties to sled hockey.

Every day, he was told, from 10:00 p.m. to midnight, Devine Rink in Dorchester, Massachusetts, donated ice time to sled hockey. Howard agreed to give it a try. When he strapped into a sled for the first time—much like his future teammates—he immediately fell in love with the familiar smells and feelings. There, he met Kip St. Germaine, who already played for the U.S. team and the Boston Blades club team.

Howard allowed all that frustration, all those defiled dreams, and all that fury to meet the ice. "I liked hitting people," he said, "and being hit." He got loud and proud. In pickup games on the Boston Blades, he played both left and right wing, and he was fast and accurate. Most of all, he had an unmatchable desire to win. St. Germaine suggested that Angelo Bianco, then the U.S. head coach, come take a look at this wad of energy called Joe.

Howard was invited aboard.

The two shared a tumultuous relationship, however. Bianco acknowledged Howard's skill and his potential to lead the team but had no patience for his unbridled temper. At the second IPC World Championship game in 2000, following the devastating defeats in the Paralympic Games in Nagano, Howard hit an opposing player a little too hard and earned five minutes in the penalty box. Next misconduct call kicked him from the game. Bianco was so furious he refused to let Howard play in the next game. This resulted in more challenges for the team: Howard was the captain, and his absence threw off the others.

That loss in 2000 added to USA sled hockey's record of failure and truly made their next event at Salt Lake City seem like the team's last chance.

As the team headed into the 2002 Paralympic Games there, Howard practiced at 6:00 a.m. four times a week. As the two fastest players on the team, Sylvester Flis and Howard grew accustomed to pushing each other to the edge. They made sure to pair up at trainings. Howard grew closer with his teammates and tried to improve his captaincy so that all of them reached the next level in synchrony. He came to be known as "Momo." The nickname evolved from Calise's original moniker for Howard: "Choo-Choo," recalling the train that got him here. Then he became "Moe" in a Three Stooges nickname for his lineup next to Calise, and then "Mo-Howard," and then . . .

Momo rehearsed shot after shot, so when the time came for him to make that end-all dash for goal in the overtime shootout, he knew he wouldn't miss.

Throughout the Games, Howard's mother battled cervical cancer. He called her every night, and one day shortly afterward, he closed her front door behind him, walked across the house on his prosthetics, found her looking up and smiling at his arrival, and placed the gold medal around her neck. Tears of happiness filled their eyes. She died shortly after.

"That one was for her," he said.

But the next Paralympic gold medal he won (in Vancouver in 2010), he admits, was his.

Howard went on to coach sled hockey and has many dogs he calls kids. He met three U.S. presidents in his time as a Paralympian: Bill Clinton, George W. Bush, and Barack Obama. He shook hands with eight-time U.S. speed skating medalist Apolo Ohno (b. 1982). But he never forgot what brought him here.

After Howard's historic victory, he returned to that bowling alley. He returned to the train tracks.

He returned to the sandwich shop owned by the man who saved his life.

Howard wanted to thank him, to tell him where the rest of his life had taken him after that day.

John had passed.

Of all the journeying Howard had done since then, that man who saved him was in the one place now where Howard couldn't get.

But maybe this story can reach anywhere.

CHAPTER FIVE

Gathering the Team

To win the game is great. To play the game is greater. To love the game is greatest of all.

—BOB O'CONNOR,
FORMER USA HOCKEY COACH IN CHIEF

ON AN EARLY SPRING AFTERNOON IN 2001, RICHARD DAVID MIDDLE-
ton (b. December 4, 1953), former NHL standout and captain of the
Boston Bruins, moved through his house. He yelled for his two boys,
Jarret and Brett, to ensure they'd made it home from school. Only the
shuffle of hockey equipment on shelves in the garage responded to him.
Brett's practice was in just over an hour, and Middleton called out again
to the eleven-year-old. His twenty-one-year-old daughter, Claudine,
would watch the house while they were gone.

Middleton, now forty-seven, was twelve years retired, aged with
lean muscle and a direct, brisk speech that reflected direct, brisk
thoughts. Pickup games on Friday nights with buddies, coaching the
boys' teams, and the occasional Boston Bruins Alumni benefit matches
kept him agile. Time equipped him with the gentleness and tempera-
ment of an athlete with enough distance from the arena now to have
perspective on it.

A right winger from Toronto, Middleton could work a puck so well
they say he could "stickhandle in a phone booth." In 1976, his teammate,
future coach, and Hall of Fame goalie Gerry Cheevers (b. 1940) bestowed

**Sledge Hockey Team
2002 Paralympic Winter Games
usa*2002**

The 2002 U.S. men's sled hockey team. From left to right: Front row—Sylvester Flis, Lonnie Hannah, Josh Wirt, James Dunham, Kip St. Germaine, Chris Manns, and Pat Sapp; center row—Brian Ruhe, Dave Conklin, Manny Guerra Jr., Joe Howard, Jack Sanders, and Dan Henderson; back row—Jeff Uyeno (equipment manager), Matt Coppens, Patrick Byrne, Tom Moulton (assistant coach), Rick Middleton (head coach), and Rich DeGlopper (team leader). Not pictured are Jim Olsen (trainer) and Brent Rich (team physician). COURTESY OF THE CRAWFORD FAMILY U.S. OLYMPIC AND PARALYMPIC ARCHIVES, 2002

on him the nickname "Nifty" for his way of making the puck a comet and he the tail, hurtling together to goal. His stick had a way of lubricating the ice and infuriating the fans in opposite colors. Although he never won a Stanley Cup, Middleton's overall points (goals plus assists) of 988 (448 goals and 540 assists) are 96th best of all time, and convert to an impressive average of 0.98 points per game. His points are 73 above Bobby Orr's, elevating him to similar ranking as Hall of Famers like Ray Bourque (b. 1960) and Maurice "Rocket" Richard (1921–2000). Middleton added another 100 points (45 goals and 55 assists) in 114 playoff games. His jersey number, 16, was retired by the Bruins in 2018 and hangs in the rafters of TD Garden alongside other gods of hockey past. He won the Canada Cup in 1984, playing for Canada on a prolific scoring line with Michel Goulet (b. 1960) and Wayne Gretzky (b. 1961). After spending time as a New York Ranger from 1974 to 1976 and a Boston Bruin from 1976 to 1988, Nifty's 1,005-game career ended in part to a cranial collision with the puck that induced a concussion he never quite kicked.

Now a single father of three, Middleton awaited life's next calling—be it parenthood or something more unexpected.

That's when the phone rang.

Middleton picked up. He recognized the caller over the din of the boys, who now moved into the living room and dive-bombed the couch. Rick tried to catch the words in the phone.

On the other line was Paul Edwards (b. 1967), captain of the U.S. Disabled Ski Team. A longtime friend of Middleton's, Edwards became paralyzed from the waist down in 1993 after an accident during a Bay State Hockey League game. Five years later, Edwards represented the United States at the Paralympics in Nagano, Japan, where he placed eighth overall in the Men's Downhill run with a time of 1:12.09 in a monoski.

The niceties lapped back and forth, and then Edwards couldn't hold it in any longer. Rick caught the barbs of the conversation, the reason for the call.

Paralympic.

Sled hockey.

We need a coach.

"I heard 'Paralympics' and 'hockey' and I said yes," Middleton recalled. "I knew it was one of those things that doesn't wait for you to chew on it. Someone else would have grabbed it."

So Rick Middleton hung up the phone in his New Hampshire home in 2001 as presumptive head coach of one of the worst U.S.-representing teams in history. Less than twenty-four hours later, he found himself on a call with U.S. Sled Hockey Association President Rich DeGlopper, where DeGlopper did a lot of speaking and Middleton did a lot of listening. The United States, seeded sixth, would be competing in the upcoming 2002

Salt Lake City Paralympics only because it was the host country. The team's previous coach, Angelo Bianco, had quit. Perhaps foreseeing his dismissal, Bianco, who was supposed to show up at a training camp, simply disappeared after the dismal Nagano and 2000 World Championship performances. He sent his friend to take over for him the way one might send a proxy to a funeral and ditch town. It's up for debate whether Mike Brito was "head coach for a day" before DeGlopper gave him the boot.

In short, the prospects for success weren't looking too good.

"I had confidence I knew the game, though," said Middleton later. He wasn't daunted.

There was only one problem. "The game" meant ice hockey. Standing up.

What the hell was *sled* hockey?

Middleton approached the arena. It was just before 5:00 a.m., and condensation frosted the glass doors. He looked around, but the glaring lights overhead pushed darkness behind them, and none of the black palm trees he had seen on the drive in were visible.

It was March of 2001, and Rich DeGlopper had invited him down to Tampa, Florida, to witness this foreign version of hockey for the first time. Here, DeGlopper hoped to solidify Middleton's commitment to becoming the new national coach. But calling in this former Boston Bruin made no headlines, and no funds from the government aided the players and staff in making their way here—plane tickets, as usual, were booked on personal credit cards.

The U.S. sled hockey team didn't need their athletes on Wheaties boxes to save them from extinction; they just needed one medal. One bronze to match Middleton's hair would do. That way, they might garner enough interest and money to continue the sport on a national level. But the silence of judgmental ice that had seen this team before pressed down on Middleton. If Team USA's miserable performance did not change, many in management feared the sport was doomed.

DeGlopper greeted Middleton. His New York accent hailed another northerner, with quick consonants and an equally quick smile after each word. A face with dark, bushy eyebrows and a round nose topped his slender frame. He often wore a blue shirt and khaki pants—but not skates. DeGlopper had little experience in ice hockey as a player, acting primarily from the management side. He was preparing once again to serve as team leader on the national team.

Of everything Middleton would see and learn that day, no image impressed upon him more than watching the sled hockey players approach the rink for the very first time. The parking lot held a few cars to the right, and a long, empty street stretched ahead. A single streetlamp showered orange light onto the asphalt. Middleton watched as half a dozen men in wheelchairs rolled down the street towards the rink. That orange light struck their tires, their prosthetics, their beards. Not a single person chaperoned them as their strong hands pumped large wheels, and equipment hung on the backs of their handlebars.

Dedication is the first thought that came to Middleton. That word would remain in his head for the next ten months. Everyone filed inside.

Clattering equipment and voices echoed in the arena as Middleton stepped up to the boards. A chill rose from below.

He spread his gaze around the rink once more. The smooth, virgin ice would soon be whipped and slashed with players eager to prove themselves at the first training camp of the season. Middleton's first test as presumptive coach wouldn't be quite so visceral. One could imagine a flashback of the puck colliding with his skull returning to him, or maybe an image of Gretzky flying along his side.

He'd been told this was just like regular hockey, with a few differences.

It was time to see how many.

The shriek of Middleton's whistle pierced his ears.

Sled hockey players whacked the ice with their barbed sticks, hanging sharp turns at his order in each of the four corners and speeding ahead. With another whistle, they screeched around in the other direction.

He studied their movements in each drill. The first thing Middleton noticed about the players was their ages. He'd expected young men just breaking their twenties. Most of the players here were older, wedding rings on their fingers. Some had stumps for legs and others used tight cables to strap their legs straight in the sled. Only one player—an aggressive man with bleached blond hair and earrings in one ear—kept on his artificial leg while in the sled.

Middleton watched this one closely. The player cried out when he speared the ice, and his gaze could burn holes through metal. Each of these men, Middleton was sure, had a story behind their injury—but the temper on this one made him wonder. The player was Joseph "Momo" Howard of Weymouth, Massachusetts, and, as fate would have it, he would one day be Middleton's captain. If he could be tamed.

After a while of warm-ups, Middleton slowly skated forward, almost into the drill.

"All right, stop!" His voice hadn't carried as loud as he'd hoped. "Stop!"

The players scraped up ice as they halted.

"Now I wanna see you back it up! Backwards!"

Silence. They all looked at him with lowered brows, confused. Was he joking?

Oh shit, thought Middleton. *They don't go backwards.*

He adapted quickly and changed drills, sending the players off in different directions. DeGlopper grinned as Middleton returned to the edge of the rink. Middleton's face was red.

A few differences.

It was August of 2001 when thirty athletes with disabilities boarded flights to Buffalo, New York, to answer the open call for tryouts.

Rick Middleton's position as head coach had been made official in June of the same year by the board of the United States Sled Hockey Association. When asked if he would work alongside Jeff Jones, the director of sports at the Rehabilitation Institute of Chicago and the locally admired figurehead of the powerful RIC Blackhawks sled hockey team, his answer had been no. Jones was right there on the call.

Middleton felt that Jones, with his close ties to the RIC Blackhawks, would have a difficult time being impartial. Instead, Middleton had chosen Tom Moulton (b. 1955), board member of the New Hampshire Legends of Hockey, as his assistant coach. His close friend since 1984, Moulton was a hockey coach and player local to Middleton in New Hampshire. He had a thickset build and a mane of black hair to contrast his blue eyes. While his voice had an endearing raspiness in speech, it boomed on the ice—exactly what was needed to relay the steady, gum-chewing silent command of Middleton. "I proposed to him in the parking lot," Middleton joked, which is true. Middleton had been walking up to the post office in Hampton, New Hampshire, and Moulton had been walking out. The two stopped outside the building and Middleton popped the question. Moulton, who had been aware of Middleton's involvement but never dreamed he'd ask him to come aboard, was honored.

Over the coming weeks, the two met for breakfast and at Moulton's office to watch footage from Nagano and the world championships and study the team's abundant mistakes. Defense was staying in the offensive zone too long and was too slow. Unnecessary penalties abounded. The team seemed to chase the puck with no plan or commitment to the division of roles and positions. And the team *had* to achieve more breakaways. Odds are greater that a player will score a goal after a breakaway than that a goalie will block it. To address these issues in just over six months and with limited time allotted for training, Middleton and Moulton would need to develop a simple, graspable system to refine that unbridled talent.

The United States had not fared much better at the second IPC World Championships in Salt Lake City.[1] They came in sixth (last) place, and then-goalie Corbin Beu lamented that the U.S. team didn't so much as put a ding on the ice.[2]

Middleton and Moulton looked at each other. "I don't think we have enough time," Middleton said.[3] Moulton pressed his lips into a hard line. It would take their damnedest effort to try.

They, too, boarded planes for the tryouts in Buffalo.

The tryouts, which would span from August 3–5, were held at the Amherst Pepsi Center (now the Northtown Center). Its floors were decked out in rubber to protect the blades of the skates and sleds. The ice rink had been adapted to allow the sleds unfettered access to the ice surface from the locker room.

Hopeful athletes with physical challenges gathered at the long, red metal benches in the middle of the foyer with equipment shops and public bathrooms flanking them on either side. Expected to try out today were players from all over the country—including a large number from Jeff Jones's Chicago program. East Coasters and even a few from Texas would contest for a place on the roster as well. Many from the 1998 team, including Victor Calise, arrived to defend their current positions, and among the collection of eager athletes, amazingly, were a man in his fifties or sixties and a man with a neck brace following a serious injury. Unparalleled determination met unparalleled strife.

Paul Edwards, who had originally called Middleton about the coaching job, was among those in search of a spot.

Traveling there by van rather than plane, the Chicago players were late. By around 7:00 p.m. on the first day, the handful of athletes already present surrounded Rick Middleton, Tom Moulton, and Rich DeGlopper next to the exterior boards of the ice rink. Some sitting in their wheelchairs, some standing on their prosthetics, they listened to the housekeeping items DeGlopper listed and then began in a circle stating their names, hometowns, and target positions.

Just as the fifth athlete took in breath to speak, the door banged open. Its loud click echoed in the wide arena. Everyone paused and looked over as Sylvester "Sly" Flis entered. He wheeled a manual chair and wore a Salt Lake City Olympics baseball cap. His grey T-shirt said USA HOCKEY, and on his lap was a maroon Blackhawks jacket. He looked around at the gathered group, his unframed oval glasses hiding his dark, Polish eyebrows and olive skin.

A little flustered, the player who had been interrupted in the roundabout finished, and then the buck fell on Flis. There was silence.

"Sly Flis." He cracked a debonair smile. "U.S. citizen."

Everyone laughed and applauded.

Flis' thick Eastern European accent represented the long and difficult process of naturalizing as an American citizen. The immigrant sled hockey star had wanted to compete for the United States in Nagano in 1998 so badly that he attempted to persuade Congress itself to enact his citizenship early. They did not. At last, with help of Jeff Jones, his citizenship was ratified in time for the 2002 Paralympics. With his debut on the national team so highly anticipated and his skill on the Blackhawks talked about around tables, many tried to conceal their eagerness at seeing him live up to the hype.

Joe Howard wasn't sure if he was looking at an enemy or a partner.

Other Chicagoans filed in moment by moment until the room was nearly half full of them. Middleton, dressed in a grey Hawaiian shirt decorated with tall black palm trees, watched their arrival from the wall. Hearsay had already circulated about the jockeying for power he'd need to expect when the Chicagoans clashed with the others. Bitterness over Middleton's shutting Jeff Jones out from the national team reached deep into the psyches of the Blackhawks. Some of them felt their beloved home coach had been robbed of the job, and they had little room in their minds for newcomers when coming from the large and impressive Chicago sled hockey program. Jones himself had made his animosity towards the situation clear.

The USSHA official "Guidelines for Evaluation" tryout sheet Middleton would have received several copies of included a 7x11 table to rank each player's puck handling, play making, hockey sense, and so on.[4] He and Moulton would fill in with checkmarks one sheet per player as they observed performances. However, the guidelines also called for considering the player's "contribution to team chemistry."[5] With the current chasm between the Blackhawks and the others seemingly insurmountable, Middleton and Moulton had little choice but to overlook that criteria and seek only skill instead.

But Middleton and Moulton had agreed to make their decisions based on absolutely nothing but what they saw this weekend on the ice. Resentment would need to be shelved, by all, if they were truly here for gold.

When it was time for tryouts to begin, what hit Middleton—and more so Moulton, who was seeing this for the first time—was the locker room. While they were used to the sight of players thumping down shoulder pads and slamming lockers closed, these thirty young men filled the room with the sound of prosthetic limbs clapping off and the straps of the sled buckles jangling across their laps. The smells of old equipment, deodorant, and sweat-stained clothing were the same, but plastic feet and legs hung where skates normally would. Each sled was unique to accommodate either two legs, one leg, or no legs.

As powerful as this first glimpse into Paralympic athleticism was, Middleton and Moulton couldn't pause to reflect on it. These players weren't interested in inspiring anyone. They wanted to hit the ice and make the team—and they weren't necessarily rooting for each other.

Players zoomed into the rink in their sleds as Middleton stood on his skates. He grasped a clipboard and wore a blue sweatsuit. Moulton eyed the athletes beside him. Yellow, green, red, and blue pinnies divided the team into groups. Middleton had the athletes skating counterclockwise-to-clockwise figure eights. Tipping over is common in sled hockey, and players quickly righted themselves, but Middleton needed to see both speed and control from those he would pick. After this drill, he placed goalies in either net and had the players in constant shot rotation.

The standouts, like Sylvester Flis and Joe Howard—superstars on opposite sides of the Chicago/East Coast rift—were easy to peg. Chris Manns's leftie shot might come in handy, too. Middleton looked for his four pillars of hockey: skating, shooting, stick handling, and passing. But the particularities he may have sought in an able-bodied tryout did not always apply here. Sled hockey players exhibited slightly different shooting strategies.

A slapshot, in ice hockey, is when the player lifts his or her stick to shoulder height and swings it down, intentionally dredging up a little bit of ice before the puck and forcing the bottom of the stick to bend backwards. The stored-up energy then releases and transfers to the puck, firing it hard and fast like a slingshot, while the player follows through until the end of the stick points towards the target. Sled hockey players possess neither the height nor the two-handedness required for this famous move. Instead, most shots are made within ten feet of the net. Middleton had to watch for accuracy as well as deftness weaving through the defense with the puck at full speed.

The rainbow of pinnies surrounded Middleton as he called the athletes in for a huddle. One yellow pinnie, just a dot near the opposite goal, rushed to meet the group. He glided in closer and closer until he wobbled, flailed out an arm, and crashed into the huddle. Middleton looked up. "All right, Doyle, yeah!" Everyone laughed good-naturedly.

Mike Doyle would be a significant name by the end of the day. He was one of the two most difficult players to cut.

The first player Middleton lamented cutting was Paul Edwards—the very same man who had recruited him to this once-in-a-lifetime opportunity in the first place. Edwards was the one in the neck brace. He had showed up to the tryouts hoping to make it onto the ice despite his medical disqualification. But by the time Edwards petitioned for an exception, Middleton had identified his selections, and he insisted on standing by them even though it meant rejecting Edwards. Interestingly, an evaluation sheet still exists for Edwards, and is filled out in the hand of USA Hockey's Bob O'Connor (1935–2015). O'Connor wrote in the "General Remarks" section, mixing capital and lowercase letters liberally,

> Paul presented to Rich [DeGlopper] and Carlo [Casarno, player representative] a doctor note saying he could not skate at the tryouts because of neck injury. In my many Olympic and national select tryouts, there as [*sic*] always been contingency guidelines . . . [but] this Coach Middleton has a vision that I have faith in. He knows what he wants . . . I could see Coach Middleton['s] vision for his last roster players[:] quick, fast[,] harassable players.[6]

Even if the injury had been excused, Edwards likely would have been cut. He had the spirit, but he could not keep up with the talent currently on the ice. Although it felt like a rotten way to thank him, Middleton had to do what was best for the team, and he and Moulton agreed Edwards would not be joining them.

Doyle was the second man cut, for quite different reasons. Slower and clearly more discordant, Doyle would later acquiesce that cutting him was a fair decision. He had overcommitted, competing on the swim team as well, and was tired by the time he arrived at the hockey tryouts.

But Doyle was the only Blackhawk Middleton dismissed. Even though the Chicago loss was just one (compared to the whopping ten players cut from the old guard of Nagano), the tensions—and the disapproval from Jones—would intensify.

After the announcement had been made on the last day, August 5, Middleton recalls someone mumbling a warning to him: "Shit's gonna hit the fan now."

FINAL ROSTER

No.	Pos.	Name	Hometown
1	F	Lonnie Hannah	Mansfield, TX
2	D	Brian Ruhe	Chicago, IL
4	D	Sylvester Flis	Chicago, IL
5	F	Matt Coppens	Richton Park, IL
7	D	James Dunham	Garland, TX
12	D	Kip St. Germaine	Sagamore, MA
14	F	Patrick Byrne	Chicago, IL
15	F	Jack Sanders	Pekin, IL
19	F	Josh Wirt	Brush Valley, PA
20	F	Dave Conklin	La Crosse, WI
22	D	Dan Henderson	Chicago, IL
23	F	Joe Howard	Weymouth, MA
33	GK	Pat Sapp	Rockwell, TX
44	F	Chris Manns	Buffalo, NY
67	GK	Manuel Guerra Jr.	Minneapolis, MN

CHAPTER SIX

Sylvester Flis, #4

"Sly"

Pos.	GP	G	A	PTS	PIM	"+/–"	GWG	GTG	PPG	SHG	S	SG%
D	6	11	7	18	0	14	2	0	2	1	29	37.93

ON SEPTEMBER 12, 1997, SIX MONTHS BEFORE THE NAGANO GAMES, Senator Dick Durbin (D-IL) rose on the senate floor. He prepared to speak on behalf of Sylvester Flis, and his own bill, S. 1172: "A bill for the relief of Sylvester Flis; to the Committee on the Judiciary." Durbin was serving his first year in the Senate after almost fifteen years as a representative for Illinois' 20th congressional district. His bill would grant Flis immediate U.S. citizenship, waiving one year of the five-year waiting period required to naturalize him. Without this act of Congress, Flis would be unable to compete in Nagano.

Durbin emphasized Flis's quintessential story of the American dream. "Mr. President," said Durbin, "I rise today to offer legislation on behalf of Mr. Sylvester Flis, a permanent resident alien from Poland, now living in Chicago. . . . Like many young Eastern Europeans who grew up during the final years of Soviet domination, Sylvester, now 23 years of age, is eager to take advantage of the opportunities offered by his new found freedom."[1] He explained to the floor that Flis was born with spina bifida and had overcome this challenge to become a world-class athlete in the sport of sled hockey.

"Sylvester is more than just a good athlete who wants to compete for the United States," Durbin concluded. "He is a young man of tremendous character who has worked hard to become part of our community."[2]

Flis had moved to the United States from Poland on July 11, 1994. His original first name was Sylwester, but, much like immigrants sailing into Ellis Island in the nineteenth century did, he found his name changed to Sylvester by a distracted official typing up his documents too fast. He welcomed the nickname "Sly."

Flis's parents, Czeslaw and Lucja, wanted more for him than Polish medical professionals could give. The country's physicians, in their experience, knew little about spina bifida, and a botched surgery at Zakopane, Poland, actually made matters worse. As Flis's left leg began to weaken in midadolescence and he no longer could walk without crutches, they hoped he'd find treatment in America to stop or reverse the progression. Flis's grandmother had been born in New Haven, Connecticut, and although she had only lived in the United States for six months, her birth certificate offered a path for Flis's family to make the overseas move around 1994. Flis's uncle was older than his father and moved first, establishing for the family a support system at the ready in the States.

Durbin's bill passed the Senate that November in a unanimous vote. Unfortunately, Congress dragged its feet, distracted by the Monica Lewinsky hearings, and time ran out. The bill was dropped, and Flis did not have the opportunity to compete for the national team in Nagano.

It was one of many setbacks in life that Flis had learned to deal with. He was born on June 20, 1974, in Stalowa Wola, Poland, and shortly after, he would fumble in attempts to walk. His family farm was surrounded by dense forests and clear, cool ponds he swam in as a boy, and he loved to watch his father play soccer. He did not realize, however, that the trips he used to take with his uncle to cut lumber in the woods were becoming less frequent. His strength was withering. Flis played soccer as well, but only in the net. Running and balancing were becoming harder.

Adding to his obstacles was a damned rooster. When Flis was around seven years of age, he was walking along a fence towards a neighbor's house when a rooster jumped from the ledge and onto Flis. It flapped its wings and squawked, and Flis fell to the ground. The rooster pecked his left eye and damaged his vision. Flis has worn glasses ever since. As a sled hockey player, he doesn't use contact lenses during games, he simply whacks a blurry puck.

For the first years of his life in the United States, Flis and his family shared an apartment with his godfather on Henderson Street in Chicago. The space was tight, and one couldn't cross a room without encountering several relatives. While his parents did find American specialists in the field of medicine Flis needed, the cost of treatment overwhelmed them. They still had to afford a living space of their own eventually. With an attitude of genuine selflessness, Flis told them it was okay; he would get used to the wheelchair. They purchased one for him at Walgreens for $300. Flis's reliance on crutches—hauling the weight of his body with his legs dangling beneath him—and his need to pump the wheels of his new chair hardened the muscles of his shoulders, triceps, and back, all of which would soon be called upon.

The Flis family eventually moved to their own small house. One day, Flis was hosing down his father's car in the driveway, suds and towels on the ground. A woman cruised her car up to the mailbox and stopped. She rolled down her window, saying something in English that Flis could not yet understand. The woman wrote it down on a note, gave it to him, and drove away. He looked at the note in his hand and lowered his brow.

Later, Flis's cousin translated it. The woman worked at the Young Men's Christian Association (YMCA) and wanted Flis to join her new dancing program for people with disabilities. Here began Flis's exploration of adaptive athletics in the States. He met a man named John in the program who taught him English on the side and connected him with the Rehabilitation Institute of Chicago. While Flis didn't mind dancing, his competitive edge, inherited from his father's passion for soccer, yearned for "a ball, a puck, or somebody to chase." While playing softball and table tennis, and even water skiing, he crossed paths with a sled hockey player on the Chicago Parks District club team. Flis was intrigued and visited the McFetridge Sports Center to give it a try.

"When I got on the ice [the] first time," said Flis, "I was super fast." He paused and smiled at me as if remembering just how good it was to be that guy. In fact, he was so fast, and so good, that the club team soon thereafter insisted he find a league at his skill level or start one himself so that the other players wouldn't be discouraged.

Once he'd found sled hockey, he said, "It felt like this is it. It felt like I found it." Here, during our interview, he looked off into a corner of the room. His expression was full of wonder. "I lost this wheelchair. I'm no longer in a wheelchair."

Now with a need to advance his game, Flis sought reinforcements. He recruited golfer and fellow RIC member Patrick Byrne to sled hockey. Garbling Irish and Polish accents together (the two often pitched their ears closer to each other in conversation), they worked to compile a team to present to the athletic director, Jeff Jones, and eventually to the NHL Chicago Blackhawks.

Flis and Byrne generated enough interest that the RIC Blackhawks, established in 1999, became an unmatchable force in the world of sled hockey. Theirs was the only club team to travel overseas to compete, including in the Malmö Open in Sweden, and the RIC both raised and recruited some of the most talented hockey players in the country. Within only one month, Flis was invited to try out for the national team.

At the time, the national team was coached by Angelo Bianco—the same coach from Team USA in Nagano. While Bianco proved to be a controversial coach, Flis remembers how he taught the players to keep their heads up and be aware of the arena before them. Bianco would hold his hand in the air with a varying number of fingers raised. The players were then required to skate towards him and shout out the number. Flis, even with his fuzzy vision, took this lesson to heart.

Around this time, Flis received his renowned #4 jersey. But he didn't realize the number belonged to the legendary Bobby Orr. The jersey was literally thrown at his face from a pile in a locker room. He stretched it over his body and thought nothing of it. Not having grown up with hockey, Flis never knew the idols (or the rules) of the sport before coming to the RIC. Today, however, he reflects on how Orr and he would one day share the unique position of being famously offensive defensemen. In other words, much like Orr, Flis decided that his speed was better suited on defense and to be used opportunistically for offensive rushes. This flew in the face of the historical practice of loading up the defense ranks with the biggest of players, and his new colleagues at the net often wondered why he was leaving his glamorous position as a forward. Little did they know the decision would become an enormous part of his legacy.

To Flis's shock, Bianco moved not to take Flis to the 2000 IPC World Championships in Salt Lake City. Bianco claimed this was because Flis was still not officially a U.S. citizen, even though the World Championships did not demand this. It is possible Bianco just had another candidate he preferred. This denial, however, only proved to make Flis's thirst for competition on the world stage that much more desperate. So when his citizenship still had not cleared the red tape by 2001, just a few months ahead of the 2002 Paralympic tryouts, Flis slammed a letter on the desk of Jeff Jones. The letter was from the Canadian head coach. It told Flis he would be welcome to play for Canada, which would grant him citizenship in a flash. Jones responded to Flis's leverage, called in a few favors, and moved Flis's citizenship case along. Within two months, he naturalized.

Flis blazed his way onto the 2002 Paralympic team. He worked well with fellow Blackhawk Brian "The Ruhester" Ruhe, #2, who had also made the team.[3] The two were intellectual partners on the ice, reading each other with ease and setting up plays as if one organism. Eventually, they needed to incorporate Bostoner Joe Howard into this ecosystem if they were truly to create an unstoppable team.

It is fair to say that in all likelihood, the 2002 gold medal would not have been won without Sylvester Flis. He holds the Guinness World Record for most goals (11) and most points (18) in one Paralympics. He was responsible for two game-winning goals in Salt Lake City. He's met two U.S. and two Polish presidents. He speaks three languages, excels in chess, and is a budding musician. As of 2022, he is both player and head coach on Team Poland for national competition, and although he is almost fifty, athletes in their twenties still have a hard time keeping up with him in the rink.

Flis is also the only sled hockey player to have his own NHL trading card. After Flis won the gold medal, team trainer Jeff Uyeno, an avid card collector, recommended Flis to Brian H. Price (b. 1947), founder of the card company Be A Player Trading Cards. Weeks later, Flis found himself at the United Center in Chicago skating around the lens of a professional photographer. He hand-signed tiny silver stickers for his card, which

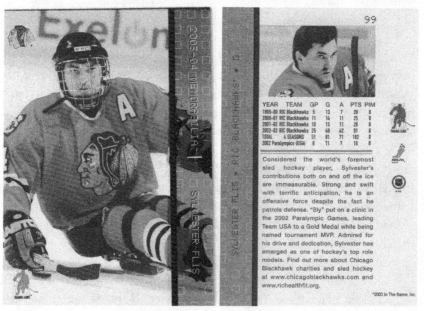

Sylvester Flis trading card, front (left) and back (right). COURTESY OF THE AUTHOR

would have been part of a "signature series" along with NHL players if the players had followed through. The card was released to the public in 2003.

I purchased Flis's card before our interview. I held it up to the Zoom camera.

He smiled a *Now where did you find that?* kind of smile.

I treasured it, and thought to myself, *Fly like Sly*—the man who would shake the U.S. Senate just to play the game that made him feel whole.

CHAPTER SEVEN

Training Champions

We know that hockey is where we live, where we can best meet and overcome pain and wrong and death. Life is just a place where we spend time between games.

—FRED SHERO, NHL

Hi Guys,

I'm sorry to have to send you this e-mail under such tragic circumstances.

What has happened today in America is inexplicable and unforgivable. In light of the magnitude of these events, along with the airports and borders being closed, our team will not be participating in the tournament in Canada.

Rich and I have been working on securing icetime [sic] for the weekend of Oct. 5–7. We recently were told that Lake Placid couldn't give us icetime [sic] on that weekend, so we're looking at either Buffalo or Boston. I should have confirmation by next week on which location the camp will be held, and will pass it on ASAP.

Again, I can't tell you how sorry I am, for obvious reasons. Keep skating, and working as hard as you have been, and I'll be in touch. If you feel a need to get in touch with me, you can reach me on my cell.

Coach[1]

Hours before, the World Trade Center had crumbled to the ground. It took with it 2,763 lives and the security of a nation.

Team USA shared the devastation and shock of its countrymen, and preparations for the 2002 Paralympics, less than six months away, froze.

While no comparison to the losses incurred on September 11, 2001, missing out on the tournament in Montreal—the Tri-Nations Cup, which would have included Canada, Japan, and Great Britain—meant the U.S. sled hockey team would have no opportunity to play an international opponent before the Paralympics. The forces working against them only seemed to strengthen.

Weeks before, on August 8, 2001, the wrath that Middleton had been warned about in response to his cutting Mike Doyle materialized as well. Jeff Jones sent an email out to five of the players, carbon copied to Doyle, criticizing the decision. The subject of the email was "The envelope please."

> Well gentlemen, if you remember I had asked you all to predict the U.S. Team and seal your list [in an envelope?] until after camp. If you did as I did and actually wrote down a list of 15 or if you had just thought it out in your head, I can guarantee two things. 1) each of your names were on your list 2) Mike Doyle was also on your list. . . . How could Middleton actually pick Chris Mann [sic] and Josh [Wirt] over Mike?[2]

In the email, Jones went on to say, "Buffalo was a disaster. You all know it," and, "It is time [for] you guys to wake up and begin to see Middleton for what he is." After stating his case and disparaging the way Middleton had conducted the drills at the Buffalo tryouts, Jones announced that he would be submitting a petition to executives at Wheelchair Sports USA demanding (a) that Mike Doyle be added to the team; (b) that Rick Middleton not be confirmed as head coach, on the basis of negligence and because he was allegedly selected outside of United States Olympic Committee policy; and (c) that Rich DeGlopper not be confirmed as team leader, also under the claim that DeGlopper neglected standard procedure. Jones's email declared that Sly Flis would be reaching out to the players personally to ask for their support.[3]

On one hand, the influence Jones attempted to exercise is alarming. His criticism of Middleton's competence with sled hockey is difficult to justify against the testimony DeGlopper gives that Jones himself coached from the bench and almost never put on skates. It is interesting to note, however, that Jones's aggression seems to be deployed primarily on behalf of Doyle. The motivation of the email could be akin to the motivation of a protective mother whose child had been benched. No one can deny he opposed the hiring of Middleton, and strangely, he had had a short-lived stint holding the title "alternative coach" (the meaning of this position is still unclear) on the 2002 team before Middleton objected. But Jones's list of demands curiously did not include replacing Middleton with himself.

Middleton was aware of the scheming. He'd gotten a look at the message after people talked, and sent an email of his own out to the players, reassuring them that he did not see Jones as a threat. "The fact is, I don't believe him for a minute," wrote Middleton.[4] He then told the players he had emailed Jeff Jones directly, offering to allow the players themselves to decide via a vote who should be head coach. DeGlopper promptly kiboshed this idea, which Jones took as Middleton chickening out.[5]

While Jones was not to find a permanent position on the team, one of his allies from the RIC would. Jeff Uyeno (b. 1962), a Hawaiian descendant, served as the equipment manager, and, to some, his placement on the team symbolized representation from the RIC. Uyeno brought helpful experience to the team, however, and had come from a position with the equipment staff at the NHL Blackhawks, aiding the professionals. In 2014, he would officially be named the NHL Blackhawks' equipment assistant. Uyeno was instrumental in the development of the RIC sled hockey program, unlocking the rink for them at 11:00 p.m. and letting them skate through the early hours of the morning. Back when sled hockey sticks were still made entirely of wood, Uyeno's colleagues would run onto the ice and scavenge pieces of carbon from broken sticks when the NHL Blackhawks practiced their slapshots. Uyeno would then collect them and use the scraps to create carbon-wood hybrid sticks, which were lighter and facilitated greater agility, for the RIC sled hockey team.

When it came to criticism, Uyeno knew precisely what the players could take—and what they couldn't. To the Chicagoans, Uyeno was a competent drillmaster and something of a mentor. He often said of self-mastery, "If you don't do it on the ice, you're not going to do it out there [in the real world]."

Middleton and Moulton were wary of Uyeno, given his association with Jones. They were concerned that Uyeno might be inclined to favor the Chicago players. In the end, Uyeno, like so many other volunteers, gave his best but felt caught between the frustrations of either side. In fact, the stressful position he was in may have contributed to a cardiac episode he would suffer only weeks after this was all through. But he'd pressed on in his role until the end.

The horrifying attacks of 9/11 no doubt stalled the meddling and redirected attentions from both sides. For weeks, everyone still looked twice as planes rumbled overhead.

With the Canadian tournament canceled, the next camp indeed ended up being again in Buffalo from October 5–7, 2001. Thousands of Americans were still scared to fly.

And yet, only weeks after the plane hijackings in September, every single player boarded flights and arrived at the training camp. Politics faded to the background, and they looked at each other with new, solemn solidarity in their eyes. This was their true first test of courage and patriotism.

On the first day of camp, Middleton's drills continued the patterns from tryouts. But conversations off the ice were more hushed. They asked each other how their airport experiences were. Some described the disturbing sight of armed soldiers and air marshals patrolling the terminals.

As the day wore on, DeGlopper gathered the team on the ice for a group photo. The staff made an effort to foster the beginnings of kinship—and players tried nicknames on for size. Middleton called a huddle and attempted to reframe the unfortunate loss of the Canadian tournament. He told the players that it could be a blessing in disguise. After all, if international teams did not have the chance to see their new lineup before the Games, Team USA would have an element of surprise. He ended his speech by saying—heavy with the fresh emotion from the attacks—"I know how important this is to you." The surrounding players, silent, looked up at him through their helmets. "And I'm right there with you. I'd love to hear the USA chant"—the serious expressions of the players turned to smiles—"and put the gold medal around your neck to the national anthem."

Now, every player—Blackhawk, East Coaster, and Texan—impromptu rattled both of their sticks against the ice. The rising thunder echoed in the rink.

That music, that noise, that pounding, said what their words could not, released the anguish the tears no longer would, and warned the world that America was on its way back.

Team USA met for six more training camp weekends: Boston from October 25–29, 2001; Salt Lake City from November 11–12, 2001 (Veterans Day weekend); Dallas from December 7–9, 2001; Blaine, Minnesota, from January 11–14, 2002; Chicago from January 24–27, 2002; and Dallas again from February 14–16, 2002.

Boston saw more of the same and the accumulation of repeated tactics. These "suicide practices," as some called them, stretched for hours. Drills included racing to the red line, blue line, or goal and back and then stopping. "That's really what hockey is," defenseman James Dunham, #7, said when recalling the practices. "Go as fast as you can until you stop, and then go as fast as you can and stop again." The repetition and simplicity of Middleton's strategies were beginning to take root.

Long gone was the Middleton who shouted for the sled hockey players to back up when they ergonomically couldn't. Middleton was now entering a groove, just as the players were.

But one player hadn't turned Middleton's rookie mistake into a running joke.

Sylvester Flis had heard about that "skate backwards" incident, laughed off by many, yet he thought about Middleton's words for days. In private moments on the ice when no one was looking, Flis actually tried

TIMING DRILL #1 & 2

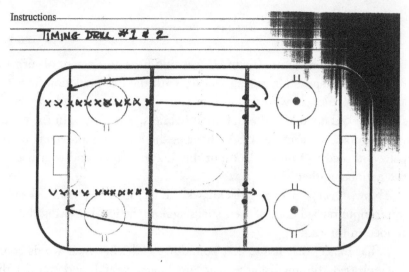

Objective____ #1 - SPRINT FROM ONE BLUELINE TO THE OTHER W/O PUCKS

#2 -   "   "   "   "   "   "   "   WITH PUCKS

Equipment Needed_____ #

Drill blueprints in the handwriting of Rick Middleton. A second version of this chart called "Timing Drill #3 and #4" exists, the only difference being players go as far as the face-off dots rather than the blue lines. COURTESY OF RICK MIDDLETON AND RICH DEGLOPPER

GAME #4

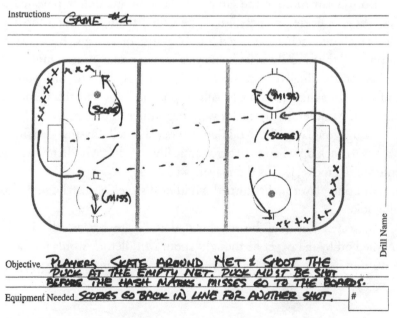

Objective____ PLAYERS SKATE AROUND NET & SHOOT THE PUCK AT THE EMPTY NET. PUCK MUST BE SHOT BEFORE THE HASH MARKS. MISSES GO TO THE BOARDS.

Equipment Needed____ SCORES GO BACK IN LINE FOR ANOTHER SHOT. #

Drill Name

Game drills and goalie drills were practiced as well. COURTESY OF RICK MIDDLETON AND RICH DEGLOPPER to do it. He tried to skate backwards. After a struggle, Flis managed to deftly skate backwards just a few inches. He would incorporate it into his offensive maneuvers by the net later on.

In his coaching, Middleton forwent staples of standard ice hockey like "always keep your eyes on the puck," which was not possible for sled hockey players, who carry the puck to their left or right rather than in front of them. He instead adapted his style to the specialization of sled hockey without losing the know-how of the NHL.

The primary offensive strategy Middleton implemented was referred to as the "dump and run." He instructed the players to fire the puck deep into enemy territory, all the way to the boards behind the net. Then, he said, send two guys as fast as you can to get it. By the time the opposition's defense reach the puck, offensive wingers are already on top of them, and the defense panics. They'll make a bad pass, get a bad bounce, or just lose the puck. When this happens, the wingers are well-positioned to catch the orphaned puck, feed it to the center, and seal the deal.

It must be noted that the "dump and run" tactic required checking in order to work. Aggressive physical play would *have* to be deployed to overwhelm the defense. Joe Howard had been kicked out of the Nagano *and* the 2000 World Championship games for overenthusiastic hitting. The RIC made checking a key component of Blackhawk training. Raw talent certainly existed on either side of the team—but it would need to be channeled.

Middleton encouraged more forechecking, using a sort of *I* formation to reduce the number of breakaways.[6] As an offensive defenseman, Flis would be a secret weapon for the team.

The November camp in Utah provided the unique opportunity for the team to preview what it would be like to be in Salt Lake City for the actual games in March. Already, preparations were underway. Team USA practiced in a beautifully renovated multimillion-dollar facility, the E Center. Moulton recalls watching workers chip away ice in a neighboring rink, replacing its layers with ionized ice instead, to ensure smoothness and clarity (such as of the logo beneath). Uyeno, the ardent hockey card collector, recalls asking Middleton to sign a card—Middleton obliged, a gesture of truce among the rivalries.

On the final day of this November camp, Veterans Day, Middleton left Moulton in charge. The head coach was needed by his family back home, and his absence provided an opening for Moulton to forge his own connection with the players and share his own wisdom. "When you're on the ice," he said, "you don't have twelve players to a team, you have thirteen. The boards can act like another player." He, like Middleton in the "dump and run" tactic, encouraged making use of the rebounding walls of the rink and harnessing what the arena had to offer naturally. Chris Manns, #44, later would argue that an enthusiastic home audience makes for a pretty powerful fourteenth player.

But when Moulton skated onto the ice that day, enthusiasm was not what he saw. *What the f— is going on here?* he thought to himself. The players were so slow they may as well have been yawning. It was clear to Moulton they were phoning it in and slacking off in the absence of the head coach. Anger built in Moulton. He reminded himself that he was sacrificing time with his family and his career to be here as well, and this excuse for a U.S. team before him looked like they couldn't care less. Around ten minutes into the practice, he called a huddle.

At center ice, Moulton reamed them out. "If you don't get your act together, if you're done here, I'll blow the whistle and you can all go home now," he said. "I don't give a shit." The booming voice for which he was partially chosen reverberated in the arena. "I don't know what you're here for. I'm here for gold."

He stormed off, leaving the team there in the huddle.

The players inched closer together and talked. As they transitioned into the next drill, Moulton immediately saw improvement. The team was alive again. At the end of the day, at least three players approached Moulton and conceded their attitudes had needed such a wake-up call.

When the team went to Dallas the following month, both coaches agreed they were moving in the right direction. Lonnie Hannah, #1, who lived in the area, invited everyone to his house for a Texas barbecue. That family feeling no drill could create was beginning to stick. However, Flis and the other Chicagoans remained reserved.

Middleton and Moulton reviewed VHS tapes of the Japanese games in their hotel room. The holiday break in December only heightened anticipation for the significant new year ahead. By the time Team USA went to its first 2002 training camp in Minnesota in January, the two coaches could tell the drills were paying off—their athletes played with more focus, and the "simple system" of lineups and role division, plus the "dump and run" Middleton sought to implement, took shape. "If you have to think about a play," said Middleton, "you're already behind the play." The team no longer hesitated.

That Minnesota camp took place in Blaine, a suburb north of the Twin Cities. The team's accommodations this time lacked homestyle barbecues. Instead, the players lodged in an army base, which looked the part with cold concrete walls and bunk beds. At the rink, Team USA was intrigued to notice a women's club playing hockey. Moulton remembers stopping and watching them. He and several of the players were touched with solidarity. Women shared with people with disabilities the desire to play at full caliber and to break the barriers currently in place which favored able-bodied men. Hockey is for everyone.

The penultimate training camp, in Chicago, rekindled tensions that may have been forgotten in the blur and exhaustion of the other weekends. Team USA's practices here were late at night. Jeff Jones arrived, looming over the rink silently and judgmentally, while the camps transpired. On their home turf, the Chicago players seemed to don an air of superiority. Such heavy energy stalled Middleton's efforts to reduce the friction and arrive in Salt Lake City with a fully unified team. He avoided Jones, however, and the sentiment was returned. The two did not collide.

The Blackhawks, with funding from the RIC, snuck in an extra "training camp" of sorts that was not on the schedule. Although the entire team was welcome, the East Coasters declined to join the Chicagoans at the Malmö Open in Sweden that February of 2002. It was a chance for a little outside competition, but small enough in scale that not all their secrets would be revealed. In fact, for this reason, it was probably for the best that the entire team did not compete together. The Chicagoans checked into their tiny Swedish hotel late at night only to find that the inn had no elevator and no rooms on the first floor. No alternative lodging would be open at this hour. The players looked at one another, then at Jeff Uyeno.

Uyeno carried them up the stairs on his back, one by one.

Finally, the *entire* team returned to Dallas for one final weekend of brutal training. Their execution was sharp, their shots clean, the system tight.

Frustrated, eager, and alive, Joe Howard barreled off the ice in his sled at the end of practice. Moulton was there before him.

"I'm ready." Howard's words were sheer anger. "I'm done practicing. I wanna play. I wanna go." *Let me at 'em.*

Moulton smiled. Middleton did, too.

Finally. It was time.

CHAPTER EIGHT

Patrick Byrne, #14

Pos.	GP	G	A	PTS	PIM	"+/–"	GWG	GTG	PPG	SHG	S	SG%
F	2	0	1	1	2	0	0	0	0	0	3	0.00

PATRICK JOHN BYRNE TUGGED DOWN THE TAP AND DARK BROWN GUINness streamed into the glass. He held the pint at an angle, ensuring the liquid hit at the perfect spot to create a thick white foam that wobbled at the top. Patrons laughed and hollered around him. He moved into the throng with drinks at the ready.

He was only fourteen. The year was 1979.

Andrew "Andy" Byrne, his father, had taught him to pull beer before his tenth birthday and had assigned him to clear off tables during the evening rush at the family pub, Andy's, in County Offaly, Ireland. They had purchased the establishment in 1970 when it was called Sullivan's, renamed it, and leveled the old bar and replaced it with a new one. They installed long couches at the walls leading to a lounge area. Darts thudded into dart boards and smoke wreathed the air above card tables.

In the same county stood the Tullamore Dew Distillery, its nineteenth-century grey stone and black shingles overlooking a canal and painting an idyllic picture of the Emerald Isle. It produced a best-selling whiskey, second only to Jameson, and was a staple at Andy's, along with traditional Irish music that specialized in foot-thumping rebel songs like "Kevin Barry" and "The Ballad of James Larken." The band was only supposed to play until 11:00 p.m. when Andy's closed, but while Byrne's father attempted to shoo out guests, his mother, Frances, would be on the stage enticing the band to play on to keep patrons buying.

Young Byrne traded full glasses for empty ones that night in 1979, trying to keep the tables clean, when he looked up at the sound of angry voices. A regular—an old man with a peg leg—sat in a chair and rested the wooden appendage straight out into the aisle. Weekends were always busy—even Sundays—but Byrne had never seen a night as crowded as this, with nearly 120 customers packing around tables. A younger man trying to squeeze through found himself blockaded by the peg leg.

"Move your leg, old man!" His Irish brogue was slurred.

"I can't!" the old man scoffed, looking up indignantly at his offender.

A jumble of curses was exchanged, and then—

Thwack!

The younger man kicked the peg leg. It dislodged from its socket and soared across the room. Byrne gasped as dozens of chairs screeched backwards and patrons leapt to their feet. The old man's friends lunged at the younger man's, and a two-sided bar fight quaked the building.

One could say that was Parick Byrne's first real interaction with disability. He had no interest in more.

Although he was born in Chicago on April 11, 1965, Byrne moved back to his parents' homeland in 1970. He was one of eight children, and one of the six who enjoyed dual citizenship with both the United States and Ireland. When asked if he could speak Gaelic, Byrne leaned in with a half-smile and a mischievous twinkle in his blue eyes and said, "Only the bad words." He resisted learning it in school, feeling, after all, more American than his full-Irish siblings.

The Byrne family genealogy originated in County Wexford and carried down a line of strong Roman Catholics. Capuchin priest Fr. Alessio Parente (1933–2000), the assistant of Padre Pio (also known as St. Pius of Pietrelcina; born Francesco Forgione, 1887–1968), was a friend of Byrne's mother. Parente cared for Padre Pio at his residency in San Giovanni during the final years of the saint's life. Pio, by then infirm, was said to have shivered and murmured at night, as if in conversation with angels, and slept no more than ten minutes at a time.[1] An exhausted Parente moved to Dublin in June of 1968 to learn English and recharge his strength, but he brought with him a devotion to Pio that spread throughout Ireland.[2] Byrne remembers his mother welcoming Parente— his black hair and beard well-trimmed, his glasses kindly, as were his blue eyes and large nose—into their home. Lovingly held in the priest's hands were the dark garments and white rope belt of Padre Pio. Byrne touched it in wonder.

It's said that no matter where you are in Ireland—even right in the heart of the island, like County Offaly—you are never more than an hour away from the ocean. The same could not be said for the frozen lakes and country ponds necessary to learn ice hockey. The sport was nonexistent in Byrne's childhood. He instead played soccer, hunted rabbits, and could bike for miles without huffing. His favorite thing to do, however, was tinker with the tractors on his uncles' farms. When not working at the pub, he earned a little money helping his uncles with chores after school. Cows needed milking twice a day and sheds needed cleaning. His maternal uncles kept pigs and sheep as well, and once a year Byrne joined them in the circus-like activity of sheep dipping. This event required corralling the sheep into a pen and forcing them into a tub of chemically treated water to prevent insects and fungus from growing in their wool that year. Byrne's job was to hold the sheep down in the bath as they bucked and splashed. Some would bolt away and jump the fence. It was always a day of laughter and frustration.

The sheep's wool would be sent to merchants and woven into sweaters and hats. Every one of his uncles' farms seemed to have that same messy clump of a woolen rug on the bedroom floor that looked more like roadkill. It made Byrne smile.

His love of farm machinery encouraged him to pursue a technical education at Mountmellick in neighboring County Laois. But by 1984, Byrne realized the same grim reality his parents had before they moved to America and gave birth to him: there was no work to be found. Byrne felt his best chance at a steady income would be to follow his parents' footsteps and move to America.

He landed in New York that year, full of energy and optimism that quickly frosted over. Ironically, the day was March 17, and probably the coldest St. Patrick's Day the United States had experienced in a decade. Byrne made his way west to Chicago, the city that seemed to juggle Byrneses across the Atlantic Ocean and back. There, he applied his passion for machinery and worked construction.

In early November of 1992, Byrne sat high above the ground in a monstruous 4300 Link Belt excavator. Its giant crimson arm extended ahead of him, ready to claw into the hard earth. He was waiting for a truck to arrive on the job site, and a woman caught his eye from across the street. She rolled along the side of the road in a wheelchair. A thought crossed his mind: *If I'm ever in that situation, I'd rather be dead.*

On November 17, 1992, he almost was.

Byrne's team labored late into the day installing a water main into a four-lane highway, two lanes on either side of the yellow line. It was damp and cold. Flurries swirled down from the grey skies, and more than once Byrne poked his head into his boss's truck and asked if they were going to start cleaning up for the day. Finally, his boss gave the okay. As the construction had closed the outermost two lanes, Byrne searched for his flagmen to control traffic while the other employees cleared out their equipment. They were nowhere to be found. Byrne entered his 960 end loader, drove up to the street, parked it, and stepped into the road with his own stop sign in hand. The first car stopped. But the second swerved around instead, just as Byrne was walking back. He jumped when he saw headlights coming at him at high speed. The car skidded as the driver attempted to brake. All Byrne heard was squealing tires as the vehicle crushed him against the machine he'd just parked.

Pain beyond all understanding swallowed his senses. A stranger ran up to him, trying to grab him by the shoulders. Byrne gagged out a request for the person to kill him. And in that moment, new pairs of hands gripped his shoulders. Strength and almost ferocity braced him. The stranger transformed in appearance to an old man—grey beard puffing out at his chin, brown eyes, and arched black eyebrows. "Irish," said the man, "everything is gonna be all right."

Byrne put his hands behind his head and looked up at the sky. *If this is the way I'm supposed to go*, he thought, *take me right now.*

The pain evaporated at the final word.

And the man was gone.

EMTs arrived and loaded Byrne into the ambulance. They put his leg—*was it still attached?*—onto the stretcher and slammed the doors. Inside, the siren wailed and the EMTs asked Byrne the same questions over and over again. Name, age, name, age. Byrne grew annoyed. He still felt no pain, only a grinding thirst now. His requests for water were denied. Finally Byrne snapped and said, "Look, pull over and I'll *buy* us a drink."

Advocate Lutheran General Hospital immediately took him into surgery—but not before Byrne's brother Richard, who had just arrived, ran alongside his gurney. Byrne remembered that old man holding him by the shoulders and his promise that he'd be all right. He told Richard not to call his parents and worry them; all the while, doctors warned Richard that his brother wasn't going to make it.

Byrne slipped into a coma shortly after.

Colors, shapes, and memories flashed in his mind. He saw his childhood. He saw rabbits hopping away from his missed shot. He saw a crowded Catholic Church and his uncle, Fr. Paddy Byrne (b. 1936), accidentally knocking over a chalice of blood red wine. His brother Joseph ran across the altar to get a new jug. He saw the garments Fr. Parente had brought to his house.

He saw the old man's face again and realized who it was standing in the snow and holding him against a semi-truck: Padre Pio.

Byrne awoke twenty-one days later. He'd bled out and somehow recovered.

His mother, Frances, was sitting at his bedside when he blinked his eyes awake. She whispered the rosary over him, and he smiles as he recalls never learning more Catholic prayers than right there in a Lutheran hospital. When he had the energy to speak, he asked her if everyone was all right, and why there was a funeral at St. Mary's Catholic Church, his uncle's parish. Confused, Frances asked him to elaborate.

"Uncle Paddy spilled the wine," he said.

Later, Frances called home to Ireland and learned that Fr. Paddy had said a powerful Mass for Byrne's recovery. It seemed the entire town had attended. Frances asked her son Joseph if anything unusual had happened at the Mass.

"Not really," Joseph said. "Well, Uncle Paddy spilled the wine."

Now that Byrne's life was secured, though, he had to face the reality under his bedsheet. His pelvis was broken in four places. One of his legs was gone. His longtime girlfriend was gone as well—she had left him while he was in the coma, saying she could not handle the life he was heading into.

But the hardest thing he ever had to do, he says, was move for the first time from that bed into the simple manual wheelchair resting beside it. No, not because of the pain—rather, because every time he looked at it, he was transported back to the inside of that excavator machine, watching that woman roll, alone, on the side of the road.

If I'm ever in that situation, I'd rather be dead.

Shame seared him. He looked again at the plain wheelchair waiting for him.

After seven months, Byrne transitioned from the intensive care of the hospital to the Rehabilitation Institute of Chicago to continue his therapy. He took an elevator to the twelfth-floor office. Without hesitation, he hobbled to the front desk on his crutches and said, "My name is Patrick Byrne and I'm here to start my therapy."

The receptionist looked up. "Okay, take a seat."

Byrne's brow pulled together. He was confused why they were not taking him right away, why they were not treating it like the emergency it still was in his head. "Oh, you don't understand," he said. "I'm Patrick Byrne and I was sent here."

Now the receptionist almost had to scoff. "I understand completely. Sit down."

Shaken with annoyance, Byrne stumped over to the waiting area and sat. Tears were in his eyes.

That's when he swept his gaze around the room and saw the others waiting with him, all with bodies twisted and torn. The woman seated across from him was smiling the widest, most compassionate smile his way. He swallowed and concealed a start: The woman had no arms or legs.

"It was the first time I had realized what I had," said Byrne. "Not what I had lost. You think you have it bad up until you see someone else."

As I typed quickly to transcribe his words, looking down at the keyboard, a cynical smile touched my lips. I paused the conversation, respectfully, to turn the tables on him and ask how *he* felt being used as an "at least I'm not that guy" comparison for able-bodied people to make, the way he was comparing his lot to this woman with no arms or legs.

Byrne paused and leaned in again, turning his head and showing me just one of his mischievous eyes, as if letting me know he was aware I'm a rotten old troublemaker, but sort of looking like he liked that about me, too.

"If you asked me that question a few years ago," he replied at last, "you'd have a lot of Patrick coming down on you." Now, he says, he tries to have a connection with people like that instead of bemoaning them.

Byrne married Kathy McNaughton in 1996. Like many of his future teammates, and with her support, he dabbled in handicapped sports through the RIC, beginning with basketball. His father encouraged him into golf as well, where he excelled. At a golf camp, Byrne crossed paths with Sylvester Flis, the Polish-born sled hockey dynamo who would one day be a star player alongside him at the Paralympics. Flis was not signed up to play. The two got along, despite having to repeat almost every sentence twice to understand each other's accents. Byrne struck a deal with him: If Flis agreed to golf, Byrne would try sled hockey.

Flis made good on his end of the bargain.

When Byrne first eased onto the ice, a twelve-year-old girl showed him how it's really done.

Erica Mitchell, disabled from birth, had been playing sled hockey since she was nine. She recalled that day in 1997 when Byrne wobbled into a sled for the first time. "My coach told me to treat him like everyone else," she said, "so he was on the ice, so I hit him."[3]

That hit from a little girl jolted something in Byrne. And he began to laugh.

Sled hockey allowed him to hurt again. That felt good.

Flis and Byrne initially played with the Chicago Blizzard sled hockey club, sponsored by the Chicago Park District. Byrne, who was used to being booted from almost every basketball game on physicality fouls, enjoyed not hearing the whistle chirp every time he whacked someone on the ice. Most hitting was perfectly legal here: "My kind of sport!"

That's when, in 1998, Byrne approached Jeff Jones, the director of the sports program at the RIC, about starting a team. While Jones liked the idea, he had no response to the issue of funding. If this were to happen, he and Byrne would need to source it elsewhere. Byrne suggested a meeting with the NHL Chicago Blackhawks owner, William Wadsworth Wirtz (1929–2007), also known as "Bill" or "Dollar Bill."

The Blackhawks owner exuded capitalism both in his style and through the media's criticism of him. Usually wearing a full business suit and tie, he boasted a stocky build and thick neck, and the skin on his face looked rough even when clean-shaven. In fact, ESPN's Page 2 (a now-discontinued section of the network's website) listed Wirtz as the third greediest owner of a sports franchise, due largely to his refusal to allow local networks to broadcast Blackhawks games in what many believed was an effort to increase the sale of his highly priced tickets.[4]

Wirtz accepted the request for a meeting. Byrne sat in the office across the desk from him. Blackhawks memorabilia hung from every shelf. He explained the sport of sled hockey to Wirtz, unconfident about where this conversation would lead.

Wirtz finally cut in. "What can I help you with?"

Byrne edged around the ask. "Well, we would need equipment, and jerseys . . ."

Wirtz spoke briskly again. "I'll ask you one more time." He looked Byrne in the eye. "What exactly do you need?"

"I need money," Byrne finally stated.

There was silence. Wirtz opened his drawer and pulled something from it. Right in front of Byrne, he scrawled out a check for $25,000.

With those funds, the RIC established the RIC Blackhawks. Jones stepped into the coaching position, and players were attracted to his involvement and dedication. He made an effort to know them each on a deep and personal level. "[Jones] could tell you how many times each individual player scored in their career. He knew their families. He knew their stories," Byrne recalled.

Byrne improved himself on the ice by making use of his ambidextrous shooting ability. He checked hard—with such fierceness that he jokingly stakes claim of the penalty-minute record. In 2000, Byrne tried out for the first time for the national team, which was preparing for the second IPC World Championship games in Salt Lake City. At the time, the national team was still coached by Angelo Bianco. While Byrne was skating on the ice, Bianco called him into the coaches' room.

Bianco did not mince words in his scathing commentary about Byrne's skating ability—perplexing to a Byrne who had spent hours refining his skill. Byrne exited the building moments later with his dignity wrapped in anger. He suspected Bianco's imprudent manner had either ignorance or ulterior motives behind it, and he brought news of this back to Jones and the Blackhawks. Possibly this early event is where the seed of bitterness between the Chicagoans and the East Coasters began. Byrne concedes that by this time, Chicago had firm dominion over the world of sled hockey in the United States, with a much more organized and financially secure program, which may have made the other programs—like Bianco's—feel the need to rattle sabers.

Nonetheless, the insult affected Byrne. He stopped playing sled hockey. For a time, chances were high that the great future and the gold medal ahead of him would disappear. Jones, his teammates, and his wife urged him to return. Still hesitant, Byrne decided to visit the rink in Chicago again. Jones wasted no time prodding him back on the horse. Tryouts for the 2002 U.S. Paralympic sled hockey team were imminent. Bianco had abruptly vacated the head coaching job. Jones insisted Byrne try again.

Byrne sat in a sled in his garage and practiced shooting with both left and right hand in the days leading up to the tryouts in Buffalo, New York. He would be selected as a right winger.

A gold medal was in his future again.

In fact, so were his three kids, and a return to construction work with the same machinery that got him here—this time under the Local 150 union.

"I lost something in my life," Byrne told me. "But I found something better."

CHAPTER NINE

Arriving in Salt Lake City

March 1, 2002

As the Olympic torch neared Lake Placid, N.Y., in 1980 . . . newspapers and magazines throughout the world offered predictions on who would win medals in the major sports. Not a single publication gave the American men's hockey team a chance against the world powers.

—DON YAEGER, ASSOCIATE EDITOR EMERITUS,
SPORTS ILLUSTRATED

TEAM USA ARRIVED IN SALT LAKE CITY ON MARCH 1, 2002, PREPARED TO upset. The opening game would be against Japan, those same bitter rivals who had halted hope of progression in Nagano, and Joe Howard was having none of it. "We're here for gold," he told Japanese newscasters before the opening ceremony.[1] And despite the failures of the last Paralympics, the American players managed to win the hopeful attention of their countrymen.

In January, the team held training camps at both the American Airlines Center and The Rink in Addison, Texas, earning the coverage of the Dallas Stars Boosters Club and building a small fanbase who at last spared a glance for the Paralympics. The article urged readers to lend their support.[2] Howard's confidence—cockiness—had some numbers backing it, too. The U.S. team's two exhibition games in Salt Lake City before the lighting of the torch resulted in a double victory: Norway, 2–1, and Sweden, 4–0.

The logo of the Salt Lake 2002 Winter Paralympics dyed into the ice. USA defenseman Sylvester Flis and Norway captain Helge Bjørnstad chase each other atop it.
DONALD MIRALLE/STAFF/GETTY IMAGES SPORT VIA GETTY IMAGES

Middleton had been careful not to reveal Team USA's deadly secret weapon in Sylvester Flis or even in goalie Manny Guerra at these preliminaries, placing Pat Sapp, #33, in goal and originally refusing Flis's request to play. But Flis insisted, as he had recently moved his sled blades to just one inch apart—a radical adaptation with the objective of speed. Flis needed the chance to test out the change. Middleton relented, so long as Flis promised to underplay and resist showing off his skill. Flis agreed—and *even then* Team USA came out on top.

Middleton withheld celebration. "I'm nervous," he said, "and that's the way I like to be."[3] He and Tom Moulton knew the odds were still against them. The United States was seeded sixth in the tournament, eligible to compete at all only because it was the host country. And Norway planned to defend its gold title from 1998. Middleton may have kept a stiff upper lip, but he knew that if the newly systemized team he'd put together couldn't beat Japan, they may as well go home now.

Competing in this Paralympics would be Canada, Norway, Sweden, Japan, Estonia, and the United States.[4] Middleton had joked that before the recent European tournament qualifying Estonia, the United States had been placed in the sixth seed after a literal "TBD" ahead of them in fifth.

As soon as they could, Middleton and Moulton perched in the arena's nosebleeds, section 122, and watched the rival teams practice. Middleton leaned back with his arms crossed, a relaxed but calculating expression on his face, and Moulton, the opposite, sat erect and alert, as would a student listening to a lecture before the hardest exam of his or her life. Moulton studied the superior speed and technique of the Japanese and insisted if Team USA had any chance of not being skated around in 8's, they'd have to focus on interrupting Japan's passing.

While the coaches strategized and rubbed their necks, the players settled into the Paralympic Village. "Paralympic Village" is a pseudonym for the complementary accommodations set up for players and staff, which this time spanned the seventy acres of the University of Utah. The U.S. team was assigned to Building 812.[5] With an uncomfortable mixture of fear and bureaucracy, security forbade the U.S. residents from displaying in their windows the American flag or other memorabilia that would announce their nationality. The attacks of September 11, 2001, had heightened anxiety surrounding a high-profile event like this, and safety officials worried that potential terrorists would seek targets draped in the red, white, and blue. The Village allowed no outsiders.

Nor did it seem to need any. It provided twenty-four-hour dining at Douglas Dining and published a daily community paper—8½ × 11 and full color—entitled *Paralympic Record*, featuring interviews, schedules, weather reports, and snippets into daily living called "Visions of the Village."[6] In this way, an intimate ecosystem quickly formed.

Close quarters did not equate to close friendships, however. The U.S. sled hockey team that arrived at the Village looked nothing like a family—it was Chicagoans and East Coasters smashed together with a few Texans thrown in for spice. Flis, a die-hard Blackhawk, had little interest in fraternizing. He made straight for his room. Out of empty disregard more than direct aggression, the East Coasters didn't hold the elevator for the Chicago players, and vice versa. This, again, was due to bitterness for a variety of reasons. Some Blackhawks were resentful that Jeff Jones had been passed over for Rick Middleton's job; others felt Middleton was just a hotshot coming in from the NHL with no business coaching sled hockey. Still others raised concerns about how the team money was being spent and particularly how much Middleton was being compensated. Money, after all, had always been scarce for U.S. sled hockey, and a well-paid head coach didn't sit well with players who were used to tightening their belts. Meanwhile, the East Coasters seemed fed up with the Blackhawks for pressing issues and distracting attention from the tournament. To them, it seemed the haughty Blackhawks were not yet convinced that Team USA needed more than Chicagoans on it. Middleton sent the team captains to visit the rooms of the Blackhawks to try to strengthen allegiances. He knew they needed to come together if they were going home with anything but laundry after this was all through.

The effort may have backfired on him, however. The captains likely tried their best to foster unity, but at least one Blackhawk, Brian Ruhe, took insult at this gesture. To him, the captains were challenging his integrity if they felt they had to knock on his door and ask if he was here for anything other than to win. Like the other Blackhawks, Ruhe was used to the hands-on style of Jeff Jones, and did not understand why Middleton sent others to deliver his message. "I do not know who [you] are. I am also pretty sure you do not know who I am," Ruhe had emailed Middleton.[7]

Indeed, Jones's familial style of coaching back in Chicago contrasted with the style typical of the NHL, where coaches and players were not friends. Warm relationships between coaches and players in the league opened the door to conflicts of interest and, much like the reason farmers avoid naming livestock, made it hard when the time came to cut or trade athletes. Without a doubt, and regardless of the problems of split loyalty it would later cause in these Paralympics, the bond Jones shared with the Blackhawks was unique. Middleton's more traditional coaching approach came off as disconnected to the Blackhawks, whereas Middleton was acting in the manner he was raised to consider professional.

At the very least, the crossed wires and frustration arising from this event imbued Ruhe with a greater drive to leave the captains dizzy with no doubt that he was here to perform.

Chris Koseluk and Cynthia "Cindy" Mulkern, the husband-and-wife founders of Never Dull Productions (est. 1995), unpacked their trunk as well. The videographers had been following the team since Nagano, collecting[8] footage for a documentary that would be called *Sled Shots*.[8] One thing they grabbed from the back of the car was a coffeemaker. The coffee in Salt Lake City, primarily populated by members of The Church of Jesus Christ of Latter-day Saints, was abysmal.[9] The pair hoped Team USA would medal and secure a thematic ending to the story they spent many days on planes and in automobiles to record while tailing the team. With all that time together, Chris and Cindy formed bonds with the players and handled the only cameras Coach Middleton allowed in the locker room.

They were not the only film crew covering the Paralympics, however. Newfound interest in media coverage at the Games continued an upward trend since the 2000 Paralympics in Sydney, Australia, which attracted an estimated 300 million viewers.[10] German public broadcasting corporations[11] sent a film crew of around fifty to cover the Salt Lake City Paralympic Games, and the Canadian Broadcasting Company (CBC) promised around fifteen hours of coverage.[12] Canada, of course, expected to win in sledge hockey and thus readied their cameras.

The Paralympic sled hockey icon, used to introduce the sport in pamphlets and head up rows of stats. A series of black-and-white icons like this existed for the other winter sports as well.

The United States was not left behind, however. Dabbling in sports programming for the first time, A&E Networks—an American multinational broadcasting company that is a 50/50 joint venture between Hearst Communications and the Walt Disney Company—partnered with the Bud Sports Productions to produce American television coverage for the Paralympics.[13] Hosts Harry Smith and Joan Lunden sat before a cozy fireplace each night at 6:00 p.m. Eastern going over highlights of the day's events. They wore wintry sweaters and stayed in theme with evergreens and antique ski equipment in the background. In the field were reporters Ian Furness and Brent Severyn, who always stood microphone-to-microphone, heads tilted together, to look into the camera and fit the square dimensions of early 2000s televisions. A&E projected the official Paralympic sledge hockey graphic as it displayed rankings throughout the week.

It was the week before the March 7 opening ceremonies. Chris and Cindy followed Team USA into the Paralympic locker room for the first time, pausing in front of the players as they unloaded their bags and filled cubbies with helmets and hooks with hats. The Chicagoans occupied a corner. Matt Coppens, #5, dragged black tape around his stick—old hockey folklore assures that'll camouflage the puck. Dave Conklin adjusted the seat bucket of his sled alongside Jack Sanders, #15. Both of their buckets were collaged with American flags of all eras from colony to modernity. Sanders tilted his bucket to the camera to reveal the navy blue carpeting that padded its bottom. "I went to the K-Mart and spent another four dollars on a nice blue toilet seat," he said, smiling.

Chris chuckled behind the camera. "'Cuz when it comes to the tush, you spare no expense."

"That's right."

Kip St. Germaine looked over at the Chicago players from across the room as he unpacked. Joe Howard didn't look up at all.

Sylvester Flis wore his spectacles and a yellow T-shirt. It gave him the rare effect of looking academic and kindly, as opposed to the wolverine on ice he was known as.

Thankfully, Team USA had other resources to ensure their comfort than just a trip to K-Mart. Dedicated and understated volunteers provided for them.

One was Jeff Uyeno. When Team USA first received their uniforms from USA Hockey, they noticed the jerseys were hand-me-downs from the 1996 women's ice hockey team. With Uyeno's tenacity and a willing sponsor in Nike, new jerseys were procured for the Games, printed with each player's name. The whites were as blinding as fresh snow.

Another, physical trainer James Robert "Jim" Olsen (b. 1948), treated the players daily. Olsen specialized in manual therapy, which involved specifically working on the small joints of the body. The philosophy was that if you focus on the little things, big things will happen. Before coming to Salt Lake City, Olsen, who had experience working on athletes in gymnastics, wrestling, and weightlifting, knew none of the players. His approach broke the norms of his field. Most physical trainers treating athletes with disabilities concerned themselves only with the care and prevention of injuries. Olsen believed in adding "enhancing performance" to his objectives. After all, enhancing performance would naturally reduce the risk of injury—statistically, Olsen claims, Stanley Cup winners are often the teams with the fewest incurred serious injuries that season.

Injuries also impact psychological aspects of health. Olsen seems to have favored patient-oriented outcomes, or patients' own reports of health and what is meaningful to them. This type of health practice improves the ability to evaluate what "recovery" means and to set goals that matter to each patient.[14]

Particularly in the case with athletes with physical challenges, Olsen insisted that game play was not the greatest adversity to players' bodies—gravity was. A game lasts roughly forty-five minutes. Gravity is constant, and wears down the players' bodies, which often suffer from unequally distributed weight intended to compensate for one ailment or another. He worked on the areas of the body sled hockey players exhaust the most: head and neck, upper thoracic, shoulders, and the mobilization of their joints. To Olsen, Team USA players were heaps of clay he aimed to shape into their finest version within.

In addition to accepting appointments with Olsen, the players had a busy schedule ahead, full of pregame rituals.

The first order of business required all players from all countries undergo "classifications" between March 1–4. Players arrived at their appointment to have their physical conditions and medical histories evaluated by officials of the International Paralympic Committee at the E Center in West Valley, Utah.[15] Brutally speaking, this was to ensure the athlete was suitably disabled. Each player, before being assigned to their appointment, received one of three possible evaluation statuses: Paralympic New Status (PNS), Paralympic Review Status (PRS), or Paralympic Permanent Status (PPS). PNS meant that the player had not ever been evaluated for the Games before and must go to the classification assessment. PRS meant the athlete had been identified as having a medical status that was fluid and could have changed for better or for worse since the time of their last Paralympic evaluation. This, too, required assessment. Only PPS-status individuals did not have to endure reevaluation, as these athletes were recorded as having a permanent qualifying disability.

A complicated appeals process was available to players who were not satisfied with the results of their assessment (which could, in fact, lead to officials saying the athlete is not eligible to play in the Games). Fortunately, none of the players on Team USA experienced classification challenges, but the process as a whole has been criticized. For one, most classifiers were able-bodied. And many were overworked. Towards the end of the 2000s, there would be a push to replace IPC officials with a "practice community" made up of athletes with disabilities and the able-bodied staff closest to them, like coaches and medical trainers. Likewise, those opposed to the current protocols favored a less dry and clinical assessment. Rather than relying on diagnoses—for instance, categorizing all cerebral palsy athletes as the same—assessments, they felt, should be based off functionality: what one can and cannot do.[16]

ESPN's Eric Adelson joined this dialogue when challenging the spectrum of disability allowed in the regular Olympics, along with the use of prosthetics. He argued that prosthetics, or any tool used to compensate for human imperfection, are in use by almost every Olympic athlete already. A swim cap, for example, is a prosthetic used to smoothen out the imperfect (relative to the task) head texture of swimmers.[17] While Paralympians are subjected to scrutiny over the level of their reliance on prosthetics, able-bodied athletes of the near future, says Adelson, might design intentional prosthetics to make them fiercer competitors as the technology to do so advances.

Athletes with disabilities fight to come back to the field, rink, or stadium after losing the use of one or more limbs. Able-bodied athletes, Adelson argues, might one day cut one off "to gain a prosthetic advantage."[18] When tested against inconsistent standards, classification becomes all the more problematic. But as the only system the Paralympics had to work with, it remained a necessary way of creating the most balanced lineup possible.

Otto the Otter, the 2002 Paralympic mascot, roamed Salt Lake City in the days leading up to the opening ceremonies and smiled from advertisements.[19] Locals enjoyed a sizeable amount of buzz. As restaurants and shops prepared to host the 416 athletes (and their families) from thirty-six countries, other Utahans purchased tickets for the games, which were being hyped up on the street. Prices for tickets ranged from $20 to $100 for the opening ceremonies, $50 for closing, and $10 for adults for each game.[20]

The aftershock of the terrorist attacks of September 11, 2001, also drew global attention to this event, as it had the able-bodied Olympics weeks earlier. Lloyd Ward, CEO and secretary general of the United States Olympic Committee, addressed the still-devastated America at the beginning of the *U.S. Paralympic Team Delegation Handbook* for 2002. "This gathering of the world's greatest athletes with disabilities in elite international competition can help our nation heal," he wrote, "and

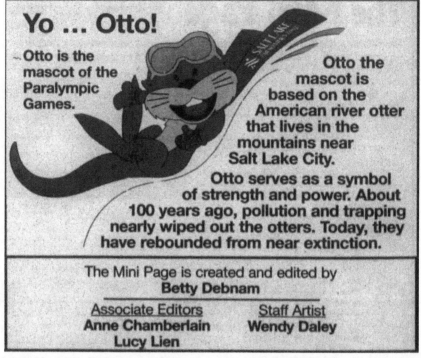

Otto the Otter, featured in the *Daily American* on February 5, 2002. © *DAILY AMERICAN—* USA TODAY NETWORK

overcome the wounds and grief suffered on that fateful day, September 11, as our Paralympians triumph on snow and ice to win the hearts and minds of our nation."[21] Utah governor Mike Leavitt (b. 1951), who had just hosted around ninety diplomatic events for the Olympics, prepared to entertain around ten to honor the Paralympics. He gave interviews expressing how inspired he was by the athletes with various physical challenges gathering in his city.[22]

Inspiration did seem to be the flavor of the Paralympic establishment. Its mission statement was simply, "Mind, Body, Spirit," and its motto read, "To inspire the world by successfully staging a Paralympic Games which sets new standards of excellence to enable the athletes to achieve their best performance."[23] Even its emblem used symbolism to represent disability's place in sports competition.[24]

The E Center. COURTESY OF KAY ROBERTSON

Salt Lake City officials made changes to the venues to accommodate the special needs of the athletes. Nearly $40,000 went into replacing the boards of the players' bench and the penalty box with plexiglass to allow the seated athletes with disabilities to see through. Another $21,000 was spent to install artificial ice around the rink so the sleds would not be damaged by crossing the regular flooring. The venues added more handicap-accessible spectator seating as well, to ensure at least 2% of the total seating capacity for the stadium accommodated fans with disabilities and their companions.[25] Teams were assigned their own accessible shuttles, which were provided by the Rocky Mountain National Park Service.[26] It seemed, for sure, that Salt Lake City matched its words of grandeur about the Paralympics with financial commitment. The E Center, where all ice sledge hockey matches would be held, was ready.

Five difficult matches stood like concrete gates ahead of the United States team. Performing well would unlock the medal game. There were reasons for the players to feel a massive ton of weight on their shoulders now, even discounting the astonishing hardship and comeback spirit of their personal backgrounds. The pressure of a grieving nation needing a reason for hope, and the legacy of defeat they needed to change—or else they would be disbanded—pressed down upon them. All would be decided after the parade of the opening ceremony, after fire leapt from the torch.

CHAPTER TEN

Dave Conklin, #20

"Ice Man"

Pos.	GP	G	A	PTS	PIM	"+/–"	GWG	GTG	PPG	SHG	S	SG%
F	5	0	3	3	4	3	0	0	0	0	5	0.00

IN THE LATE 1960S, DAVID PETER CONKLIN WRESTLED A BEAR NAMED Sascha. Black fur pressed against his face and the odor of a hot, over-sized mammal filled his nostrils. He could feel her powerful muscles moving against him as she turned and flung him away. She reared on her hind legs and swiped at him. Conklin jumped back fast. The ground shook as her front legs landed. When her teeth snapped too near to Conklin's face, his brother taunted her aside and tackled the creature. Roars ripped from deep within the animal's chest as her heavy paws flailed. The brothers took turns.

Of course, Sascha was in on it. All the kids at the campground watched the show from behind a fence, Clear Lake lying like a mirror in the grass beyond. They hooted for Conklin and let out cries of "Whoa!" as Sascha's black nails tore up the ground beneath her as she rolled.

Sascha slept her winters away on that campground in Wisconsin, and when she woke in spring, Dave Conklin and his brothers ushered her from her cave and into the lake for a bath to wash her matted fur. They watched as the bear cut through the water fast as a sailboat, leaving a V-shaped ripple in her wake.

Conklin's father—a teacher during the off-season—owned the camp, and he employed all ten of his children there each summer. Dave was the eldest, born in Edgerton, Wisconsin, on September 22, 1955. In his own words, his childhood can be summed up with the phrase "concussions and Catholic school." He served as an altar boy as a youth, and when he was barely eight, pushed his way onto the fields of football games the older boys were playing. Kids twice his size held nothing back, knocking him to the ground and shoving him away from the ball. The plastic Green Bay Packers helmet he wore to every game was cracked by the time he was ten.

You might say Sascha was just one in a long line of those trying to get a bite out of Conklin.

The accident happened in late autumn of 1981. Conklin was twen-ty-six, working as a diesel mechanic. He revved the engine on a borrowed Kawasaki motorcycle. It was grey, and glared off rays from the sun. Conk-lin and the bike hurtled down the road before sliding on loose gravel. He swerved and hit a guardrail, flying off the bike.

Conklin lay on the ground with a broken back—and, of course, another concussion—for at least fifteen minutes before anyone came along. A car braked in the street—the accident had blocked the road—and Conklin could hear the driver's door slam shut.

"Can you move me?" he remembers croaking to the stranger.

"I'm not going to touch you," the man replied. But he ran to get help.

Immobilized with pain, Conklin arrived at the nearest hospital only to be turned away due to an insurance dispute. He then waited more than forty-eight hours to undergo surgery at the next hospital: Their only surgeon was on vacation. Not even considering the excruciating pain Conklin endured, this delay meant the doctors were unable to reverse the effects of his injuries and Conklin was left partially paralyzed.

Conklin entered the dark and trying days of recovery during a time and in an area where rehabilitation resources were limited. He encountered various adaptive sports as a way to keep alive the competitive spirit of his youth, beginning with wheelchair races and including everything from bowling to softball and basketball. Then he found sled hockey at the Bloomington Ice Garden in Minnesota.

Joined by his future Paralympic teammate Manny Guerra, Conklin fell in love with the sport at this clinic. Hardly anyone had heard of the game at this time, and even here the clinic was only a subprogram of the Ski for Light event hosted by the Sister Kenny Institute.

Conklin met sled hockey advocates John Schatzlein and Mark Schmidt at the clinic as well. Passion for the sport bonded the men, and Conklin soon found himself acting as an ambassador for expanding sled hockey all over the country. He filled a trailer with sleds Schmidt had built by hand and accompanied Schatzlein on tour of the northeast, establishing clinics wherever possible. In Boston, Conklin was among those who proudly watched Kip St. Germaine skate the arena for the first time since his own accident. St. Germaine was wearing a full work suit in the sled.

Conklin also allied with the RIC Blackhawks sled hockey team, coached by Jeff Jones, to expose the sport to followers of the NHL Blackhawks. During the quick intermissions between periods at the NHL games, Conklin and a few others soared onto the ice and demonstrated the sport in front of massive audiences.

Advertising the sport came hand in hand with playing a whole lot of it. Conklin honed his skills and lifted weights year-round. He took up cross-country skiing to mimic the motions of sled hockey. Twice a week he traveled the 460 miles round trip to Chicago to practice with the RIC Blackhawks.

But Conklin's greatest skill of all, as Sascha the bear would attest, was still his ability to take a hit. He earned a reputation in the arena as a sort of tank, absorbing damage off his teammates and using his body to clear their way to the net. "Ice Man" became his nickname due to all the injuries he was constantly pressing ice packets against in the locker room. Decades later, Conklin speaks with a stammer. He's lost his depth perception.

Conklin was moved by passion to try out for the 2002 United States team. He made the cut and would later describe the buzz of euphoria during the last fifteen minutes of the gold medal game as he watched his team win the shootout. It would not have been possible if Conklin hadn't taken a few heavy hits from the Viking-sized Norwegians in earlier periods. After I interviewed this man, I knew I'd never forget the slow, gentle smiles that fluttered on and off his face as he managed to recall these moments.

The 2020 Tokyo Paralympics (held in 2021 due to COVID-19), were the first to be aired as part of NBC's main broadcast. Prior to this, news coverage of the Paralympics was sporadic at best. Word of the 2002 victory for America, therefore, spread slowly. No fans awaited Conklin at the airport as they had for the able-bodied Olympians returning home— none, that is, except his sister Cathy, who had driven nearly three hours from Steven's Point, Wisconsin, to his homecoming airport in La Crosse to hold up a sign.

Conklin continued to play for Team USA through the 2006 Torino games, where his injuries finally forced him to retire. His sled from the 2002 gold medal game now resides at the Olympic Museum in Park City, Utah.

Since retiring from competition, Conklin has remained involved with the sport professionally, coaching and organizing clinics as well as lending out equipment, which he still has in that same large trailer he used to tour the country with. On the side, he learned to teach downhill skiing. He may have even snuck in a few more concussions.

Conklin finds joy in retirement in the eight freshwater aquariums that bubble throughout his house. They are full of catfish and cichlids. Why does he like them? "They stay alive," he answers.

Like him.

CHAPTER ELEVEN

Game One—USA vs. Japan

March 8, 2002

Half the game is mental; the other half is being mental.
—JIM McKENNY, NHL

THE DOORS OPENED TO AN ALMOST EMPTY ARENA. IT WAS BEFORE 9:00 a.m. on March 8, 2002, moments away from the kickoff game against Japan. Team USA, dressed in their dark-blue-and-red uniforms, looked around at the bare stadium seats on the upper levels and the sparsely occupied lower sections. It must have seemed perplexing to some, and offensive to others, that the hype and fanfare surrounding the previous day's opening ceremonies failed to translate to numbers at the early morning game. Then again, there was still important work to be done to earn the true adulation of fans.

Around 7:00 p.m. the night before, it seemed all of Utah had gathered to watch the cauldron ignite at Rice-Eccles Stadium. Monoskiers Muffy Davis (b. 1972) and Chris Waddell (b. 1968) had the honors. They watched as Erik Weihenmayer (b. 1968) jogged up the steps to the stadium to cheers and whistles, holding high the torch.[1] Weihenmayer was the first blind man to summit Mt. Everest, and his German Shepherd guide dog, Seigo, forged ahead of him.[2] Waddell and Davis guided the torch to the base of a tall tower of artistically twisting metal

Artificial mountains pierce the sky at the dramatic Opening Ceremonies on the eve of the first game. COURTESY OF KAY ROBERTSON

rails that resembled a strand of DNA. The flame burst upon meeting the cauldron. Then, interior mechanics slowly and dramatically raised the brazier to the top.

Nearly forty-six thousand people attended the sold-out event.[3] Commuters waited as long as an hour to catch the train to the stadium at the University of Utah.[4] The sky had progressively darkened, and many of the spectators eyed the enormous artificial mountain on stage with apprehension. The mountain and other stage equipment were constructed of metal, and lightning flickered behind thick black clouds over the unroofed venue.[5] When rain finally collapsed onto the ceremony, it met a crowd refusing to be deterred. They donned ponchos and umbrellas, and the night continued with performances from musicians Stevie Wonder, Wynona Judd, and Donny Osmond.

Wherever the onlookers had gone overnight, it was not to the E Center. Nerves replaced yesterday's euphoric energy. Not counting the preliminaries, this would be Team USA's first official Paralympic game under Middleton. They—and he—had a lot to prove.

The Paralympic games would operate bracket style, with one round robin sending the two highest-scoring teams into the gold medal game and the third and fourth best-performing teams to wrestle for bronze. But Middleton wasn't thinking about gold now, only dignity. Wearing a USA baseball cap and a zipped-up Nike jacket, he chewed gum at the players' bench and sized up the ice in his head. Tensions between the RIC Blackhawks players and those from Boston were still high. He was flying on a prayer that his efforts with Moulton to discipline and train the team had succeeded, that the prelim triumphs were not a fluke. A real, ranking-impacting win would melt away differences between the players faster than anything.

Middleton's first change for the better (he hoped) focused on Joe Howard. He had reassigned Howard, the team captain, from his normal position at center to left wing. Middleton hoped this would force Howard down from the stratosphere of his own self-confidence and into the troposphere of his teammates. Howard played damn well but needed to learn to not do it all himself. "You gotta pass the puck so you can get open and get the puck *back*," Middleton intoned. Howard needed to move the puck down the ice by letting go of it now and then. Doing it alone wasn't getting anyone anywhere. Middleton also knew that if Howard was removed from center, he'd be less at risk of opposing players knocking into him and revving up his temper. In fact, opposing players familiar with Howard made it a strategy to get him mad and sloppy. Middleton needed to avoid the devastating penalty box charges of the 2000 World Championship, where Howard was ejected from the game for getting too riled up.

Middleton and Moulton gave their best pep talk to the team as the Japanese athletes filed into the other side of the rink. Japan wore white jerseys with what looked like a comet enclosed in a circle around their country name in bold italics.[6] On their helmets streamed the red-and-white rays of the rising sun, and re-creations of *The Great Wave off Kanagawa* reared up on either side of their ears. Japanese head coach Hiroshi Ohmura appeared alongside his team. He knew the Japanese, with their smaller figures, couldn't hope to out-muscle the Americans one-on-one.[7] Instead, they planned to pin two, even three bodies to every one American with play potential in an attempt to annoy and overwhelm. And while the two nations had played each other before, Japanese assistant coach Katsuhiro Takase warned reporters that the United States should expect an even harder team than the one they'd lost to in Nagano.[8]

The time for talking about it was over, though. Both sides had cockiness to prove right. When the puck fell, they held their breath and watched.

Japan held true to Ohmura's strategy: The puck seemed to disappear into their bodies and sticks each time Team USA attempted to carry it into enemy territory. They checked hard at the blue line and buffeted back the American offense. Middleton shook his head as he saw his players forcing aggressive passes that weren't there instead of retaining possession by making safe passes into the neutral zone.[9] These chaotic passes invited turnovers to Japan. Frustration built on the ice as neither team could score.

On either side, it seemed to be a goalie's game. Japanese goaltender Mitsuru "Mits" Nagase, #39, stopped two shots in the first period: the first at 4:07—so easy it looked like a pass meant for him—and the second at 14:44, when he bumped the puck around his knees and arced it behind the goal. Guerra saved one goal at 6:23 of the second period by colliding with a Japanese player a few feet out of the crease. The puck slid outward as the two players tumbled. He saved another at 11:16 of the same period by lifting a hand and knocking down the high-flying shot.

By the end of the second period, the score was still 0-0.

Middleton stood at the huddle. "There are fifteen minutes left." He swept his gaze around his players, each of them sweating and panting but their attention pinned on him. "If you want to win the gold medal, it starts *right here*."[10]

Just before four minutes into the third and final period, defenseman Brian Ruhe slid a long-distance pass to Matt Coppens inches from crossing the blue line. The puck soared diagonally across open ice and onto Coppens's stick. Coppens charged for the goal, but Japan's defenseman Satoru Sudo, #68, hooked him with his arm and swung him awry just as Coppens's arm swung for the shot.

Then Chris Manns pulled a miracle. He rushed up and claimed the open puck, at least two white Japanese jerseys on his tail. Finding an angle only a leftie could achieve, he launched the fifteenth shot of the game and converted it to goal in the top right corner of the net at 4:09 of the third period. The crowd roared and waved American flags. Middleton's controversial choice placing Manns on the team over Doyle had just proven itself.

Now momentum chose a victor. At 9:18, Sylvester Flis shed a single Japanese defenseman and streaked to the net. He waited patiently, gliding just past the goalie on the left before flinging his puck into the net at the last moment. It went in almost horizontally.

Team USA set up a final play with only 22 seconds left on the clock. Manns and Conklin fed the puck to Jack Sanders, who was sliding in to almost exactly in front of the goal. A quick flick of his wrist sent the puck flying in at 14:38 of period three to end the game at 3–0.

With the first American triumph at the 2002 Paralympics in the books, media crowded the likes of both teams. Team USA complimented the Japanese. "They're fast, they're everywhere you turn," Sanders said. "It's tough to get away from them."[11] But admiration for their opponents gave way to smiles and celebration.

Japan, on the other hand, admitted they hadn't expected even an ounce of the ferocity Team USA showed that morning. "The American team was excellent today," Takayuki Endo, #10, conceded.[12] Endo had begun his career in sledge hockey in 1999 after the Nagano Paralympics, and after a difficult decision to sink his time into athletics rather than the alto saxophone. He was a forward in Salt Lake City but would in fact later switch to defense, specifically citing being inspired by watching Flis and his charismatic antagonism as a defenseman. As for the comments of Japan's overworked goalie, Mits Nagase: "We just got tired at the end."[13]

Manns was awarded the game puck for that momentum-winning first goal—and his crucial left hand. He proved to his RIC Blackhawks teammates that they needed the East Coasters to win, too. Middleton knew just how much this victory meant, sure as he knew a failure would have suffocated the last breath of morale in the management of Team USA. That might have been it—for the tournament, and the fate of the American team forever.

But it wasn't.

Now, he needed to see if the magic today could be repeated against Canada: the giants seeded to win it all.

Final score: 3–0
USA game MVP: Sylvester "Sly" Flis
Fans in attendance: 2,073

CHAPTER TWELVE

Chris Manns, #44

Pos.	GP	G	A	PTS	PIM	"+/-"	GWG	GTG	PPG	SHG	S	SG%
F	4	1	2	3	6	2	1	0	0	0	6	16.67

IT WAS APRIL 11, 1991, AND CHRISTOPHER AMADON MANNS WAS thirsty. He sat in a recliner surrounded by family in the living room. There was talking and rubbing of backs, and sports played on a small, square TV. Relatives had gathered to welcome him home from nearly a monthlong stay in the hospital after the train accident on March 16 of that year. The ten-year-old Manns had lost his left foot and his right leg above the knee. He was bandaged up and weak.

The young boy didn't have the strength to transfer himself from that recliner back into his wheelchair. He addressed the room at large: "Can I have a glass of water?"

Immediate movements to oblige were made, and then everyone froze as the confident, steady words of his father cut through.

"Get up and get it yourself."

Silence followed. The air was thick with embarrassment and pity and the shock of an entire room of company suddenly sucked of noise. Only the colors of the sports channel flashed on the television.

Manns saw the serious edge in his father's eyes. He winced and dragged himself to the wheelchair. Then he pushed the large rubber wheels towards the kitchen and reached for the sink. Tears of anger and exhaustion burned as he blinked.

In the next room, his parents argued. His mother, Michele Halbert, contested her husband's harshness. The wounds were still fresh, and a community stood ready to lend Manns any aid he required. "You'll be his own worst enemy, Michele," came his father's stern retort. He believed Manns needed to figure this out himself. "And if you want to keep bumping heads, we can. I won't let you do that to him."

Albert Manns Sr. stood a short 5-foot-7, but something about the way he held his chest made him look bigger. He had thirty years' worth of grease under his nails from working machines in the Outokumpu American Brass factory. There he made almost thirty thousand pounds of copper coils, and he collapsed each night at the dinner table with Chris and his three other children seated beside him. A long tradition of upstanding, faith-based surety rested on his shoulders. Grandfather Manns had attended Mass daily. Albert Manns encouraged daily rosaries and soup kitchen service on weekends. Young Manns, born on June 30, 1980, spent his dinners looking up from his plate at the quiet dignity of his father, who was spearing food with a fork across from him, and wanting to be like that.

The family resided in Buffalo, New York, and on a night when the Sabres cut up the ice particularly well on his TV, Manns stared at the screen with a little bit of that white light reflecting in his eyes. His dad sat nearby. "That's what I'm gonna be one day," said Manns. "I'm gonna be on TV and make you and Mom proud."

His father was quiet for a while. Then he said, "You can. You try and don't succeed, that's okay. But don't be a quitter. Once you quit, you'll always be a quitter."

On the day the train took away Manns's legs, however, his father's directive was a tall order.

Grey clouds stretched across the sky and buried the sun like a marble under a mattress. Manns and his brothers were eager to break in the new bikes they'd recently received, and a few of the neighborhood kids were getting together a game of football for later that afternoon. After breakfast on weekends, the Manns kids were permitted to play anywhere in the neighborhood—anywhere save the train tracks, that is—so long as they were home before Albert returned from his shift. This Saturday, however, he'd been called in for overtime, and their regular playtime schedule was disrupted.

The Manns boys failed to convince their parents to allow an exception to the rule today, and they wore pouts as their father entered the front door and set down his car keys. He thumped upstairs and the rush of shower water could be heard moments later.

Michele, her already tender heart softening, reminded her boys that tonight she and Albert would be leaving to play euchre at a restaurant three blocks away. Albert's best friend would be babysitting—and he usually had a looser grip on their leashes.

As soon as the Manns parents left and their babysitter arrived, Chris Manns and his brothers got the nod of approval they were looking for. They flew out the front door and sprinted for Thompson Street, where they just might make the team pickings for that football game.

At the end of Thompson Street loomed the train tracks. The whistle of trains chugging in from Canada could be heard blocks away. Although his father warned him never to go near the tracks, Manns and his friends frequented the rails to flip over funny-looking rocks and chase the snakes that liked to bask on the hot metal in summer.

When trains rolled in, the Manns brothers tried to get close. Sometimes the conductors shouted at them to back off. One even squirted a Bug-A-Salt gun at them once. But when the train sped up or turned a bend and the conductor was out of view, the game of the season was to run alongside the train, grab the ladder, and jump on it, then jump off.

Chris Manns would watch his brothers, Albert Jr. and Len, do this day after day. He never could bring himself to it.

Until today.

The train glided along at three or four miles per hour. "If I were an artist," Manns recalls, "I could draw the face of the conductor." The two had made eye contact. Manns waved.

When the conductor could no longer be seen, Manns grabbed the ladder of the moving train car. He swung his right leg over and it slipped off. The rung was moist. And the wheels caught his leg.

Manns was dragged 397 feet, the rough earth scorching his back, and the monstrous jaws of the train sucked him closer and soon would swallow him. He kicked against it with his free leg, but the wheel snatched that one too. The train was picking up speed, nearing fifteen miles per hour.

Len stood frozen. The other neighborhood boys ran off screaming into the fields.

Al Jr. ran after Manns.

He jumped on top of his brother, trying to lock arms. The momentum of the train flung him away. He jumped a second time, then a third. Each time, the force buffeted him off.

Both brothers looked ahead and saw a viaduct—a narrow tunnel leaving no room for Manns's body to follow—a hundred yards ahead. Terror seized both of them.

"Listen!" Al Jr. yelled above the roar. "When I jump, jump onto me, too! Hug me! Don't let go!"

Manns's vision went black as his brother covered him once more; he grabbed hard, and then he heard a tumble.

Three blocks away the phone rang. Len had finally shaken off the paralysis and run for help. When the nearest bar refused him entry on account of his age, he threw a rock through a shop window and shattered the glass. This was to get the attention of the barkeeper—and access to his phone, once the emergency explained the behavior. Manns's father received the call at the restaurant, calmly walked back to the card table, and said to his wife, "We need to go."

Manns felt no pain as he lay on the ground awaiting the ambulance. Al Jr. grasped his clothes and pulled him to a stand, but he collapsed back down. The leg was hanging on by tendons. "It'll be okay, Chris. I love you," said Al.

"Alby," Manns replied, "my left foot is burning." He requested his brother remove his sneaker. When he did, the whole foot came off with it.

Al turned white. "Does that feel better?"

Manns nodded.

Tree branches brushed his face as the EMTs carried Manns's stretcher through the woods and into the ambulance.

Ten minutes later, they arrived at the children's hospital. Nurses twirled around him and hooked him to machinery. Al Jr.'s neck was covered in blood. His parents and grandmother arrived as well.

"Do you want to see them?" a nurse asked.

"No," said Manns. "Mom will be mad at me. These were new jeans and sneakers."

Then he caught sight of a priest. "Why is he here? Am I gonna die?" he asked. "I don't want to see him."

The nurses tried to shush him. Manns still felt no pain. "Can I have some water?" he asked. "If I'm gonna die, I don't want to die thirsty." How meaningful his thirst would be, still there, weeks later.

Michele and Albert Sr. entered the room then and came to his bed, one on each side. When Manns locked eyes with his father, Albert Sr. crumpled into tears.

And that's when the agony finally hit.

Manns returned to Black Rock Academy in prosthetics. He still had ghost feeling in his legs, looking down and reminding himself they were plastic. That thirst—first for water, now to make himself and his father proud—drove him to push aside his self-pity through school and into early adulthood.

In 1993, when Manns was only thirteen, he sat in the bleachers of a Notre Dame football game. Pam Maryjanowski, director of the New York State Games for the Physically Challenged, recruited him to a sled hockey demonstration that was happening that same afternoon. Manns, intrigued, and frustrated from failed attempts to reinvolve himself in sports of any kind, agreed. As soon as he cruised onto the ice and smelled the cold air, goosebumps shuddered onto him. He knew this was where he wanted to be.

Maryjanowski and team manager Rich DeGlopper directed him to the new program that was forming and connected him with players who felt and sounded a lot like him, although they were of all different ages and backgrounds. He played his first real game in 1995 against the Kitchener Sidewinders in Canada. Dark green Kitchener jerseys seemed to make a forest on the ice, and the Americans were pummeled, 20–0. They never even got the puck out of their zone.

Manns and his Buffalo club team took that embarrassment as a lesson. He realized the unique assets he brought into the arena—his bulkiness and his left-handedness—were not enough. Manns upped his stickhandling training. He pushed his body to the limit in ways that still provoke aches twenty-five years later. At the next formal game in London, Ontario, the Buffalo team beat the Swedish Paralympic team, 2–1.

Manns's training and the new success of the team seemed to pay off in 1997, when Manns was invited to try out for the 1998 Paralympic team. Of the twenty-five players who tried out for the fifteen available slots, Manns was ranked seventh in statistical analysis, but he was nonetheless cut. He attributes the surprising decision to favoritism—and the fact that he was only sixteen at the time.

"Use this as motivation," he was told. But those are words no one wants to hear. He hung up the phone.

A basketball was still clamped under one of his arms as he moseyed out of the driveway. He had been shooting hoops before the phone rang and his dad had been in the garage with the TV on. Manns announced the news.

Albert Sr.'s hand gripped his son's shoulder. "You remember what I said when you were younger." Manns recalled that night around the TV while the Sabres played. "Once you quit, you'll always be a quitter. I'll give you one week off. But then it's back on the ice."

"Someday," his mother added, "you are going to do something special."

Manns picked up his stick again the next week. His team expanded in skill and recognition, winning official sponsorship from the NHL Buffalo Sabres in 2000. For the next four years he trained while balancing a job at a steel company, much like his father, and pursuing a degree in sports management at Niagara County Community College. Pressure from all sides weighed down on him, yet somehow he kept finding himself on ice, learning to improve his mastery of the sled—going faster, cutting sharper turns, and shooting on the fly—all with one goal in mind: Team USA.

That cut made him a better player. That glass of water, always in the next room, made him thirstier.

Manns's sled hockey career in total would include a 2005 World Championship win, a 2006 bronze medal in Torino, and a term as team captain in 2008. His marriage to Shoshana Milich in 2007 would last four years and yield three apple-of-his-eye daughters, Ariana, Miliegh, and Carissa. He retired in 2009 to be there for them each day, giving up his place on the national team after what was one of the "hardest decisions of [his] life." But the right one. Manns still competes on the Buffalo Sabres club team.

The memory of that ultimate victory in 2002 will stay with him forever, though.

Chris Manns lifted a gold medal on the ice. Cameras drank up his face and bright lights shone on his sweat-sheened skin.

"Mom," he said to the world, "I hope this was special."

CHAPTER THIRTEEN

Game Two—USA vs. Canada

March 9, 2002

The grandest game of all is ice hockey. It is the fastest, roughest, most dangerous sport engaged in by human beings.
—CANADIAN REPORTER, NAME UNKNOWN[1]

ON THE SAME DAY THE UNITED STATES DEFEATED JAPAN—TEN HOURS later, to be exact—nearly sixty-four hundred fans crowded into the E Center. It was the largest audience to date for a sled hockey match, and Canadian and Norwegian flags were flying. Many considered this showdown of the two top-seeded teams to be a preview of the gold medal game. The Canadians, dressed in deep red jerseys with a single white maple leaf on the front, and the Norwegians, wearing white jerseys with a simple but confident red NORGE written diagonally across the front, crashed into one another on the ice—literally. The game excited fans with multiple group collisions and aggressive checking to be expected from the top two teams. At the second period, the score was gridlocked at 1–1, but Canadian forward Billy Bridges (b. 1984), just eighteen years old, scored the game-winning goal in the third period.

It was looking like Canada would make good on its first-place seeding.

Bridges, #18, the youngest player on Team Canada, had been recruited to the national team at only age fourteen, the youngest ever in history. He was born in Summerside, Prince Edward Island, with spina bifida, but proved himself as a formidable athlete. Bridges idolized right-winger Guy Lafleur (b. 1951), who won glory first on the NHL's Montreal Canadiens and later on the New York Rangers and Quebec Nordiques.[2] Lafleur's was an era in hockey where blond- and brown-haired heads gliding around the ice were more common than white-helmeted heads, before modern safety standards. Lafleur refused to wear a helmet even during his final years, where he made use of a grandfather clause exempting him from the new standards. He was holding on to a belief—or even a superstition—that ditching his helmet in his fourth season helped usher in his record-breaking goal statistics and five Stanley Cups.[3]

Lafleur was known for finding openings. One of his most famous goals occurred in the 1979 Stanley Cup semifinals. His Canadiens were trailing the Boston Bruins, 4–3. (Our own Rick Middleton skated the ice as one of those Bruins battling Lafleur during this game.) Lafleur cruised in from the right wing with an air of defeatism, no sign of steely determination in his posture. Then, just moments after crossing the blue line, he unleashed a wicked slapshot from what seemed like miles away and sent the goaltender flipping backwards with his glove in the air. The net bulged outward, the goal was good, and the Canadiens extended the game into overtime, where they eventually secured their victory. They'd go on that season to win the Stanley Cup.

Bridges admired Lafleur's shot style and channeled that radar for an opening in his game-winning goal against Norway. He was a figure Middleton and the rest of the U.S. team had their eyes on. But Canadian head coach Tom Goodings studied the United States favorites as well. He had watched the Japan–USA game and noted Joe Howard and Sylvester Flis as the preferences. After Canada defeated Norway, Goodings said the team would eat, rest, and then in the morning "discuss what players we need to take care of on the U.S. team—what systems they use and what systems we need to use against [them]." Goodings dealt with the additional pressure of his country's having defeated Team USA—in both men's and women's hockey—in the able-bodied Olympics weeks earlier, and the expectation that he continue the trend. "I'm not thinking about the pressure," he said. "We cannot think about the gold medal right now."[4]

In fact, like Lafleur and helmets, superstition abounded thanks to a 1987 loonie—a Canadian one-dollar coin—placed under the ice at the E Center. The "lucky loonie" had been embedded half an inch below center ice by Edmonton ice maker Trent Evans for the 2002 Olympics, where men's and women's ice hockey would be held in the same arena.[5] Canada promptly won the gold over it in both. By the time the Paralympics came, the rink had been reflooded and the loonie had been removed. It now holds a revered place in the Hockey Hall of Fame in Toronto. But some feared the Canadian sled hockey athletes had been cursed without their country's good luck charm.

Meanwhile, Middleton had been prepared to revise his team strategy if the game against Japan had ended in defeat. But the opposite had happened. Their victory made the front page of the local news.[6] As Team USA had yet to be scored against even once, Middleton assured reporters he was sticking with this lineup.[7]

The USA–Canada game took place at the E Center on March 9, 2002, at 7:00 p.m. Both teams warmed up in the exercise rooms in the hours leading up to the match. Bridges was pedaling on a stationary bike when Josh Wirt, also only eighteen, entered. Wirt was the youngest member of Team USA and had not yet seen playing time. The closeness in age between the two players positioned them perfectly for a man-to-man rivalry. When they met, Bridges, revved up for the game, lost sight of his manners. He sized Wirt up and said, paraphrased, "You must really suck if you can't even play on the worst team in the world."

It was just about the worst thing Bridges could have done for the Canadians. Wirt, scoffing and fuming, took those words—and maybe some hyperbole—to his teammates in the locker room as the clock ticked down to the face-off. Everyone on Team USA pledged to hit bodies a little harder than they would have otherwise. Anger is the world's best steroid.

Looking back, Bridges doesn't remember the incident, but he doesn't refute it. "I was an eighteen-year-old punk kid in a death metal band," he laughed. "I probably said stupid shit."

Canada donned the home uniform. It was another packed arena, as had been for the Canadian game against Norway the day before.

International Paralympic Committee president Sir Philip Craven (b. 1950) was in attendance.

U.S. center Lonnie Hannah met his Canadian counterpart in the middle of the Paralympic logo at center ice. They both faced the audience, nets to their left and right, as the referee crouched behind them. Hannah and the Canadian fist-bumped, then the referee dropped the puck. Their sticks clashed together like chopsticks fighting over the last morsel. The puck escaped them both, drifting forward, and was swallowed by their teammates.

As promised, Team USA's checking was ruthless. Howard rammed a crushing hit into Bridges the moment opportunity arose—and when he bumped over the ice back into the player's bench where Wirt was cheering for them, he said, "That one was for you, buddy."

The audience and announcers may not have known where all this U.S. fury was coming from, but they sure saw it.

Forty-four seconds into the first period, Guerra saved a shot, only to be followed by a second shot five seconds later. He stopped that one as well. It was shaping up to be another goalie's game. Howard and Flis, however, sought to change that. At around 57 seconds, Flis brandished his sticks on either side of him and, rowing frantically, followed the puck at a charging pace across the blue line on the right wing. His momentum caught up with him, though, and he arced wide behind the net. Two red jerseys sandwiched him against the boards and the puck flew away. With two Canadians distracted by the aggressive Flis, Howard swooped in and caught the loose puck, flinging it into the goal at 1:08 of period one. The crowd erupted.

One gets the impression Flis wasn't entirely content with that turn of events. When he had the chance, at 5:09, he repeated that same berserk rowing after the puck and took the same course down the right side of the ice as he had before. This time, however, with greater control, he arced sooner and shot the puck solo into the net for Team USA's second goal at 5:15 in the first period. The Canadian on his tail bumped into him just then, and Flis twirled and somersaulted over, his stick nonetheless raised in triumph.

By now, Canada would have been concerned. The game was not going in the right direction, the Americans seemed angry as *hell*, and early goals always swung the favor of morale. They had seen Team USA win against Japan, but Japan was not the strongest foe in Salt Lake City. How could a team that had never medaled or won a single championship be dominating the first period against Canada?

Coach Goodings resolved not to let the first period end without a counterstrike. At 11:23, four red jerseys advanced on the U.S. goal and spread out wall-to-wall in almost perfect synchrony, the way a pod of dolphins spreads to cover the sea. One broke past the net, and another, Todd Nicholson (b. 1959), #19, centered right in front of it. His Canadian teammate on the far end fed the puck to Nicholson, who popped it past Guerra at 11:29 for Canada's first goal.

Nicholson, the Canadian team captain, had been a defenseman in Nagano but switched to forward in Salt Lake City.[8] Even without shoulder pads—which he never wore—he was massive. This versatility and imposing build had forged a reputation for him since he began his playing career in 1988 with the Ottawa Sledgehammers following a car accident.[9] Alongside Bridges, he was another player the United States needed to look out for. With the score at a close 2–1 now in only the first period, there very well could have been more where that came from at the hands of Nicholson or Bridges.

Team USA wanted to avoid playing into a tie, where the shifting momentum could frustrate either team until one got tired and sloppy. They set up another offensive rush at 12:02, not even a minute after Canada's goal. Matt Coppens pushed the puck gently towards the net as two of his teammates neared. Hannah skidded in from the left at high speed and almost lost balance. It's hard to say he even took possession—rather, he nudged the puck with just a tap in the right direction as he streaked past and fell onto his side, sliding the rest of the way on his shoulder and into the boards.

But the score, at 12:06, was good. 3–1.

The Canadian goalie cursed, and the coaching staff, wearing frowns, shook their heads amid the thundering of the crowd. The ferocity of the United States was becoming a spectacle.

Flis rendered the lead insurmountable by the third period. He scored twice more—at both 10:30 and 13:06—registering a hat trick (three goals in one game) and setting the score at 5–1. He made good on what he had told reporters before the game: "We are a third period team."[10] By the way they were performing, though, one could argue Team USA was shaping out to be an every-period team.

With seconds to go and the audience counting down, Bridges shot a Hail Mary from behind the blue line. It went wide. The horn sounded, fans exploded in cheers, and Team USA raised their arms in victory. Wirt may have cheered the hardest.

The first United States win against Canada in the history of sled hockey had just been realized.

"It may not be a miracle in 1980," the announcer intoned, speaking loudly to be heard over the roar of the crowd, "but it's a huge win, the biggest ever, [for] the United States in ice sledge hockey."[11]

Little did he know the miracle was still in the making.

Final score: 5–1
USA game MVP: Sylvester "Sly" Flis
Fans in attendance: 6,400

CHAPTER FOURTEEN

Josh Wirt, #19

Pos.	GP	G	A	PTS	PIM	"+/–"	GWG	GTG	PPG	SHG	S	SG%
F	1	0	0	0	2	–1	0	0	0	0	1	0.00

JOSHUA LEE WIRT'S RIGHT HAND SWELLED UP LIKE A MICKEY MOUSE glove. A bee had stung him in the backyard of his Brush Valley, Pennsylvania, home. It was springtime, and he had been out practicing for baseball, as usual.

Wirt, born October 9, 1984, in Johnstown, Pennsylvania, spent most of his childhood sharpening himself into a better athlete. He threw tennis balls against the side of his two-story garage to practice fielding and dreamed of playing for the Pittsburgh Pirates. His mother, Karen McClure, attended every game he played.

The sting throbbed. It was hard to close his fingers around a baseball. When Wirt arrived at the game the next day, he pitched to a few opponents and then complained to his coach, Regis Mytrysak, between innings. Coach Reg was the father of his best friend, Brandon, and a disciplined motivator. Since there was nothing a visit to the doctor could do, the coach looked Wirt in the eye and said, "You gotta play through it."

Those words became Wirt's mantra.

On August 12, 1994, Wirt lost his ability to walk at only nine years old. His sixteen-year-old sister, Carrie Jo, had been driving with a fresh license on a sweltering summer day. With her were Wirt and his friend Ben Harley, who she was babysitting. The windows were down, blasting air into the car, and the money their parents had given her for an errand was wedged between the driver's and passenger's seats. A gust of wind blew in and ripped the money from the floor of the car. Carrie Jo lifted her right hand to try to catch the green bills flapping around her and lost control of the vehicle. She swerved right, overcorrected left, and launched across the oncoming lane of the narrow road. The car careened over an embankment, went airborne, and then hit a tree.

Wirt and Harley had both been wearing seat belts, but unfortunately only the type that draped across their laps. They whiplashed hard. The force broke their backs, Wirt's worse than his friend's. Carrie Jo was able to crawl, dragging a broken foot, to the side of the country road to flag down a family friend driving by. Minutes mattered, as emergency surgery was needed on Wirt to stem internal bleeding.

After more than two weeks in Allegheny General Hospital and three months at HealthSouth in Erie, Wirt accepted that his dreams of becoming a Pittsburgh Pirate were over. The doctors managed the pain, removed some of his intestines, and equipped him with braces and a wheelchair. Harley recovered fully.

Wirt came home unsure of his new identity—or if he even had one anymore without sports. Coach Reg insisted he stay a part of the baseball team and assigned him to keep score. It wasn't the same. But his mom still sat in the stands.

He continued to be a competitive student in school. Brush Valley, with a population of only about two thousand at the time, pooled children from several surrounding towns, and yet Wirt's graduating class was still a minuscule ninety-six students. In other words, there was little chance of his accident going unnoticed by his peers. Most were kind, and the few who weren't quickly learned to be. When one kid made a teasing comment about Wirt at the water fountains, Brandon punched him in the face. No one made any comments after that.

Wirt credits his introduction to sled hockey to Sue Birkmire, a nurse at Shriners Hospital for Children. During one of his follow-up appointments at the hospital to check on the rods in his back, Birkmire, whose son played hockey, mentioned how many young men she had treated would be perfect candidates for an adaptive team. One of those patients was Brad Bowden (b. 1983). Bowden would go on to have an impressive resume in sled hockey himself. He played for the Kitchener Sidewinders at only thirteen years old and would later compete on the Canadian national team, winning three Paralympic medals and multiple World Championships alongside the likes of Billy Bridges. Wirt would play against him at both the 2000 World Championships and the 2002 Paralympics.

Nurse Birkmire had joined forces with Bowden to begin a sled hockey team in Erie and one in Pittsburgh a few years later.

As his school did not offer the sport, Wirt had never played ice hockey. He didn't watch it, either. But his mom, aware of Birkmire's and Bowden's efforts, pushed him to try it. After all, maybe having not played hockey before the injury would be an advantage—there would be no painful "not the same" to put a damper on it.

The first time he glided on the ice, he said, he "felt free for the first time, like I could live my life again."

The new team was called the Pittsburgh Mighty Penguins. The NHL Penguins would not officially get involved with the team until the 2010s, but a young Wirt was starstruck when Penguins right winger Joe Mullen (b. 1957) showed up at practice a few times. Mullen had learned hockey as a boy on rollerblades in the Bronx. He became the first American to score five hundred goals in the NHL and was called the "quiet killer" by his teammate Bryan Trottier (b. 1956), referring to his surprise shots from the corner.[1]

Wirt didn't quite emulate Mullen, but he became all the more inspired to invest himself in the ice. He played center and focused on being a two-way player, someone who can be effective at both offense and defense.

In March of 1999, at the age of fourteen, Wirt played in his first sled hockey tournament. The tournament was held in Kitchener, Ontario. Angelo Bianco, the national coach at the time, noticed Wirt's skill playing for the Mighty Penguins. Bianco combed through the crowds, forcing spectators to crane their heads around him, in order to find Wirt's parents. He asked them about Wirt coming to play for the national team. After the game, when Wirt's parents asked if that was something he'd like to pursue, Wirt was ecstatic.

After officially securing his spot on the national team, Wirt attended his first camp in April of 1999. At fourteen, he was the first teenager and youngest ever to play for Team USA, holding that record even when the next-youngest players ever, Brody Roybal (b. 1998) and Adam Page (b. 1992), both joined the team at the age of fifteen.

The camp was held in Lake Placid, New York, and players skated on the same ice—the 1980 Rink (now also called the Herb Brooks Arena)—where the "Mircale on Ice" game took place. Having little history with hockey, and skating on it before Disney's 2004 film *Miracle* was released, Wirt was too young to fully appreciate the experience. That ice is also where he was quickly humbled into realizing how big a difference there was between playing against kids in Pittsburgh and playing against men.

That same weekend, Team USA scrimmaged against Team Canada. On one of Wirt's first shifts, he was thrilled to actually manage touching the puck and moving towards the net in the offensive zone with it.

The excitement didn't last long, as he soon found himself looking up at the rafters of that hallowed arena, on his back after being heavily checked by one of the Canadians. Up until that point, he hadn't been exposed to the true physicality of the game, as hitting wasn't as practiced in junior-level sled hockey.

Wirt was hit so hard his plastic bucket—the seat of the sled—cracked. He remembers a split second of dwelling on the pain in his back, and then a new thought replaced the agony: *I need to pop right back up like nothing happened and show the team I can play at this level.*

At that moment, Wirt righted himself. He forged right back into the play. Another player, Mike DiPasquale (b. 1968 or 1969), was on the bench for his first-ever national team experience. DiPasquale was a double leg amputee and a goaltender. When he and Wirt got back to the dorms that night, DiPasquale laughed and said, "I thought for sure you were dead."

Wirt's responding laugh was a little unsteady. "I might've been for a second."

At the end of the weekend, Coach Bianco presented Wirt with a USA Hockey shirt, his first of what would be many pieces of USA apparel. Bianco invited Wirt to play with the team anytime they held camps. He commended him specifically on his ability to take a crushing hit and jump right back in the play. Wirt had to smile.

For the second IPC World Championship in 2000, Wirt tried out again and—again—made the team. This was the qualifier tournament for the 2002 Paralympic games, and the United States finished last out of six teams. Wirt was pleased to represent his country but acknowledged that the team needed improvement. He focused on his own areas for improvement as well.

One of his key mentors was fellow player Victor Calise, a Team USA veteran from Nagano in 1998. He and Wirt also played together in 2000. Calise was instrumental in teaching Wirt: He would sit next to Wirt on the bench and explain everything Wirt was seeing. Wirt believes he would never have made the 2002 team without Calise—which is ironic, considering Calise himself did not make that team. The two joke that Wirt stole his gold medal and that Calise must have taught him too well.

When the national team invited players across the country to try out for the upcoming 2002 Paralympics, Wirt went for it and secured a place on the roster as the youngest player. He was so young, in fact, that his mom was required to chaperone him anywhere the team went. Just as she had supported her son at every baseball game, even when he could no longer play, Karen McClure poured her heart into Wirt's new dream. Once, when the two were traveling for the team, Wirt's wheelchair did not arrive at the terminal of the plane he needed to board. McClure carried him up the stairs into the aircraft herself.

She became quite popular among the other boys. Meanwhile, Wirt's father, Donald, stayed behind working at Penelec, the local power plant, to finance Wirt's travels. He had not often been able to attend Wirt's childhood baseball games, but on those rare occasions he could show up, Wirt recalls playing harder than he ever had. He'd wanted to prove to his dad that showing up was worth his time. Donald promised he'd make it to Salt Lake City.

Being the youngest player on the team had its moments of "young and dumb," of course. Wirt is a Christian, but with a wry smile said he "didn't always act that way." Like any adolescent, he was feisty and tunnel-visioned.

Wirt remembers attending the training camp in Minnesota two months before the Paralympics. The ice rink was a mile away from the dorms, with no shuttle available. Leery of the frigid, fifteen-minute trip pumping his wheelchair, Wirt accepted an invitation from Manny Guerra to "hold onto the back of his car" and hitchhike to the rink. All the seats inside the car had already been claimed by other teammates. Once, while zooming down the street behind Guerra's car, his wheelchair caster hit a manhole and jammed. Wirt went somersaulting into oncoming traffic. Guerra slammed the brakes. Luckily, Wirt avoided serious injury and pulled himself off the asphalt with only a sprained tendon. Guerra opened the driver's door and was laughing himself sick.

Despite his youth, Wirt worked hard to make the team proud to have chosen him. Vigorous practice helped him persist as a well-rounded player adaptable to any position. He developed an admiration for Mario Lemieux (b. 1965) of the Pittsburgh Penguins, because of both his skill and his health struggles, which Wirt found relatable.

At the pinnacle of his NHL career in 1993, Lemieux was diagnosed with Hodgkin's Lymphoma. Yet he caught a plane and competed in a game against the Flyers the same day he received radiation treatment.[2] Lemieux's cancer progressed and produced intense, symptomatic back pain, so much so that he said he could not even bend down to tie on his own skates: "I couldn't tie my shoes and I couldn't tie my skates. We had one of our trainers come in before every game and tie my skates. That's how I got on the ice."[3]

Wirt sympathized with those subtle tasks that posed unsubtle challenges. But he learned that to make it on the team, he'd have to find ways to figure it out. Lemieux would go on to own the Penguins, become a Hall of Famer, and trail only Wayne Gretzky in average points scored per game. In Lemieux, Wirt found who he considered to be the best role model to look up to: one capable of knowing the dark places he himself had fought his way back from.

You gotta play through it.

Wirt played one game in the Paralympics, against Estonia, and cheered for the team at the gold medal match. His dad was there. His mom, siblings, aunts, uncles, and all four grandparents filled the stands as well. When the USA won gold, Wirt knew just how meaningful that medal was to not only him, but to those Mighty Penguins back in Pennsylvania. He brought the medal with him to the first practice they had after the Paralympics. Young, hopeful players with disabilities encircled him off the ice as he held it up to them in the light. One of those enamored faces was nine-year-old Dan McCoy (b. 1994). McCoy, forever changed by that day and that medal, would later perfect his game and go on to win his own gold on the U.S. national team in Sochi in 2014.

Wirt graduated from the University of Pittsburgh with a degree in communications that he did "not a darn thing" with. On September 29, 2007, he married Katrina Kester, who he had begun dating just weeks before going to Salt Lake City. Wirt was unable to have children due to his injury and instead is a foster parent with Katrina. They have helped raise five children and counting. In the professional world, Wirt made his living as a store manager at Sportsman's Warehouse, overseeing eighty employees.

Wirt continued in sled hockey on the development team, which is a team that pushes against the national one and trains players with national potential to meet the threshold. His teammate from the 2002 gold medal cohort, Kip St. Germaine, eventually took over as the development coach. Throughout every stage of his playing career, Wirt never lost that driving voice in his head. He "played through" each new obstacle.

Wirt maintains great admiration and gratitude for his supporters and teammates, even as their sometimes young-and-dumb little brother.

When asked if he had been given any nicknames, he laughed and said, "No. Did anybody tell you otherwise?"

Chapter Fifteen

Game Three—USA vs. Norway

March 11, 2002

Hockey is figure skating in a war zone.

—Unknown[1]

Norway reigned as the defending gold medalists from Nagano, and they intended to keep it that way. Their team boasted the likes of defenseman Tommy Rovelstad (b. 1972), goalie Roger Johansen (b. 1973), and forwards Helge Bjørnstad, the captain, and Stig Tore Svee (b. 1963).

Team USA first encountered these men at the inaugural IPC Ice Sledge Hockey World Championships in Nynäshamn, Sweden, in 1996. The Americans took an 11–0 beating at the hands of the Norwegians and overall came in fifth out of six places. They lost to them again at the Paralympics in Nagano, and a third time at the second IPC Championship games in 2000, also in Salt Lake City. However, the fresh victory against Canada seemed to erase these failures in the heads of the American players.

"Norway doesn't scare us at all," Sylvester Flis had told reporters.[2] His confidence was echoed by the Canadian reactions to the recent upset.

"The U.S. has been hiding for the last couple years," Canadian captain Todd Nicholson commented after the game, "and now I see why."[3]

That defeat had sent the Canadian coaching staff into an emergency strategy meeting immediately after the game. Rick Middleton, on the other hand, allowed Team USA to soak in a taste of euphoria before getting back to work. He felt that was, at last, the game that made believers out of his players.[4]

On March 11, 2002, both teams filed into the E Center for the 9:00 a.m. game. The early hour drew a smaller but no less enthusiastic audience. Norway's coaching staff wore traditional Norwegian sweaters—frosty white patterns intricately knitted into a black base—while the team sported the home uniform in red. Head Coach Morten Haglund was younger than most of his players, and handsome, with broad shoulders, symmetrical features, and youthful complexion. He had held the position in Nagano as well and shared his team's thirst for another gold medal. Blond hair curled out from beneath helmets. Blue eyes pierced through face guard cages. Team Norway, known informally as "The Polar Bears," looked as fierce as ever.

Lonnie Hannah and Stig Tore Svee, #8, took the center of the ice. They faced opposite directions and tensed up as the referee leaned forward.

He dropped the puck.

Although Hannah came away with it, he fell onto his left side and flung the puck towards the defensive zone. Flis skidded forward and attempted to take possession, but Svee's desire for a second chance was stronger. He scooped up the puck and streaked for the goal. At only 9 seconds into the first period, he shot at Manny Guerra.

Guerra denied it.

Both sides attempted to recover control of the puck. It hugged the boards around the arena and slowly bumped from stick to stick, making its way back to middle before a clear battle for it began in the neutral zone. There seemed to be open ice on Guerra's end now. When forward Rolf Einar Pedersen, #3, acquired the puck, he shot it almost halfway down the rink at a chance for goal at the 32-second mark. Guerra seemed surprised. He knocked it down at the last moment, however, and now clamped his stick protectively beside the puck.

Guerra passed to a teammate, and the struggle down to the opposite end resumed. Joe Howard tried to carry possession into the Norwegian defensive zone, but three red jerseys bumped him off. The broadcast camera following the puck again changed directions. So far, Norway was proving itself as a gold medal team. The U.S. team failed to retain possession for more than a few seconds, making for a game that appeared to jerk side to side. This frustrating opening demonstrated to Middleton and the American players that victory would not come to them as seamlessly as the last two games suggested.

Then a penalty whistle blew. Svee was sent to the sin bin for two minutes on an interference call. With the Norwegians down one player, a power play conversion might be found at last. Hannah lost the resuming face-off—deep in the Norwegian defensive zone, he quickly became surrounded by red and spun a dizzying almost 360 degrees before letting the puck go. Norway fired it down the ice back towards Guerra, but there seemed to be no teammate there to collect. American defenseman Brian Ruhe adopted the orphaned puck and cautiously skated towards the middle again.

A red jersey dived at Ruhe from his left. He reacted with a forced pass at the two teammates he saw ahead with their backs to him. Those teammates didn't respond. The puck, unclaimed, slid fast along the wall and all the way to behind the Norwegian goal. But Flis had a plan. While Norway recovered the puck and prepared to catapult it to the opposite end, as was their style, he positioned himself at a strategic angle in front of the goal. As expected, Pedersen fired the puck towards Guerra—who was just a dot on the end of the arena from where Pedersen was—and Flis intercepted. Norway tackled him, but not before he released a shot towards the net at 1:25.

Save by Johansen.

The American power plays, drummed up with great anticipation, were not cashing out.

Frustration was mounting. Hannah again lost the face-off in the Norwegian defensive zone. Atle Haglund, #10, skated the puck towards center ice, where he met Flis and danced in circles for control at around 1:37. It was two gladiators fighting right atop the Paralympic logo. Captain Helge Bjørnstad, #11, joined the brawl, but Flis got away with the puck. He made for the Norwegian net, being constricted tighter and tighter by defensemen against the boards.

At 1:51, he fed the puck across several bodies to Matt Coppens, who was coming in hot towards the goal. Coppens's left stick touched the puck and then he lost balance and tipped over. The puck drifted away as he looked backwards at it, careening down the ice. Howard assumed it in the next instant and shot it at Johansen. It flew high, but not high enough. At 1:55, Johansen, once again, made the save.

Norway got its chance at last to repel the puck far down the ice, as the red jerseys always seemed to want. Both teams watched the puck wobble and glide with speed towards Guerra. It was a breath for reflecting on the exhausting first two minutes of game play that already felt like twenty. At this juncture, it seemed neither team would ever score.

Flis only grew more ferocious with frustration. He zoomed down the ice once more, abandoning others in his wake and keeping the puck close at his side with deft, expert movements of his stick. He was quickly suffocated against the wall by two defensemen, and he passed, almost backwards, to Coppens, who was perfectly aligned with the goal. Coppens pulled his left arm back to fire the puck, but Haglund swooped down and batted it in reverse instead at 2:24.

Ruhe, hovering at the blue line, caught the puck. He tentatively shot it past four red jerseys at the 2:30 mark of the first period. Johansen saved it but couldn't be everywhere at once. The puck rebounded to Coppens, who was just a couple feet away. He fired, and the goal was good at 2:32! The announcer howled and Coppens raised his arms, all the while Johansen was still pushing himself up off the ice from Ruhe's shot.

Finally, no more snake eyes on the scoreboard. Howard crashed into Coppens with a hug. Norway panted and exchanged glances with each other.

That hard-fought first goal remained the only crack in the scoreboard. Both teams continued the struggle for possession halfway into the second period. They wrestled in the Norwegian defensive zone, with heavy checks knocking the puck from one player to the next. At around 8:33 of period two, Howard flew in at high speed and rammed his sled into the side of a threatening Norwegian. The offended Norwegian jabbed his stick at Howard, who jabbed back, and a fight was about to break out when the whistle shrieked. Howard actually nodded—he knew exactly what he had just done, and sometimes it's worth it. Howard was guilty of the only penalty unique to sled hockey: T-boning. The dramatic move squandered Norway's chance at taking off with the puck, but it cost Howard two minutes in the penalty box. He teased the fish-eye lens inside the penalty box by leaning forward and giving it a mischievous look. Little did he know T-boning would come full circle on him before the Paralympics were all through.

Dave Conklin readied at the offensive zone face-off. The referee threw the puck onto the ice, where it reverberated and sprang like a bouncy ball behind both centermen. Kip St. Germaine caught it and seemed to gather his thoughts as he made one circle around. Then he fired a wobbly shot at the net at 8:48. It missed.

Norway took possession. Pedersen paraded down the left wing with what looked like uncontested ease, all the way to being eye-to-eye with Guerra. He shot at 9:09, and Guerra deflected the puck. But the rebound floated at the crease, and he scrambled to put a glove on the loose puck, stopping it before an embarrassing goal could sneak in.

Phew.

The rest of the second period transpired without a goal. Tug-of-war continued until 10 minutes into the third and final period. At that mark, Sylvester Flis charged down right wing, pushing and chasing the puck. The Norwegian defense curtailed him just before the net, but Flis shoved the puck towards the goal nonetheless. Flis, the defenseman, and the goalie tipped and twirled on the ice. The audience watched as the slow, aloof puck seemed to tiptoe across the goal line at 10:06 of its own accord. Johansen's reaching fingers could almost brush it. The quiet goal was good.

Now the score was a decisive 2–0, USA.

Howard rammed into Flis with a hug, beating his back as they both tipped over. The division between Chicago and East Coast literally disappeared in the cold arena air.

As the clock ticked down to the end, the puck spent the thirteenth minute of the third period ricocheting off boards and sticks. The Norwegians made long, smooth diagonal passes. The rink momentarily looked more like a pinball machine.

Pedersen occupied Flis at the blue line. Then Bjørnstad accepted a pass from left wing to his center position. He outskated two white jerseys and launched for Guerra. Guerra braced himself far out of the net, as if to tackle Bjørnstad instead of catch his shot. Bjørnstad cut right, shot, and scored.

Norwegian flags waved.

With Bjørnstad's 13:51 goal in period three making the score 2–1 with more than a full minute left in play, anything could happen.

A fresh face-off over the Paralympic logo was set up one more time. Conklin met his Norwegian opponent at center, and he flung the puck airborne towards the American defensive zone. Last-push adrenaline coursed on either side now as forces collided in the final 45 seconds. Team USA played a cruel game of keep-away around the Norwegians, flicking the puck to-and-fro in the neutral zone.

The last opportunity for Norway arose at less than 15 seconds to time. Norway fired the puck towards the offensive right wing. Tommy Rovelstad, #4, chased it with everything he had. It would have been a clear shot into goal manned by a lonely Guerra, but Ruhe beat him there by a fraction of a second. He pounced on the puck and lost one of his sticks, which went soaring down the ice.

But Norway would be denied.

The seconds drained to zero, and the horn blasted. Team USA had just defeated the defending gold medalists, 2–1.

Coach Haglund could hardly make sense of the upset he was witnessing. "I can't really explain what went wrong with Norway today," he told reporters.[5]

With three out of three games won, the United States had earned a guaranteed position to play for a medal. Inside their team locker room, a large whiteboard counted down each game until gold, with Moulton's juicy dry-erase marker slashing ink through each win like a hit list. But this would not, in all certainty, be the last time the Americans went head-to-head with these fierce, panting Norsemen with angry tears in their eyes. The insult Team USA had just dealt would have to be answered for.

Matt Coppens, who'd scored the game's first goal, knew there may as well have been a price on his head.

"This isn't over."[6]

Final score: 2–1
USA game MVP: Brian Ruhe
Fans in attendance: 3,317

Chapter Sixteen

Brian Ruhe, #2

"The Ruhester"

Pos.	GP	G	A	PTS	PIM	"+/-"	GWG	GTG	PPG	SHG	S	SG%
D	6	0	7	7	0	13	0	0	0	0	6	0.00

Brian L. Ruhe, born September 6, 1974, took his first solo flight at the age of sixteen, before he even learned to drive.

Ruhe and his father, Frederick, spent their evenings rebuilding personal aircraft in his father's shop. The small planes were high-wing propellers such as the Cessna 182 Skylane and the 172 Skyhawk, or the slim low-wing Piper Cherokee 180. Learning precision sheet metal work while working on the aircraft sparked Ruhe's love for engineering and science, and soon led him into the cockpit.

He remembers the peaceful hum of the engine and the beauty of looking down on the earth through a curtain of clouds. The ground control tower fed him information. But what meant the most to him up there was agency.

All the gauges and needles obeyed his will. Ruhe controlled his tilt, rise, and fall.

That sense of autonomy would be robbed of him only two years later. A car accident took both his legs above the knee and the life of his girlfriend.

The exact circumstances of what happened have never been agreed on, but what Ruhe does remember was that it was a cold night on January 30, 1993, at 10:27 p.m. He'd been traveling on a country road in Greenville, Ohio, where he grew up, heading to a friend's house to play cards before the next day's Super Bowl.

The vehicle slammed into a tree and split in two. The transmission gears exploded and ripped into him. His legs were amputated on site.

Ruhe's memory of the event is spotty. He suspects the involvement of another driver, citing skid marks and inconsistent witness accounts, but after strenuous legal battles, he paid the fee of his nonfelony court charge to put the event behind him.

The mystery of it still seems to haunt him.

His vital monitors beeped and sighed for six weeks as he lay unconscious in the hospital. He then came to at around 2:00 a.m. The room was empty of people. Cards, balloons, and flowers surrounded him. Ruhe looked down and saw his legs were gone, and of his girlfriend, he says, "I think deep down I knew what happened to her." He picked up the phone next to his bed, miraculously remembering his fourteen-digit calling card number, and dialed up his mother, Belinda "Lynn" Ruhe, a registered nurse, so that she could tell him everything.

Doctors had given Ruhe a less than 5% chance of survival in the first forty-eight hours. On top of the amputations, he had a punctured lung and a traumatic brain injury. Short-term memory loss had him greeting his father with enthusiasm every time Frederick returned to the room from getting a glass of water.

Ruhe's aptitude towards science, circuited into him under the wing of a plane, and his aspirations to become a researcher, allowed him to recall his medical condition in a procedural tone. Describing his return to consciousness after six weeks, he supplied that "the cerebral fluid in my brain started to release, so my memories came back." Discussing this with him was like speaking to his doctor rather than the man himself. I noticed a framed original *Star Wars* poster on the wall behind him, though, and wondered if there might be a little nerd (used as a compliment) inside this scientist, too.

Recovery involved up to seven hours of therapy a day over several long months. As Ruhe's amputations were above the knee rather than below, managing prosthetics was extra challenging. The balance and energy consumption depleted him. His goal, however, was to get back to college at the University of Cincinnati and to prove the doctors and the world wrong by figuring out a new course for achievement.

He owed that much to his late girlfriend.

As Ruhe's father returned to his job as a schoolteacher and his mother continued nursing (certainly both needed to work to pay for his medical bills), Ruhe witnessed a breathtaking act of selflessness. Retired family friends formed a coalition to drive Ruhe to and from the hospital three days a week for his rehabilitation treatment. It was an hour's drive each way, with the appointment itself lasting more than two hours. This act of love sanded off some of the bitterness of those hard appointments, but not all of it. Ruhe was still attempting to transition from wheelchair to prosthetics, and the world before him suddenly had curbs he never noticed and stairs he never thought he'd stare up at from the bottom. The challenges of relearning how to maneuver his own weight would prevent him from abandoning the chair until well into 1994.

He returned to college—a different one, though. After experiencing firsthand the frustration of problematic prosthetic equipment, Ruhe wanted to switch his major from aerospace engineering to biomedical engineering. He ended up at Wright State University to complete his bachelor's degree, and eventually earned a master's and a PhD in engineering from Northwestern University.

Northwestern happened to send Ruhe to the research lab at the Rehabilitation Institute of Chicago. It was there that Ruhe, one fateful day, ran into Sylvester Flis in the gym.

Flis gave Ruhe one look up and down—his stocky build, his missing legs—and said, "You'd be great at sled hockey. Come try."

Ruhe had attempted wheelchair basketball and adaptive swimming but never felt anything like he did when playing sled hockey.

He and Flis soon became defensive partners. Flis played offensive defense, with Ruhe the traditional defensive defense. In standard hockey, defensemen usually align themselves east-west inside the blue line. Flis and Ruhe made up their own rules, and it seemed to work. In this approach, which harmonized well with Middleton's, Ruhe patrolled closer to the middle of the ice, leaving Flis free to play like a modern rover (a discontinued position in ice hockey from the late nineteenth and early twentieth centuries that tasked the player with roaming the entire ice as-needed). Ruhe likened it to a tactic called the "Russian defense." When asked what their code on the ice together was, Ruhe laughed and said, "The code was let Sly do his thing and I cover everything behind him." Flis was the world's leading player, and practicing with him in drills was like running a blade on a sharpening stone each day. "If I could stop Sly some of the time, I could stop anyone else every time."

Ruhe was a key balancing component to Flis as his defensive partner, and Ruhe called his role on Team USA the "last line of defense." The two had a pact each shift to deny the opposition any shots on the net. Ruhe attributes his background in geometry as a secret ingredient to success in his zone. "I could read angles, read lines, and know the shortest distance between things." Indeed, his well-trained role performance would be critical in advancing the team to gold by maintaining a strong defense and enabling Team USA to outscore its opposition, 22–3, over the course of the 2002 Paralympics.

At the first game against Norway in Salt Lake City, where Ruhe earned MVP, Ruhe's friends formed a row in the stands, waving giant letters that spelled RUHE-STER. It was his childhood nickname—a derivative of his surname—and they included a picture of a rooster and his number. It made the news.

After the gold medal victory, Ruhe stayed involved with the RIC Blackhawks for a few years. He remembers a time when just he and four other U.S. players went to the Islanders International Sled Hockey Tournament in Canada around 2003 and, having no goalie, recruited Japanese national goalie Mitsuru Nagase (b. 1976), the same Nagase who played opposite them in Salt Lake City, to occupy their net. The six of them played every minute of every game, having no extra players to offer them breaks, and ended up beating every Canadian team to first place on Canadian soil. They laughed in disbelief and pride on the van ride home.

Now, Ruhe says sled hockey is a chapter of his past. He does not coach or play, and his gear is boxed in a Store-N-Lock somewhere in Las Vegas. When asked if he'll ever play again (perhaps by way of the new NHL team, the Seattle Kraken, which sponsors a sled hockey program near him), the slightest hint of nostalgia touches the expression of this direct, calculated scientist.

"Maybe someday."

Chapter Seventeen

Kip St. Germaine, #12

Pos.	GP	G	A	PTS	PIM	"+/–"	GWG	GTG	PPG	SHG	S	SG%
D	6	1	1	2	2	1	1	0	0	0	4	25.00

THE CLASSIC IRONY APPLIED TO FRANCIS X. "KIP" ST. GERMAINE III (b. April 3, 1965)—he wasn't supposed to go in that day.

It was an overcast summer morning on June 15, 1989, when St. Germaine debated heading into work. Before leaving the job site the previous afternoon, he had told his boss that he would be taking the day off. St. Germaine was a student at Norwich University studying economics, and he'd planned instead to spend the day preparing for an upcoming mathematics midterm. But the clouds blocking heat from the sun and the promise of a little extra money for beer convinced him to get in his car and work the construction site until noon.

St. Germaine earned around $600 a week at a home construction company that doesn't exist anymore. He and the framing crew attended a site in Falmouth: a single-family home that today needed a wall on the second floor raised. It was a gabion wall, 28 feet wide by 20 feet high. St. Germaine and his coworkers eyed it after a cup of coffee and decided to get the task over with.

A mist and light drizzle set in as seven men joined him walking this enormous wall up into position. Together they attempted to raise it, muscles taut. But with only about 20% left to go, the gargantuan wall began to creak and slipped loose. With a deafening crash, it knocked men into the opening for a stairwell and through openings for windows.

All St. Germaine saw was darkness.

He knew immediately that his back was broken. The entirety of the wall's weight bore down on him. Shouts and curses pierced his ears. It sounded like hundreds of feet thundered forward to help him. The others lifted the wall to about waist height; St. Germaine saw only the shins and the high-top Converse All Stars of the man to his right. The coworkers yelled for him to crawl out, but when St. Germaine tried to move, his body did not respond.

A colleague crawled under the wooden frame and dragged St. Germaine from beneath the wall. His coworkers rushed to call for help, and soon Falmouth Fire Rescue arrived to take St. Germaine away. Before the ambulance doors closed, he asked the men around him to call his dad, but to not tell him what had happened—not yet, anyway.

Everything was about to change. But St. Germaine wanted more time before he had to believe it.

St. Germaine learned to play ice hockey on the frozen cranberry bogs of southeastern Massachusetts. Each winter, two local farmers, husband and wife, flooded thousands of cranberries and delayed spreading on sand until the end of the season, postponing the melt to watch St. Germaine and his friends weave past one another in pickup games after school.

Hockey culture connected everyone in Bourne, Massachusetts, the little town along the Cape Cod Canal where St. Germaine grew up. The oldest of three, St. Germaine took to the ice as early as age five, followed shortly after by his brothers, Kevin and Kyle, who joined him around the television to revel at the Boston Bruins and the speed of #4, Bobby Orr. For a young St. Germaine, who also donned a #4 jersey, there seemed no better athletic role model. Orr, a Canadian defenseman, commanded the arena with cool confidence that made him look more like a statistician than a warrior. He earned a reputation for setting up plays that smartly conserved energy, only to lunge at the opportune moment. Orr was the first and only defenseman to win the scoring title in the NHL with two Art Ross Trophies: one in 1969–1970, when he scored a record 120 points, and again in 1974–1975 with 135 points, including an incredible 46 goals. Orr's prowess aided the Bruins in securing both the 1970 and 1972 Stanley Cups—and St. Germaine was enchanted.

Throughout high school, fittingly, St. Germaine played as a defenseman. His father, Francis "Butch" Jr., coached his various youth teams while St. Germaine's mother, Bette Jane, a schoolteacher of English, held court in the aluminum bleachers. There, she and the other hockey mothers networked and problem solved. If the kids needed new uniforms, she'd organize a bake sale. Family trips included attending hockey tournaments throughout New England, and for a little extra cash, St. Germaine worked the scoreboard or as a skate guard.

In some ways, it was hard to convince St. Germaine to do anything but hockey. He rode the bus home from school each day and there, jostling in the leather seats, planned games with his friends—which meant run home, grab skates, and head to the cranberry bogs. He remembers the exact bog where he learned to skate backwards and do crossovers (the maneuver used to accelerate in corners by crossing one foot over the other), perfecting his edge control, and he remembers the exact bog where he mastered stopping both to the left and right, equally well.

Parenting this competitive spirit, Bette Jane attempted to enforce a stable routine—such as homework before play—while Butch enforced everything else. Butch was a retired Marine and former state police trooper with a strict, disciplined disposition. He was bald and narrow, with a long mustache that trailed to the top of his chest. A symptom of both a small town and a history in the police force, Butch's phone would ring from a neighbor or colleague any time St. Germaine ran into trouble at school or in the community. By the time St. Germaine would arrive home and close the front door, his father's stern silence told him the misdeed had already been reported.

Looking back some years later, St. Germaine wondered if that was why he didn't want his dad to know a wall had fallen on him at work. But when he arrived at the hospital, it was only moments later when his father rushed in—having likely broken the speed limit on the 75 miles of highway he'd just traveled, guilty as anyone he'd ever ticketed.

At first, St. Germaine thought his injury was as simple as a broken bone. Broken bones to a young athlete were nothing new. He thought it would heal and he would move on with life. Under that wall, he recalled being "basically in a split position with my chin on my left knee," but never did he think it was bad enough to completely change who he was.[1]

During the initial recovery of his battered body, hospital staff tried to teach him how to relearn basic tasks such as getting dressed, showering, and transferring between the bed and a wheelchair. When he finally came to understand the severity of the injury, he said, "All right, fine."[2]

And then fought it every step of the way.

He refused to tell the Registry of Motor Vehicles that he no longer had use of his legs. He refused the idea of relearning how to drive with hand controls, saying he'd rather snap a hockey stick in half and operate the pedals that way.

One day, not long after returning from the hospital, he decided to make himself breakfast without any help. This ended with cracked eggs on the floor, milk all over, dirty dishes and bowls, and St. Germaine spending the whole day cleaning.[3]

It took months for the truth to settle in: St. Germaine would never walk again. And more importantly—his words—he would never play hockey again.

At least, that is what he thought.

St. Germaine had finished college in the hospital and earned his bachelor of science. He entered the work force with New York Life Insurance Company and tried to move forward, suppressing the dream of the ice he left behind. Surrounding loved ones noticed his melancholy, however, and annoyingly but with good intentions placed in front of him a constant stream of magazine and newspaper articles advertising various sports for athletes with disabilities. Roughly four and a half years after the accident, one article finally landed in his lap that caught his attention.

In Boston, a local organization was putting together a sled hockey team. The advertisement hit him like an ex-lover knocking at his door, and he paused in front of the paper. The call-to-ice lingered in his mind until one day, finally, he decided to use his lunch break to go to the rink and check out the team. No promises.

St. Germaine thought at most he'd sit in the stands, eat his lunch, and watch a few players with disabilities practice in the rink.

A short while later, he found himself strapping into a sled, lunch left unfinished in the stands. Unsure and half in a daze, he hit the ice in his sled and glided forward for the first time since the accident. The familiar cool breeze caressed his face.

Soon, he was circling the arena, grinning, in a full suit and tie.

He had found his calling.

St. Germaine skated in four one-hour sessions over the following three weeks. There he connected with the players and dusted off what he remembered from those cranberry bogs. He struggled at first with the question of whether this was "real hockey," whether he was truly back. All the ingredients were there: the chill, the competitiveness, the camaraderie, the ice, and the sounds. It may not have been exactly as before, but it felt familiar.

The club team, called the New England Ice Picks, consisted of a mix of disabled and able-bodied athletes. Two local groups sponsored them: Northeast Passage and the Wheelchair Sports and Recreation Association. Because sled hockey was still a developing sport, the early teams did not require players be physically impaired. They needed bodies, and this hybrid roster attracted St. Germaine, who saw it as a good sign the sport would be equalized and mainstreamed.

Perhaps the greatest learning curve for St. Germaine from standard hockey to sled hockey was balance. Balancing in a sitting position after his accident was "like balancing a pin on a pinpoint," and it was even harder in a sled. Many nights, St. Germaine lay a piece of cardboard on the floor of his living room (to protect the flooring from the sled blades) and just sat in his sled with the television on. He figured if he could maintain his balance in a sled while distracted by the TV, he could balance anywhere.

But what St. Germaine lacked in sled control, he made up for in strategy, harkening to the legacy of Bobby Orr and those evenings glued to the television watching the Bruins. St. Germaine's teammates admired his ability to see an enemy play developing and interrupt it. He never forced a play that wasn't there, and he created space for his teammates. He had an instinct for the game. Great heads, not great bodies, make great players.

Not long after joining the club team, St. Germaine traveled to Toronto to participate in a sled hockey tournament. It was there that he first saw "Team USA"—quotes intended. The "national" team and sled hockey itself had not yet been adopted by USA Hockey, the governing body for organized ice hockey in America and in Olympic representation. Instead, they were recognized as the USA team by merit of showing up with the right accents and wearing hand-me-down jerseys from the able-bodied USA team. Despite playing without national power behind them, St. Germaine sensed a whole other level about these players as he watched them contest Team Canada. He kept that awe in the back of his mind while returning home.

The rest of the summer of 1994 passed quietly. St. Germaine focused on his career and for a time allowed sled hockey to occupy the background of his life. Then, come late autumn, a teammate notified him of a tryout taking place in Minnesota that December. It would be for the U.S. national sled hockey team.

St. Germaine's ears perked up at that. But doubt and excuses set in. He had, by that time, only spent less than twenty hours in a sled, and he could not afford the plane ticket to Minnesota. Encouraged by his family, St. Germaine was finally persuaded to take a train from Boston to Minneapolis to attend the tryouts. Manny Guerra, the man who just a few years later would be his goalie in the gold medal climax of 2002, picked him up at the station.

St. Germaine spent four days in Bloomington, Minnesota, where he played Team Britain. That sharp game intuition his teammates admired did not go unnoticed by the observing U.S. sled hockey national team staff, including John Schatzlein and Bob Facente. They noted how St. Germaine never fell for the lure of the puck lodged into a corner, chased after by four jerseys. Instead, he'd stay on open ice, waiting for when the puck would inevitably fly back out—and right onto his stick. Impressed, the staff pulled St. Germaine aside at the end of a game. He was offered a position on the U.S. national team that same month, in December of 1994.

Years of hard practice, sacrifice, and face-offs led up to that fateful 2002 Paralympic gold medal game. There, in the roar of the crowd, St. Germaine thought back to those cranberry bogs. He thought back to everyone he played with as a boy, his coaches, and even rivals he once hated. He thought back to that fallen wall, to medical staff at his bedside—and to friends and family, some of whose voices joined the buzz of the air now. All of them were part of the resilience forged in him, and he wished they were all there to see this moment.

St. Germaine stayed with the national team for another eight years, adding a World Championship silver medal (Sweden, 2004), a Paralympic bronze medal (Torino, 2006), and another World Championship gold medal (Czech Republic, 2009) before it was all through. During the season of 2009, he developed an advanced-stage pressure sore and tried to play through the pain. The injury overcame him in 2010, however, and a young, upcoming player, Josh Pauls (b. 1992), assumed St. Germaine's place on the United States team.

Kip St. Germaine would go on to coach the U.S. men's national development sled hockey team, otherwise regarded as the farm system for the national para ice hockey team.

His gold medal hangs next to his jersey on the wall.

CHAPTER EIGHTEEN

Game Four—USA vs. Sweden

March 12, 2002

You've got to love what you're doing. If you love it, you can overcome any handicap, or the soreness, or all the aches and pains
and continue to play for a long, long time.

—GORDIE HOWE

NOW HAVING EMERGED VICTORIOUS AGAINST BOTH CANADA AND NOR-
way, Team USA was hailed in the media as something to the likes of
giant slayers. Rumors were beginning to circulate that the team was
"unbeatable." Swedish players preparing to face them sounded annoyed
by the buzzy questions reporters pegged them with. They of course
answered in the negative—certainly Team USA was not unbeatable.[1] But
their unenthused tones betrayed them a little.

Sweden's head coach, Björn Ferber (b. 1951), who had experience
coaching since 1985, was well trained at identifying threats.[2] He showed
the greatest trepidation for Sylvester Flis. "You have to control him if you
still have a chance," he said.

Middleton, when asked about Flis, echoed the sentiment, telling
reporters that Flis was probably the best sled hockey player currently
in the world.[3]

On the reverse, when asked about Middleton's performance, Flis
simply said, "I'll let you know at the end."[4]

Sweden enjoyed a noteworthy history with sled hockey. It founded the sport near Stockholm and won gold in the first-ever Paralympic sledge hockey competition in Lillehammer in 1994, playing against four other countries: Norway, Estonia, Great Britain, and Canada. Those five teams inaugurated the sport on the world stage. The gold medal game, however, was a frustrating shutout until overtime, when Sweden closed it out at 1–0. They went on to win bronze in Nagano in 1998. Sweden had also claimed gold at the first IPC World Championships in 1996, securing bronze at the second in 2000. Sweden was well decorated—the opposite of Team USA.

So far in this Paralympic year, Sweden had won two of its three games, defeating Estonia and Japan and losing to Norway.

The United States and Sweden met at the E Center on March 12, 2002, to compete in a 7:00 p.m. game. Sweden wore the away uniform— pale yellow with black stripes on the jersey sleeve cuffs and the bottoms. On the front was the Swedish *tre kronor*, or "three crowns," the national emblem of the country. The Americans looked confident in their bold dark blue and red. Coach Ferber on the Swedish side wore a stately sports coat over a yellow turtleneck. He donned a dignified pair of glasses and a calm expression harkening to his background as a federal judge.[5] Middleton stuck with his baseball cap and gum.

The first goal of the game occurred at 5:42 in the first period. Matt Coppens, carrying the puck down the right wing, hooked sharply behind the offensive net. He looked up, searching for an open ally, and then dished the puck several yards past the goal to Jack Sanders. Sanders caught it but barreled immediately into a throng of Swedish defensemen. The players who bottlenecked there, including Sanders, lacked any momentum and clawed at the ice with their picks to get moving. Somehow Sanders found a pocket to pass the puck through nonetheless. It sauntered into the net at a leisurely pace, but notched a goal for the United States all the same.

Flis seemed determined to score in the first period as well. At around 8:07, he made deadly gains towards the offensive zone from almost all the way across the rink, zigzagging to avoid the Swedish. Whatever great plans he had were interrupted by the cry of a whistle, though. The penalty was on Sweden's #16, Dedjo Engmark (b. 1979). Engmark, a forward, had mahogany skin and black, curly hair—a striking contrast from the silvery blond

Swedes he called teammates. Adopted from India at the age of seven and suffering from severe effects from polio, he had been playing sled hockey since 1995.[6] Today, Engmark swigged water in the penalty box, where he sat for two minutes for T-boning Joe Howard, who had skated ahead of Flis. The assault looked more like an accident, as if Engmark lost control of his speed as he raced to cover Flis. Then again, sometimes "accidents" like that in sled hockey are strategically placed; Sweden may have considered being a man down worth it in order to stop Flis from feeding to Howard.

Flis would soon have another chance, though. Still in the first period, Brian Ruhe, Howard, and Flis read the ice ahead of them and worked out a plan to move the puck out of their own zone. Flis took off on the left wing, Howard to the right. Ruhe passed to Howard as Flis continued to rocket up the sideboards. At 8:26, Howard pushed a diagonal pass in Flis's direction. But the pass asked a lot of Flis—he saw it coming in from the corner of his eye and needed to power forward twice as fast to make the catch in time. It was a move epitomizing the words of Wayne Gretzky: "A good hockey player plays where the puck is; a great hockey player plays where the puck is going to be."[7]

By the time the puck was safely on Flis's stick, a whole two seconds—an eternity in playing time—had passed. He then raced ahead with speed eliciting what must have felt like blizzard winds in his face. He eased to the right, leveled center with #14, Swedish goalie Kenth Jonsson, and shot the puck at 8:41. It flung high into the net.

The monstrous crowd roared. Flis raised a hand in triumph and skidded against the side of the rink as he cruised back towards the neutral zone. Jonsson leaned his back against the post of the net and closed his eyes, processing what had just happened. The announcers hailed the power play conversion to Flis's credit. The score was now 2–0.

But in the second period, it was Team USA's turn to spend time in the clink. Coppens got two minutes for hooking. He took off his helmet in the penalty box to reveal an American flag bandana. Then he leaned in and stared playfully into the fish-eye camera lens. Next, Lonnie Hannah dove into the box, beating his chest. He earned two minutes for slashing. Hannah held up a handwritten sign to the camera that read CALL MY LAWYER.[8] The announcers laughed.

This time, however, being down in players did not stop Team USA from maintaining their momentum. At 4:16, still in the second period, Flis motored towards goal once more. Swedish defenseman Niklas Ingvarsson, #3, a leukemia survivor, chased hot on his tail. He reached out an arm to interfere with Flis and fell forward on his face. Flis executed one of his signature moves: swishing in the puck while passing by the side of the net, almost parallel. It lit the goal lamp at 9:17.

Wild applause.

The camera zoomed in on Flis as he cruised back to center. Breathless, he cast his dark eyes from the cage of his helmet, gave a tired but cocky smile, and winked to someone off-screen. It was a look that could slay the easily tempted.

In period three, Jack Sanders approached the goal with three yellow jerseys pressuring him. He appeared to scoop the puck with upwards force and sent it airborne into the net at 8:10, making the score 4–0. Sanders curved around in a sharp *J* movement to face his zone again. He pumped his fist and two of his teammates crashed into him in revelry.

The game seemed to be heading for a shutout.

Third period arrived with no Swedish comeback. Conklin met Engmark, long freed from the penalty box, for an offensive zone face-off. Engmark's large frame overshadowed Conklin's—saying a lot, as Conklin was himself known as a tank on Team USA. The puck bounced away, however, and scooted into the possession of Ingvarsson. Despite coming

Sly Flis cruising away confidently after his second goal against Sweden.
COURTESY OF NEVER DULL PRODUCTIONS

away with it, Team Sweden could not penetrate the American defensive zone without dissolving like motes of dust caught in a filter. "You see the U.S. just smothering defense," said the announcer. "They can't even get in the zone."[9]

Ingvarsson's pass to Engmark just ended up striking an unprepared Engmark in the back. Ingvarsson skated forward to reclaim his own botched pass. He bravely streaked ahead but became overwhelmed by three Americans all at once. His shot was physically blocked by the body of Dan Henderson.

A hat trick in ice hockey is when a single player scores thrice in one game.[10] Flis was about to achieve it for the second time in the tournament. He ignored the wave of yellow jerseys surrounding him as he sped up to the net from center right. With a flick of his wrist, he popped the puck into the air and over the head of the Swedish goalie, who could never seem to meet the altitude of the Americans. The goal was good at 11:30 minutes into the final period. Fans in the NHL traditionally throw hats onto the ice when this occurs. This may not have happened at the Paralympics, but Flis egged on the crowd by gesturing for noise with both arms. Team USA capped off the game with one more goal in period three by Howard at 13:22. The final score was 6–0.

Jonsson, solemn, unstrapped his goalie mask and let it fall with his glove. While the American players celebrated on this ice, and while assistant coach Tom Moulton clapped, Middleton leaned on his elbows on the rails and continued chewing. He only turned when someone came up to shake his hand.

Afterwards, the excited players gave interviews. Flis held the visibly distressed game puck up to the camera. He smiled and said, "Six goals. That's what it takes. Six goals took the paint off."

Perhaps Team USA was, in fact, unbeatable.

But Norway still had a say in that.

Final Score: 6–0
USA game MVP: Manny Guerra Jr.
Fans in attendance: 6,400

Chapter Nineteen

Dan Henderson, #22

"Hondo"

Pos.	GP	G	A	PTS	PIM	"+/−"	GWG	GTG	PPG	SHG	S	SG%
D	6	0	1	1	6	−1	0	0	0	0	2	0.00

Dan Henderson popped up on screen. He was framed in a Zoom rectangle and smiled upon seeing me. His white hair was askew, his scruff on the verge of being a beard, and his eyes were wide behind black horned glasses. He wore a plain grey T-shirt and had a tattoo of roman numerals—the birthdate of his daughter—along his forearm. In the background of an empty room, a flatscreen was playing a movie, which I could only assume he forgot to pause.

When I asked him to tell me something meaningful about his childhood, he brought up the farm. Daniel Blaisdell Henderson was born January 4, 1965, in Boulder, Colorado, but his family moved to Sparta, Wisconsin, three years after his accident. They bought a hundred-acre farm with cows, sheep, pigs, horses, and chickens.

"I bought a calf once," he said. "A jersey cow. You know, the cute ears and big eyes. She was sitting on my lap in the car on the way home, and my grandmother said, 'Look at all those teeth, pearly white.' So I called her Pearly. I loved her. She was my pet, basically. She was just a milk cow, but I loved her."

I took notes fast. He seemed to really be lost in memories about this beloved animal.

"Then I sold her."

I looked up. He laughed a party boy sort of laugh. "I sure enjoyed that motorcycle I bought with the money."

And thus I *really* met Dan Henderson. He was mischievous, fun-oriented, and, when it came right down to it, violently honest about himself. He assured me, at least, that Pearly probably did not become a hamburger. She likely continued her role as a milking cow, but I would have preferred to see some proof.

I thought the story of Pearly was heading for a lesson somewhere: responsibility, friendship. But in Henderson's house, feelings were not talked about.

Instead, Henderson tried to learn by observing. The farm was a hobby, not a career; both his parents still worked regular jobs. However, his stepfather, Ephrem Gelfman, marched around the farm with a handful of tools, fixing things. He whacked fences into shape and repaired tractors. Once he spent two days meticulously forcing objects into the mud under the tires of a stuck farm vehicle, digging long grooves to haul it out through. Young Henderson often followed him and watched the quiet and self-reliant man work. He absorbed the qualities of independence and levelheadedness.

By this time, at the age of ten, Henderson had almost gotten used to his prosthetic leg.

On March 4, 1972, when Henderson was seven, his mother had pulled too far into an intersection. It was night, and orange construction lights blinked everywhere—likely the reason his mother had been confused about where to stop. Another car slammed into the side of the vehicle. Everyone was ejected from the car, but none as far as Henderson. He cannonballed into a farmer's irrigation ditch and, after landing, bobbed in and out of consciousness. If there had been water in the ditch at the time, he would have drowned. If his sister had not asked the EMTs where he was before she herself was loaded into the ambulance, he would have also died. No one would have seen him near the crash.

He woke up wrapped in so many bandages he looked like he belonged in an Egyptian tomb. One leg was elevated in a pulley. Everything below the waist was crushed and bleeding. A nurse wheeled his mother into his hospital room, and she—bandaged up herself—grabbed pretty much the only bits of uncovered skin available, his toes, and began to weep.

After several failed operations that summer to save his foot and reestablish blood flow, the foot died and was amputated four inches above the ankle. Without the foot, he recalled his leg feeling buoyant, like it could rise into the air, free of the weight of another body part. When asked if he remembered anything else about the accident, he shook his head and let out that mischievous laugh again. "My brain is protecting me from reliving it. Nah."

His recovery was angry and awkward. His mother didn't want to discuss what happened, and didn't want to process the emotions. She wanted Henderson to hurry through rehab and get back to their lives as normal. But they were, with painful obviousness, never going back to normal.

At first, Henderson had to relearn his boundaries—which, to a seven-year-old, seemed limitless. He still believed he could jump on a pogo stick and run as fast as before. When he fell or lagged behind, he frowned more, and that distinguishing spark inside, the one with which we all are born, flickered.

As a teenager, Henderson refused to go out in public without his prosthetic covered by long pant legs. God forbid he wear shorts or go to the pool. By the age of eighteen, however, he realized how much this self-consciousness was holding him back. He slowly forced himself to go out in public with only his stump or with a visible prosthetic. That was when it became clear to him that people didn't care as much as he thought they would. They were too wrapped up in themselves, after all.

In the same spirit of growing himself, and at the same age, Henderson showed up to a high school in La Crosse, Wisonsin, to try wheelchair basketball. He met another athlete with a disability there who played sled hockey, and . . .

You know the drill by now.

Henderson was a skilled defenseman, with the eye-hand coordination capable of lifting a glove and knocking the puck away midair. "I should have been a goalie," he said. "You open a cupboard and something falls out—I always catch it." He didn't follow hockey off the ice and couldn't name last year's Stanley Cup MVP. But he lived for the thrill and the camaraderie. Dave Conklin, his teammate, inspired him the most. Henderson admired how Conklin pushed himself to the edge of bodily harm for the sport, almost to the point of masochism. "He's paying for it now," said Henderson, in his blunt, irreverent way. "Have you tried talking to him?" The effects of Conklin's severe concussions made it necessary to have a translator (someone close to him) present for any interviews to interpret his slurring and fill in gaps.

Henderson's earliest game memory came from his first travel tournament in Canada. His team was lined up on the blue line for introductions, and one of the less-skilled players moved forward and raised his stick when his name was called. When he tried to get back into position, however, he tipped over onto the player next to him, which set off a domino effect, knocking all the players over one by one.

During Henderson's 1998 Paralympic experience in Nagano, he recalls a Swedish player Team USA nicknamed "Hamburger." Hamburger, says Henderson, was a "very large hunk of legless meat on a sled." He had the puck at the boards deep in the U.S. zone, so Henderson skated out of the crease to challenge him—it looked like Hamburger was setting up to shoot. When Henderson hit him, it was like hitting "a very large piece of frozen hamburger." Immediately his ears starting ringing, his jaw tingled in pain, and his face burned. Henderson couldn't close his teeth together properly. After a bit it subsided, but his jaw has never been the same.

Perhaps teeth are bad omens for Henderson. The last anecdote he shared occurred at a team camp in Boston. After practice was over, Henderson had invited a "nice-looking young woman" from the stands down to the ice to try out a sled. As the Zamboni doors opened to let her in, someone took a final practice shot at goal. The puck went sailing above the net and hit her smack in the mouth. She took off running with her hand clamped over her face to stanch the bleeding. Henderson got out of his sled, picked up two whole teeth from the ground, and hopped down the hall to the ladies' bathroom. As she cried, he sat down next to her, apologizing and handing her the two teeth. He has always wondered what became of her. "Needless to say," said Henderson, "I was not allowed to invite any more women down from the stands."

In 1992, Henderson graduated from the University of Wisconsin with a major in geography and a minor in earth science. He moved to Washington, DC, in 1994 to pursue a career in digital cartography, but arrived to find a dry work environment. President Bill Clinton had just downsized the government, and this put a freeze on hiring. Instead, Henderson picked up a job as a bartender, where at least drunk guys couldn't remark on his prosthetic hidden behind the counter. Eventually, Swank Audio and Visuals (which would later merge with AVI, its only competitor) hired Henderson. His job was to set up the sound systems and projectors at high-end hotels to support business conferences. He met President Clinton once at the Ritz-Carlton while servicing an exclusive event hosting only twenty-five people or so. As Clinton's Secret Service agent passed by Henderson, his microphone interfered with the one Henderson was hooking up, causing a deafening beep in Clinton's ear. The president winced, and he turned to give Henderson a look. Then Clinton laughed.

There was less laughing, however, when Henderson accidentally dropped an enormous screen on a chandelier worth tens of thousands of dollars at the same hotel. Crystal showered onto the floor. Managers came running in, mouths dropping at the sight of glass fragments covering the ground. Henderson wasn't directly reprimanded for the costly mistake, but he also wasn't sure Swank was sad to see him leave town. In 1999, he relocated to Chicago in order to more closely practice with the RIC Blackhawks sled hockey team, preparing for the 2000 international championship. Swank did, however, continue to employ him over there—where the Ritz-Carlton staff couldn't run into him again.

That same year, 1999, Henderson married German native Sandra Leibrich, who would be the mother of his only child, Lela. The marriage wouldn't last, but it ended cordially with Henderson making his final move alone to Denver, where he currently resides. He is a business owner and founder of a green energy company called Green Tracks Colorado.

During the 2002 Paralympic season, Middleton awarded Henderson the nickname "Hondo" because he knew a baseball player named Henderson who had the same nickname. It was the only pet name for Dan Henderson to ever stick.

A shadow box on the wall displays Henderson's gold medal from Salt Lake City. I asked him to think about that medal and tell me what he would say to a teenaged Dan Henderson now, if he could—that same teenager who was hesitant to go out in public without layers of clothes disguising his wounds.

Henderson thought about it for a long beat. A smile grew on his face that I just knew would be misbehaved. "Stop skipping class," he said. Laughed at himself. Then he sobered up. He talked to that teenager for real this time.

"Look, it's gonna work out." He nodded again and again. "It's gonna work out."

CHAPTER TWENTY

Game Five—USA vs. Estonia

March 14, 2002

I went to a fight the other night, and a hockey game broke out.
—RODNEY DANGERFIELD, COMEDIAN

ALTHOUGH THE GAME AGAINST ESTONIA WOULD BE INCONSEQUENTIAL
to the impending gold medal game, one thing was for certain: When
Estonia touched the ice, sleds came away in pieces.

Their last game against Canada on March 11, 2002, resulted in Canadian captain Todd Nicholson's sled breaking in four places. Nicholson's
injuries throbbed long after the final period, and Estonian forward Leonid
Zubov, #9, did time for T-boning. The country's other forward, Maksim
Vedernikov, #13, admitted to the match being "maybe a little dirty."[1]

It was in fact dirty enough that the *Deseret News* wrote an article covering the physicality of sled hockey, particularly as displayed in this game.
The article called into question the safety of letting such aggression go
without penalty or only lightly penalized: "It's not unusual to see players
go full bore and lean back to lift the unpadded end of the sled just as it
crashes into an opponent."[2] Estonia seemed to be especially good at this,
said the article.

But the *Deseret News* also acknowledged how quintessentially
"hockey" this brutality is. The article's tone thinly veiled its favoring of
excitement over safety—and may have even sounded a little proud.

That Estonia versus Canada game spurred dialogue not only for its bruisers, though. The match was the 2002 Paralympics' first frustrating draw at 3–3—and if not for a controversial call, the game may have gone to Estonia.

In the third period, an out-of-control Canadian crashed into his own net with what seemed to be possession of the puck. The net dislodged. Referees called no goal as they thought the net moved before the puck entered. A furious Estonian coach ran out onto the ice. Replays show that the call was probably misplaced, and if reversed would have made for an astonishing victory for Estonia. It was, however, an era before the practice of sending replay footage to off-ice officials who would review every angle and ensure the "right" call was indeed made. Even the NHL "war room" in Toronto did not yet exist for reviewing calls on a nightly basis during NHL games. The lack of replays at this Paralympics had been an issue among many players across national lines—and this outstanding example perfectly represented why.

The score stood at 3–3, though, and Estonia moved on with steam whistling from their ears. What better team to take that anger out on than the United States, glistening in its first-place ranking?

Team Estonia and Team USA met at the E Center on March 14, 2002, for a noon faceoff. Estonia wore bright blue with a yellow shield crest in the front, three black lions stacked in the center. For this game, Middleton decided to dress defenseman James Dunham and forward Josh Wirt, #19, to grant them playing time in the tournament and rest a couple of veterans nursing injuries in preparation for the medal game. He even allowed Manny Guerra a reprieve, placing Pat Sapp in the net. Middleton did not excuse Sylvester Flis or Joe Howard, however, needing to ensure Team USA did not let up on offensive pressure. And unbeknownst to Coach Middleton, Howard had other reasons for making sure he was in the lineup that day.

The choice allowed the Americans the first goal of the game at 4:15 from the stick of Flis. The crowd chanted "SLY FLIS! SLY FLIS! SLY FLIS!" repeatedly.

Team Estonia did a good job of chasing the Americans into the boards for the rest of the period and deep into the second. Their aggressive tactics resulted in Wirt's sled breaking. The bolt that held the blades onto his seat bucket snapped after a hard check, and the sled was wobbling. Wirt had to bump his way back to the bench, and Howard played in his place for seven minutes straight while equipment manager Jeff Uyeno fixed Wirt's sled.

Estonia tied USA at 1–1 with a goal from Juri Tammleht, #12, a forward. The time recorded was 9:42 into the second period.

At 13:49, Team USA struck back. Howard had been circling the offensive net like a shark and attempting to assist Matt Coppens perched at center. He grew frustrated by the congestion Estonia had produced at the net, which denied Coppens an opening. Team Estonia failed to dump the puck towards the neutral zone, though, and Howard arched around to reattempt. He sped towards the net, dragging some of the Estonians away from the gridlock at the crease. Howard jounced against enemy forward Kaido Kalm, #18, and Kalm staggered aside, freeing the puck. Then Howard turned, tossing the puck to Coppens. Coppens flung it into the net with his left arm. The goal was good, and the crowd erupted as he raised his other arm in victory.

Defense was still the name of the game, though. By now, Team USA had made thirteen shots, putting two of them on the scoreboard. Sapp had saved five out of six.

The horn blasted to announce the end of the second period. Although the score stood at 2–1 in favor of the Americans, Middleton paced the locker room and intoned strong warnings. "We're getting caught way too much," he said, referring to players caught out of position. "Do that against Norway tomorrow, we're gonna get our f--ing ass kicked." The players, listening raptly, panted and drank Gatorade while a muffled version of "YMCA" sounded through the walls from the crowd.

"Fifteen minutes," ended Middleton. "That's all that's left in this Olympics [sic] until the gold medal game. Let's go out and win these fifteen minutes." His use of "Olympics" rather than "Paralympics" may have been just a slip of the tongue, but perhaps it was a Freudian one. To him, there was no distinction in magnitude or importance.

Helmets on now, Howard called the team to a circle, and everyone laid forward their sticks, creating a nest of wood and black tape. Next to them at the door was the large whiteboard which had GOLD! written on it in red ink. On three, the team chanted USA thrice. They rowed out the door. Conklin, not dressed, lovingly smacked the back of Brian Ruhe's helmet. Ruhe made up the end of the line. The crowd grew louder as the Americans funneled back out onto the ice.

That second-period Estonian goal would prove to be their only. A late goalie change for the Estonians from #1, Valeri Falkenberg, to #20, Vladimir Karandasev, proved of little use.

Flis, Howard, and Dunham advanced as a wave towards the net. While skidding in at a tilt, Flis lobbed the puck in and secured a goal at 5:05 into period three. Howard would make the score 4–1 a minute and a half later, at 6:35. Fans waved full-sized American flags and shouted their approval. Middleton, standing with one hand down against the rink wall, blew bubble gum and refused to look pleased. Tom Moulton leaned in and whispered something in his ear. He kept chewing.

Arvi Piirioja, #6, on the Estonian defense, fell forward trying to stop Flis's next advance. After that, only white ice lay ahead. Flis forced the puck past Karandasev at goal. The clock read 12:30 into period three. Flis had just achieved his third hat trick in only five games.

Team USA claimed its final goal at 13:08 thanks to Coppens. His teammates piled onto him. The score, 6–1, would stand until the end of the game.

Sapp tallied a total of twelve saves. Thrilling, this moment was "the fruit of being on the ice by 5 a.m. and sleeping out of [his] truck so [he] can play hockey."[3] Any nerves he'd felt at the beginning of the game had dissipated once he realized nothing here fell back on just one player—he was part of an organism. Kip St. Germaine echoed this sentiment to the press, commending Howard for having calmed down as a player, it seemed, and allowing Flis the chance to score more goals.[4]

The players were eager to get back to the locker room and slash a line through Estonia on the whiteboard. Only one game to go.

But an announcer told the crowd not to leave yet, and an alarming siren rose and fell through the speakers. Howard faced the stands and ran a hand through his undercut bleached blond hair. His many earrings shimmered. He looked as if he were trying hard to control his nerves and smiled a demure no-teeth smile.

The announcer had found Howard's girlfriend of nearly five years, Carol Tribuna, a young woman with long, curly red hair and glasses, in the audience. He turned her attention to the Jumbotron and pretended to challenge her to a game of trivia.

On the board appeared the following question:

Which member of Team USA hopes to get engaged at the Salt Lake 2002 Paralympic Winter Games?

1. Rick Middleton
2. Kip St. Germaine
3. Dave Conklin
4. Joe Howard

Tribuna smiled and her eyes sparkled. She laughed and shook her head in awe as the announcer read the question. "Gee," she responded, "I hope it's Joe Howard."

"He wants to talk to you down on the floor," said the announcer.

Howard cruised over to meet Carol, and she crouched to his level. With thousands of onlookers surrounding them, he pulled out a ring and placed it on her finger. They beamed at one another. The Jumbotron read: SHE SAID "YES"! and projected their image across the arena. She wrapped her arms around his shoulders, and they kissed as Billy Idol's "White Wedding" played through the sound system.[5]

Finally, Rick Middleton allowed himself a broad smile. He had no idea that this was the reason Howard had insisted upon playing Estonia.

The proposal was a welcome intermission before the pressure would bear down on them again the next day. Gentle snow began to swirl through the air outside.

Hopefully, it was not the last moment of ecstasy Team USA would celebrate on this ice. But Middleton, walking back to the locker room and leaving the cheering fans behind him, was not all that sure.

The Jumbotron making a celebrity couple out of Joe Howard and his fiancée.
COURTESY OF NEVER DULL PRODUCTIONS

Final score: 6–1
USA game MVP: Sylvester "Sly" Flis
Fans in attendance: 5,400

Chapter Twenty-One

James Dunham, #7

"Diesel"

Pos.	GP	G	A	PTS	PIM	"+/–"	GWG	GTG	PPG	SHG	S	SG%
D	1	0	0	0	0	2	0	0	0	0	1	0.00

In the summer of 1982, James Gordon Dunham III (b. November 22, 1963) awoke to the thundering of aircraft. Helicopters the size of dragons chopped through the night sky, and F-16 jets boomed past overhead. The ground shook.

Dunham had been sleeping in a tent atop a roof in the Beqaa Valley of southern Lebanon. The house below was like all the rest surrounding him: made of twelve-inch-thick concrete walls acting like an oven in the Arabian heat. The roof was the only place he and the other missionaries could sleep, their skin caressed by the cool evening air. Silvery green trees outlined street blocks against the camel-skin color of the boxy buildings and dry earth.

Tonight, cries of terror pierced that block. Dunham watched as the Israeli military invaded Lebanon.

The conflict would be known as the First Lebanon War (1982–1985) to the native Lebanese. Although the building Dunham slept atop survived, the one beside him exploded in a blast of fire and stone. A bomb had been dropped.

Israel called the war Operation Peace in Galilee.

The next day, Dunham, only nineteen at the time, sifted through the debris. Locals carried away a few dead bodies from the site. Then the day went on as normal.

Dunham's father, James "Jim" Dunham Jr., had been reluctant to give his blessing to young Dunham. Not only was the Middle East again in violent motion, he also did not want to relive the horrors of Dunham's first mission.

Decades before, in 1966, Dunham had accompanied his parents on a mission to Mexico when he was only two years old. There, a mosquito bit him. He contracted viral encephalitis, which takes a deadly path from the bladder to the bowels, the diaphragm, and eventually the heart and brain, arresting functionality and rotting the body along the way. Some call it the "sleeping sickness," as those suffering from it eventually reach the point of vacating their minds and staring into space. They remain statuesque until the virus advances to the cranium, where inflammation as high as 107 degrees fries the brain to death. Doctors fed pain relief medicine into the toddler but told his parents there was nothing more they could do.

Dunham's mother, Kay Jones Dunham, wasn't raised to believe in miracles. She hoped no one was looking when she knelt in prayer anyway and asked for one. There at his bedside, she pleaded with God until, at around 3:00 a.m., a voice spoke in her head.

Don't you know I love him more than you do?

At that time, Dunham woke. His fever of 102 had broken. He remembers wanting food, wanting water. Wanting is a pretty good sign of life.

The virus began to reverse, and doctors could not explain how he ever left that hospital alive.

But he did not walk out of there. He hobbled, on wooden crutches. Irreversible damage had been done. The playful young boy would get used to those crutches—sometimes even letting them double as baseball bats with his friends or using them to hook onto a tree branch and climb it. "Things will be harder," his dad had said, "but you have to figure it out." He assigned Dunham the same chores as his two sisters had.

In Lebanon, Dunham crutched and limped through the streets as he helped rebuild residences and install water filtration systems. His disability did not stop Lebanese fathers from offering their daughters to him in marriage almost once a week. They yearned to send their children anywhere but here, and they knew that Dunham's four-week missionary program through the Christ for the Nations Institute would eventually call him back to his Texas hometown.

Israel was not at war with the Lebanese people; rather, they targeted Hezbollah and the Palestine Liberation Organization that occupied the land. It was ironic and painful all at once that as soon as peace finally touched the Lebanese factions from within, war arrived from without.

On either side of the Beqaa Valley rise two snowcapped mountains. Atop the mountain of the west live the Orthodox Christians. The east mountain hosts Jacob's Well, the Sunni Muslim village where Dunham served. For thousands of years, the fertile Beqaa Valley, with its checkered rows of deep green fields and chestnut-brown earth, was soaked in blood as the two tribes fought. Either side tipped warriors down into the bowl—some bodies remaining there and others returning to enrage their people more with tales from the battlefield. In recent years, though, the fighting had stopped. Then the Palestinian-Israeli conflict moved in.

Relations were, in fact, safe enough that Dunham traveled to the western mountain during his mission. He looked up in wonder at the village's ancient Orthodox church, with its smooth, pale domed roofs and glittering gold icons inside. The priest wore black robes, and his white beard fell past his chest. Dunham sat in a pew during liturgy as the clergyman mumbled words at the altar in a language he could not understand.

Then, the walls rumbled. The chandelier above shook and showered the ground with dust. Everyone in the church dived under their pews. Dunham closed his eyes. After around thirty seconds, the vibrations faded. Worshippers stood, brushed off their clothes, and sat back down in the pew. The liturgy resumed.

In Dunham's village, men wore *thobes*—tunics down to their knees—and loose pants. Some wore turbans. Dunham does not remember the Muslim women wearing hijabs or burkas. The colors were earthen—tan, or grey—unless an exciting visitor arrived at their homes, in which case the host would rush for a colorful scarf to drape around him- or herself as a way of showing the guest they were worthy of dressing up for. Dunham received such hospitality in the home of a Muslim woman in her sixties. Expecting his company, she had slaughtered a goat for him—a gesture of immense importance, as goats represented livelihood. He remembers the elderly woman kneeling on the floor, surrounded by broken tile, and battering the cutting board of meat with a wooden mallet. The process took hours, and she talked to Dunham with friendliness the entire time, then served him the meal and some Turkish coffee. He smiles as he remembers the coffee just being shot glasses of boiled-down syrup mixed with half a cup of sugar. The locals had thirty to forty shots of it a day.

Although his mission once involved smuggling himself from one town to another in a windowless white van to avoid being apprehended by a local hate group, Dunham never saw troops in his village. The closest encounter came as he was working on a house with a handful of his missionary companions. A woman walked his way as if straight out of a James Bond film. She strutted with her long legs and shining blonde hair. On either side of her were two beefy men with squashed, unwelcoming faces. They wielded AK-47s. Dunham turned to watch their approach, and some of the darker-skinned locals paused as well to stare at the white trio patrolling the streets. The gunmen stopped in front of Dunham, looked him up and down, then kept moving.

Dunham learned later that they were KGB agents in search of Americans meddling in the war. He says his disability likely saved him from abduction. "[When they saw me, t]hey probably thought: *Eh, not special forces. Just special.*"

The mission trip was risky to both his life and his physical condition. But the risk is what made him feel it was real. "Love is always expensive," he said. "If you are truly loving in your heart, it will cost you something."

When he returned to America, any self-pity he had left over from his illness dissipated. The experience of seeing people live in a war zone, in poverty, and still finding joy opened his eyes to the blessings of life in the United States.

Dunham moved to Hawai'i in his twenties and ran his own radio station. When he joined, the station was worth about $250,000. He catered to conservative audiences among the diverse ethnic groups of Hawai'i, including Japanese, Samoan, and native islander. He mixed music and interviews. While the AIDS epidemic raged, Dunham broke barriers and invited LGBTQ+ individuals onto his show with the objective of inspiring empathy. He lost several viewers and gained as many hate letters. In Hawai'i, he also participated as the only person with a disability on an outrigger canoe team, oaring in the predawn hours and admiring the flying fish splashing alongside the canoe, and occasionally the terror-inspiring shimmer of barracuda scales below the water.

By the time Dunham left the station, its worth had grown to nearly $2.5 million. He moved back to the mainland. In Dallas, he went to work as a repairman, and later fell in love and married. The decade before he found sled hockey transformed him into the man he is today—carefully worded, intelligent, and gentle. His wisdom comes at you not with the rapid chimes of a cuckoo, but the calm slowness of a grandfather clock. He is heavyset and bald, with a thin beard trailing down to his chin.

When Dunham hit thirty, his legs buckled from the physical damage that his childhood disease left behind. The effects were called post-polio syndrome, and he found his joints no longer able to support his weight.

Doctors recommended he move, permanently, into a wheelchair. He fathered children and balanced the challenges of parenthood in a chair.

Two years before he won the gold in Salt Lake City, Dunham found media attention on *The Oprah Winfrey Show*. While cleaning the kitchen on St. Patrick's Day, Dunham asserts that he heard a voice in his head say, *Take out the trash now*. This struck him as strange—taking out the trash was usually the last thing he did when cleaning the kitchen. It didn't make sense to take the trash out early only to fill more bags with trash after. He tried to ignore the intuition. But it persisted, more emphatically: *Take. Out. The. Trash. Now.*

Dunham relented, confused, and with a kitchen full of garbage still to go through, he grasped the top of the trash bag in his teeth and used his arms to propel his chair to the dumpster outside.

When he threw the bag into the dumpster, he heard a muffled mewing sound. His heart dropped.

In the dumpster was a human baby.

Dunham ripped open black bag after black bag. Then the worst possible thing happened—the crying stopped. He hastened his digging, and finally pulled out the very bottom bag. Inside, covered in discarded Picante salsa, was the baby. Dunham saved it. Oprah invited him into the studio to tell his story and underscore the Baby Moses Law, also called the Safe Haven Law, which allows parents to drop newborns off at the ER or a fire station, no questions asked, to avoid infanticide.

From that day at the dumpster on, Dunham's faith resounded. He considered adopting the baby boy but was unable to access the infant's records at the court. The baby developed cerebral palsy due to the temporary lack of oxygen, and Dunham wishes, as his rescuer and as a fellow person with a disability, that he could meet him and remind him that his life has purpose.

While his faith and experiences prepared him for life in the wheelchair, and for debilitating physical transitions, mentally, he could not reconcile losing one of his great passions: athletics. Crutches never deterred him as a youth, after all. He simply sat on skateboards and used his hands or sat at shortstop and threw the ball from the dirt. As an adult he longed for that same physical outlet.

And thankfully, he soon would have it.

A friend introduced him to wheelchair tennis, and later, when rumors circulated that a new adaptive sport was coming to town, invited him to Addison, Texas. There, sled hockey would be offered as an exhibition.

Rich DeGlopper, the national team manager at the time, had taken the sport on tour. The owner of the Dallas Stars, Tom Hicks (b. 1946), purchased twenty sleds and twenty sticks to accommodate a game. Dunham was told to bring gloves—he brought ones for gardening.

Despite the ragtag style, Dunham was lovestruck the second he boarded a sled and glided onto the ice. "Imagine you can fly for the first time," he said. But according to Dunham, Texans look at hockey as just "football on ice." After getting comfortable, he wasted no time before going after opponents and attempting to tackle them. No doubt his bulkiness was useful here. Seeing Dunham coming at you was a frightening sight.

Lonnie Hannah and Pat Sapp played alongside Dunham and would later join with him to make up the trio of Texans on the 2002 U.S. national team. They broke the news to him, however, that tackling wasn't quite legal here.

Dunham earned the nickname "Diesel." His heaviness made him slow to accelerate, but once he got going, he hurtled over the ice like a runaway Mack truck. Two key skills landed him that spot as a right defenseman on the national team: (1) he, along with Chris Manns, had the hardest shot; and (2) Middleton could use him as an enforcer to take out threatening opposition. Little previous exposure to ice hockey disadvantaged Dunham's ability to strategize, but he had a coachable attitude and a knack for adaptability. Middleton had him train in both defensive and offensive positions so that he could understudy any of the starters if they were injured.

His family—parents, wife, sisters, nephews, and in-laws—traveled to Salt Lake City to watch him compete for gold. Coming from a struggling financial situation, they slept in sleeping bags on the floor of a generous church member in the area. Dunham, who frequently received complimentary food from Paralympic administrators, smuggled snacks into his suitcase and brought them over to his family.

The most profound memory of the Games he cherishes is rolling through the tunnel towards the field of the Paralympic Opening Ceremonies. The United States was the last nation to enter, and Dunham advanced a few rows behind the flagbearer. From his low position, he could only see the starry blue tip of the flag ahead over everyone's silhouettes. Dimness covered him, those around him only shapes hidden beneath the arch of the tunnel. He could not yet see the crowd ahead, but he shivered when the moment came that the thousands gathered must have seen the flag emerge from the darkness. The sound was "like the roar of a jet engine" that filled the tunnel. Mere months after 9/11, the crowd cheered loud enough to echo the words of President George W. Bush on Ground Zero when a fireman shouted that he couldn't hear him—"Well, I hear you," Bush had replied.

Tonight, the crowd ensured the world heard their cheers.

Tears streamed from Dunham's face. His eyes redden looking back on that night. In fact, looking back on his life in its entirety thickens his voice, too.

"Whenever I fight depression," he says, "I just go and start helping people." The darkness doesn't stay long then. "Go find them."

CHAPTER TWENTY-TWO

Pat Sapp, #33

"Lt. Dan"

Pos.	GPT	GKD	GP	MIP	MIP%	GA	SVS	SOG	SVS%	GAA	SO	W	T	L
G	6	6	1	45:00:00	16.07	1	12	13	92.31	1	0	1	0	0

ROBERT PATRICK SAPP, AGE FOURTEEN, TWISTED THE KEY IN A CAR that wasn't his and slammed the gas.

The car jolted and he drove into the night. Ask him why and the reasons might vary. He'd been a good student up until then and went to church like any of the other boys. His parents fed him and clothed him, but the house still felt empty more often than not. His mother worked around the clock to support her three kids.

Sapp was born April 12, 1953, in Columbus, Ohio. And he wasn't sure he'd ever get out of there, especially when he looked in the rearview mirror and saw red and blue lights twirling.

Sapp jerked the wheel, hit another car, and flew into the front window of a grocery store. Glass shattered. He opened the door and ran like hell. For two days, he sprinted, hid, and sprinted some more. But the cops, eventually, were faster.

The jail doors clanged and that was it. Sapp was sent to juvenile detention, where the only tastes of the outside world permitted were an alternative school and a few shifts as a linen boy at a hotel. He carried towels to the maids and tried to keep his head down. All his earnings went to paying off the damages caused in the carjacking.

Only five years earlier, Sapp had shivered in the ten-below weather and held a fishing pole on a frozen pond. He looked up from the hole in the ice he'd chiseled and saw a handful of dark figures holding shovels and walking onto the pond. He pulled up his fishing line, breathed out a puff of visible breath, and approached the group.

Sapp stood far enough back that they wouldn't notice. Even under heavy jackets and red faces, he recognized a few of the boys from church. They used their shovels to fling snow off the ice and carve lines into the surface.

They were making a hockey rink.

Sapp watched, enraptured, as the boys stomped their feet into skates and glided along the homemade rink. There was no body checking, no keeping score. No helmets, either. But there was speed and laughter and the satisfying scrape of blade on ice.

Every day that winter, Sapp returned to observe the games. The boys noticed him now, of course, but Sapp kept his distance. He didn't know the sport and was too embarrassed to ask questions. It seemed the teenagers had their own language when they played, full of slang and funny words.

Instead, Sapp flipped through the black-and-white channels on his home TV and stopped on ice hockey. He studied it. Read about it. That little round puck moved around in his head when he closed his eyes at night.

So when he lay in bed in juvenile detention at fourteen, he thought about how he wished he'd picked up a stick instead of stolen car keys for fun. This track was going nowhere fast.

Sapp continued to struggle with the law, and at the age of eighteen, he was given a choice: finish his sentence, or join the United States Marines Corps.

Well, an American flag in the background of a photo sure looked a lot better than a white wall.

The Marines chose jobs for Sapp and taught him authority. Harsh as it was, the structure and support are what the young man needed. It was the first time he felt like something bigger than himself had his back.

Sapp began a successful career. He worked hard, showed up, and soon found himself with a White House clearance working directly alongside the commandant of the Marine Corps, General Robert E. Cushman Jr. (1914–1985), at the 8th and I barracks, the oldest active post in the Marine Corps.

Things were looking up. Until Sapp took a hard fall down. On April 2, 1974, Sapp, four other Marines, and a few FBI agents steadied themselves in a CH-46 helicopter. The cargo helicopter flew over Quantico, Virginia, for a routine training. All were to jump.

Sapp jumped, air rushed, and he jerked out the cord of his parachute. It fired out and deployed. Air thrust into the canopy above him and tugged his harness upward, but then something collided into him.

It was another Marine, with no parachute.

They tangled together and tumbled in the air. Moments later, Sapp was on the ground. He couldn't see. Nausea lurched through him. Voices shouted.

He remembers the hospital next.

The accident caused severe neurological damage, and stitches covered his body. As a form of physical therapy, he pushed a lawnmower down hospital hallways to a symphony of beeps and machinery. Pain was his existence. Eventually, doctors put him into a wheelchair, and he remembers being told that those wheels would be his new legs for the rest of his life. The Marines had medically discharged him as a sergeant E5. He was told to go home to Ohio, live with his parents, and apply for disability income from the government.

Well, that lasted about a week. As his legs were weakened and torn, Sapp dragged himself into a car by his upper body and used a cane to operate the pedals with one hand; he held the wheel with the other. He drove straight to Wisconsin to live with a friend and acquire a job at the United States Post Office. Around this time, in 1981, the post office had established an initiative to hire veterans who could pass an exam.

Sapp worked in the mail room for thirteen years. He married and had a daughter, and time took its toll on his struggling body. The mail job required standing on his feet most of the day, and soon Sapp resorted to doing whatever it took to kill enough pain so he could keep working and prove wrong everyone who encouraged him to collect disability checks and do nothing more.

At first, doctors attempted reflexive sympathetic dystrophy (RSD) surgery, a process that burns all the nerves coming out of the spinal cord to eliminate pain but leaves the patient without any sensation there at all. It wasn't a great success. The medical professionals encouraged him to stop working, but Sapp resisted yet again. He continued to grind his body down to the wire under bags and bags of mail.

So Sapp found the bottle, the pills, the stupors—and his wife found the door. She took his daughter with her.

Distraught once again, Sapp left the post office and retreated to an isolated cabin in the Wisconsin wilderness. He boarded up for three years. With bitter irony, Sapp realized that he had lost his family and his health doing what he'd set out to do—keep a job and never succumb to federal support—and he still ended up jobless.

One day, sometime when Sapp allowed himself to see people again, he drove in for an appointment at the local Veteran's Association. It was there, in the hallway afterwards, that he met Tom Wheaton, a U.S. Navy veteran, who was way too enthusiastic about handicapped sports. Wheaton had served on the USS *Fort McHenry* before sustaining a spinal cord injury in Perth.[1] He was friendly and persuasive, and he invited Sapp to a winter sports clinic in Crested Butte, Colorado.

Four hundred veterans with disabilities gathered in Crested Butte to compete. Like at that pond as a kid, Sapp stood far back, wore a tight expression. He crossed his arms a lot. While others around him buzzed with the adrenaline of excitement, Sapp avoided talking, sizing up the people in the room and wondering if this really could be him one day.

"One day" came pretty fast. Somehow, Sapp was convinced to sign up for a single day of skiing. He was handed a number and told to wait in the lodge for the able-bodied instructor to show up and meet him.

Up walked a large man with the confident stride of someone who's seen a lot of things and tackled a lot of crooks. He was over six feet tall, with hairy arms that hung down to his ankles. His barbed Manhattan accent proved he was NYPD better than any badge could.

Sapp looked at him, then at the two other men beside him—enforcers!—who would be there to heed his command and wrestle Sapp into his equipment.

Words lodged in Sapp's throat. Before he could say anything, however, the cop kneeled down, gripped Sapp's wheelchair with both hands, looked him in the eyes, and said, "Listen. I'm gonna take you up to the top of that mountain, and if you ski down that mountain, you can do anything in this world you want to do."

Sapp blinked rapidly. Up the ski lift, into the frigid wind, and approaching that mighty peak they went. And then, just moments after they reached the summit, a jolt of force pushed Sapp forward and his monoski careened down the slope. The cop, on skis as well, was tethered to a safety cord yards behind him. In a blur the world flashed by and snow hissed beneath Sapp. He felt he might die again. But he also felt something coming alive.

With a bump and a wide, turning arc to slow their momentum, the team reached the bottom. It was done. Panting, the cop stomped through the snow and stopped in front of Sapp. He said, "Today is the first day of your life, right now." And dammit, heart pounding and mind racing, Sapp finally nodded. "You're gonna start talking to yourself," said the cop, "saying 'I can do anything I want to do.'"

And that day, Sapp swears, is the day everything changed.

Not long after, he founded an adaptive ski program in Bend, Oregon, where six mono- and bi-skis were purchased. To this day, the United States Paralympic ski team practices at the very program Sapp created. He got remarried. Together with his new wife, he relocated to Texas, where Sapp participated in wheelchair racing and the annual Veterans Wheelchair Games.

He was even invited by the renowned 3rd Battalion of the Marine Corps to run with the soon-to-be boot camp graduates—an honor all but unheard of. A newspaper article captured a photo of Sapp, in his slick manual racing wheelchair, in the lead ahead of a column of uniformed cadets trying to keep up. He outpaced them, traveling three miles in under five minutes.

In 1997, Pat Sapp met sled hockey. A fateful clip popped up as a suggested video on the internet. He clicked on it and spent the remainder of the night frying his computer watching footage. Sapp noticed there was a U.S. team preparing to head to the 1998 Paralympics in Nagano, and the very next day, he drove to the Dallas Stars training center in Arlington, Texas.

Sapp wheeled into the office of Robert "Bob" Gainey (b. 1953), former NHL player for the Montreal Canadiens and then general manager of the Dallas Stars. Gainey boasted a successful playing career, with five Stanley Cup championships and, arguably more impressive, four consecutive Frank J. Selke trophies. The Selke Trophy seeks to recognize a very particular type of player: forwards—those whose main objectives are to score—who demonstrate unprecedented defensive skill. This unique combination screamed Gainey's name when the Selke Trophy debuted in the 1977–1978 season. Gainey leaned on consistency as opposed to aggression, providing a steady ally near the net for the Canadiens' attack dogs. Brawls on the ice with Gainey were rare. He retired in 1986 and transitioned to managerial and coaching positions amid the tragic death of his wife to brain cancer in 1995.

Sapp approached the secretary desk. "I need to speak to Bob Gainey."

"Really?" The secretary's brow rose. "Do you have an appointment?"

To this Sapp replied with confidence, "I don't think I need one. I want to play hockey."

The secretary stood and disappeared for fifteen minutes. She returned, and said, "He wants to talk to you."

Sapp must have felt a sense of unreality hit as he entered the office of Gainey and sat across from his desk. The man greeting him had curly auburn hair that was just beginning to recede, revealing a tall forehead. His blue eyes were hooded, and a rosy complexion gave him a sense of friendliness.

"Mr. Gainey," Sapp said, once the formalities had been dispensed with, "I'll clean bathrooms if you give me one hour of ice time and a goalie coach."

Gainey sat back in his chair. "You want to play hockey."

"Yes, sir."

"How do you play hockey in a wheelchair?"

Sapp introduced sled hockey to Gainey, who listened, asked questions, and listened some more. By the time Sapp was through, Gainey was quiet. And then he started to nod.

Sled hockey intrigued Gainey. He agreed to grant Sapp ice time in exchange for Sapp chartering the first Dallas Stars sled hockey team. Lonnie Hannah and James Dunham, who would eventually be Sapp's teammates at the 2002 Paralympics, joined the team. One was greener than the next. The men slammed into each other on the ice and wobbled themselves steady in their sleds. They pitched the team to anyone—able-bodied or disabled—who would listen, trying to grow the program.

Less than a year later, Gainey invited the U.S. sled hockey team, fresh from the 1998 Nagano Paralympics, to play Sapp's Dallas Stars. Rich DeGlopper, manager for Team USA, watched Sapp from the sidelines. He pulled him aside before he could reach the lockers.

So Pat Sapp, at the upward age of forty-five, was invited to try out for one of the two goalie positions needed for the United States sled hockey team.

Sapp took the position seriously. Still in Texas, he rotated between Duncanville, Addison, and Arlington ice rinks daily to play pickup games during his lunch break. At home, he spent hours sitting in his sled and shifting his body, studying the ways he could compensate for his weight to achieve perfect balance.

One night, Sapp waited in the lobby of a hotel before a Colorado Avalanche game, hoping to catch #33, four-time Stanley Cup goaltender Patrick Roy (b. 1965), with whom he shared a jersey number. The professional appeared, walking across the foyer. He sported a blond beard and thick, Nordic brows. In Sapp's forward way, he cornered Roy, but Roy didn't need much coercion. The NHL goalie sat down in a chair to speak with Sapp for roughly twenty minutes, answering Sapp's questions about the art of puck-stopping. Roy had earned a reputation for expanding the role of the goalie beyond the crease in ice hockey. He roosted at the net like an eel, darting out and lunging for opposing players if he could reach them. Roy was also known for falling to his knees to stop a shot—what would come to be known as "butterfly style"—ushering in a whole new trend of goaltending. Finally, Roy contributed to defense by covertly signaling to his teammates when an opposing player was about to swoop in from behind. He shared with Sapp his strategy of using advertisement signs around the rink as mental point markers to help measure how much he needed to back up or shift to perfectly align with the net. He stressed the necessity of closing the angles opposing players might find, and—true to character—claimed that coming out of the goal was the best way to do this. Inside the net, the goalie is only a small dot in a large square. The geometry doesn't work.

The conversation was easy, but Sapp took note of every word. At the end, Roy stood and said, "Someday I'm gonna ask for your autograph."

Sapp continued to hone his craft until realizing, much like fellow goaltender Manny Guerra had, that he simply wasn't going to achieve optimal performance without a custom-made sled. His regulation equipment was simply too awkward.

That's when Sapp decided to knock on the door of a factory in Rockwall, Texas. A woman answered the buzzer, and Sapp cold-pitched his problem—and his idea. She let him in. I asked Sapp how he managed to, literally, open doors as if by magic, how he got person after person to lend him their aid when, to many, the world often seems determined not to help. "If you believe in what you want to do," Sapp reflected, "people respond to that."

The factory belonged to none other than the Indianapolis 500 Extreme Team. And Sapp asked to meet with a racecar engineer. He rolled in to find model racecars parked in the warehouse, their bright paint jobs reflected against spotless floors. Moments later, the engineer's footsteps echoed as he approached Sapp. He bent down to speak eye-to-eye and said, "What can I do for you?"

Sapp repeated his predicament and requested the engineer build him a custom sled.

Fortunately, when an engineer is presented with a problem to which the solution is bolts and blueprints, his or her schedule swiftly clears. The racecar engineer agreed to help, and he called in a few coworkers. They laid out graph paper, and one took notes from a computer on sled hockey regulations. The bustle and energy surrounding Sapp would have been fit for spacecraft designers in a NASA hangar. Sapp came into the factory once a week so the engineers could measure him and test which parts of his body were weaker or stronger. In the end, Sapp received an ideal custom sled, free of charge. The engineers even arranged to put a United States Sled Hockey Association sticker on their racecar that year when it raced.

The new sled gave Sapp the edge he sought, but there was one thing no piece of equipment could change: his aging body. Sapp outranked, by age, his teammates by an average of ten years. His body suffered pressure sores and urinary tract infections. The teammates nicknamed him "Lt. Dan," like the character from *Forrest Gump* (1994), fusing his previous military service and his grizzled physical history. He pushed past the pain, believing the only way to success was to train harder than the enemy, to be physically and mentally *more* than the enemy.

That, and he plain old loved hockey. "It's no god," he said, "but it's awful close to heaven."

He admired how head coach Rick Middleton looked at the team not as a charity but a challenge. He didn't flinch away from the scars some people couldn't deal with. Sapp, who was used to not removing his shirt in public to conceal his injuries, felt the pleasant and unfamiliar feeling that Middleton might not mind. That acceptance, to Sapp, meant everything. Acceptance of self, of what you are, of what you've been through, meant that when doors open, you're *ready* to walk through.

Sapp retired at the age of fifty-one, "so old everyone thought I was the coach," he laughs. He knew when he was breaking bones that were no longer healing it was time to slow down. Every minute in the sport was worth it, though. "There is no greater honor," Pat says softly, "than to serve my country twice."

Sapp has continued to watch hockey and run clinics in Dallas. He donated some of his gear to a display case at the historical Colorado Springs Olympic Training Center, and the rest of the memorabilia he left to his home office, a place where he goes into quietly, shuts the door, and looks around the walls and shelves to feel whole again.

In 2002, during the Paralympic games, Sapp dyed his hair gold, long before the team had the medal in reach. The team laughed and teased it, but Sapp gestured to his locks of shimmering gold and assured them that in thirteen days, they'd "have this around [their] neck." He wanted them to remember what he learned in the Marines: You don't win something and become a champion. You were a champion before you won.

"They needed to see that," says Sapp. "They needed to know they can win."

CHAPTER TWENTY-THREE

The Storm before the Storm

I've been gifted. But the world is full of people who've not been gifted. Not only haven't [they] been gifted, but they've had things taken away from them. All I have to do is see one of them . . . some little girl that can't walk and yet she keeps on smiling at me . . . and then I don't think I'm such a big hero anymore. I think that compared to those people, I'm a very small article. . . . It knocks me down pretty bloody fast.

—BOBBY ORR[1]

WHEN THE U.S. TEAM ARRIVED IN SALT LAKE CITY, NO ONE HAD looked their way. Estonian assistant coach Ollie Sildre, when asked by reporters what teams he had to look out for, had answered Norway and Canada.[2] No mention of the United States.

Now, he struggled to explain his loss to them. "We hoped if we changed the goalie it would light up the game," he said, referring to their switch in the third period, "but it didn't happen today."[3]

Aleksander Jarlokov, game MVP for Estonia, said, "We played the best we could until the end. Just those little, light goals that they hit—the puck just went slightly in. That makes us unprepared and feel nervous."[4]

An angrier Juri Tammleht blamed his team for phoning it in. "We should have won the game," he declared. "Each player didn't play the best that they could have." He went on to mention how much more blessed with opportunity the United States is. "USA is a large country with freedom, and they can do what they want to do. Estonia is a smaller country, and we have less advantages. We didn't have anything to lose in this game, but it was a sharp fall and it hurt."[5]

While pleased with its victory, Team USA recognized that Tammleht's words held truth. Kay Robertson, who worked for the U.S. team, had also graciously accepted the responsibility of making sure all participating teams had their laundry and towels taken care of. She had visited the Estonian locker room after the game and was taken aback by the conditions the players dealt with. Team USA may have been underfunded, too, but not like this. The Estonian goalie glove was riddled with holes. Robertson, with a lump in her throat, took the glove back to the United States team. After seeing it, U.S. team members—and a few referees—split open their wallets and pitched in to purchase a brand-new glove and other supplies. Robertson and a few U.S. players returned to the Estonian locker room to present the glove to the team. "Tears flowed unashamedly from [the Estonians' faces]," Robertson said.[6]

Meanwhile, one final hurdle stood in the United States' way to victory against Norway, and it came from within. When Rick Middleton decided not to dress Patrick Byrne for the gold medal game, Jeff Jones sent a message out to all seven RIC Blackhawk players. He called on them, in the name of loyalty, to refuse to play in the game unless Byrne was dressed alongside them. The Chicago players today are tight-lipped about what that email and the conversations considering the demand looked like. What is clear, however, is that Jones's final attempt to exert control over his Blackhawk players from afar was unsuccessful. No one agreed to boycott the game, and they played without Byrne in the lineup.

A few weeks later, on April 3, 2002, Jones would chastise the players for this. He wrote in an email,

> As far as loyalty, Patrick is the only one who really understands the meaning of loyalty. True loyalty can't be used only when it is convenient. I realize that you were faced with two types of loyalty. Obviously your primary loyalty while you wear a Hawks jersey is to RIC. Based on the level of commitment RIC has made to this program over the past 3 years, all of you should be pissing RIC green....

I am convinced that if the 7 RIC players went to Middleton to give up their jerseys he would have had to play Patrick. You all know Patrick deserved to dress. He earned it in each and every camp. Patrick stuck by his conviction to the end, he has [*sic*] expendable and he got screwed. And to some extent, you as his teammates let it happen.[7]

This was the second time that Jones's intrusion into the national team asked for unprecedented sacrifice from the RIC Blackhawk players. If they had complied, they would have lost their own opportunity to play in a once-in-a-lifetime gold medal game—and probably would have cost the entire team the victory that inspired this book. It cannot be overlooked, however, that just as with the case of Mike Doyle being cut, Jones's ire was actually in the defense of another person. One would think that by this point, when it was clear Jones would not be granted Middleton's job just hours away from the last game, Jones would have lost interest in trying to line up his allies or meddle in the business of the team at all. For this reason, his actions do suggest a motivation of genuine passion for Byrne's good. At the same time, one has to wonder how much Jones viewed Byrne as an individual as opposed to as an extension of the program Jones ran. He is a complicated figure.

Of course, a chief reason the Blackhawk players ultimately rejected Jones's appeal was probably due to an awareness that it would be a bad personal and career choice for them. Sylvester Flis had attempted to change the very laws of the United States just so he could compete. The decision to put that dream ahead of torn loyalties may have been painful for him. But his ambition had never once been inconsistent, and making that choice could be seen as the final test of Flis's resolve.

He was here to play.

Another reason for rejecting Jones's proposition that can't be discounted might have been the feeling of family and camaraderie that had at last grown between the players, whether they noticed it happening or not. At this point in the Paralympics, they'd rallied together against the Canadians' insults; they'd pummeled through a rough, low-scoring first game against Norway; they'd shared the close quarters of the Village and the early-morning bus; they'd joined forces to bless the Estonian team with goodwill; and they'd congratulated Joe Howard on his engagement. (Howard joked that now he *and* his fiancée would be going home with gold.) Not a moment too soon, the U.S. players finally embodied Sidney Crosby's famous quote: "I promise to play for the logo on the front, not the name on the back."[8]

The men shared the cameras, too, in interviews after every game, and now, before the gold medal match, all as one team in the locker room. A&E's Harry Smith, the host, no longer sat in that cozy ski lodge by the fireplace for the television—he leaned forward on a folding chair, surrounded by equipment, cubbies, and hooks, and faced the entire U.S. team, asking them "How the hell did we get here?"–type questions. The men laughed together and exuded confidence together.

They were Team USA.

The daily publication *Visions of the Village* lightened the mood by showing warm interactions among even the bitterest rivals. The front cover of the March 15 issue showed a Canadian sled hockey player grasp-

Team USA gathers in the locker room for a group interview before the gold medal game. Finally, they shout true unity. COURTESY OF KAY ROBERTSON

ing a crutch under one arm and throwing a snowball with the other.[9] "We play against them," said Pat Sapp, "but off the ice, we're all human beings, all black and blue."[10] In another issue, a service dog, Ehreth, from Canine Companions for Independence, could be seen playfully tugging the tail of mascot Otto the Otter.[11] The newsletter built friendly and positive anticipation for the gold medal game in sled hockey.

Even Middleton and Tom Moulton noticed the decrease of tension between the players, despite Jones's final interruption. Moulton thought they all seemed a little more focused and a little more down to earth—which was hard to be, considering they already had at least the silver medal in the bag. "I call them the lunch-pail kids," Moulton told *New York Times* reporter Christy Karras. "They're a blue-collar bunch of guys who bring their lunch pails to work."[12] Karras's article was one of many hyping up the showdown for gold. At last, the American media seemed obsessed with sled hockey, if only for the moment.

So, with Jones no longer looming godlike over the RIC Blackhawks, the team finally seemed ready to end this story as one unit. Talks already insisted it would be the hardest game of all.

"We will have to fight, fight, fight," said Tommy Rovelstad of Norway. "It is going to be a very hard game."[13]

"I expect it to be low scoring," Sapp said, "and the U.S. will prevail."[14] Moulton offered a deeper pregame analysis:

This is going to be a grinding, hard game. We need to stay in their face and have great position play. We've played three kinds of games. The Japan game was a morning game and we call it our wake-up game. We didn't play well until the third period. With Canada, we were so well prepared; we played three excellent periods. Norway's game was grinding. We can draw from these experiences tonight. It won't be easy. Norway is the defending gold medalist and a good team. We have great speed and mobility. We haven't come this close not to win, but if we do end up with silver, we have everything to be proud of. We were in sixth place and the only reason we're in the tournament is that we're the host country. But we won't end up with the silver.[15]

Defenseman James Dunham found he couldn't sleep leading up to the game. He paced up and down the hallway past midnight. Jim Olsen, the trainer, heard him and woke, approaching him with a hushed voice and guiding him through breathwork. Olsen knew the difference between the regular injuries of the body and the lasting ones of the mind. Dunham soon went to sleep.

The hour was finally at hand. Game day reached a high of 39 degrees Fahrenheit, and the sun hid behind observant clouds. Even the sky was standing room only. The E Center had sold out, with 8,317 fans in attendance.[16] Otto the Otter found a seat among them. Her Highness Märtha Louise (b. 1971), Princess of Norway, was there as well, wearing an elegant white jacket and brown-and-black checkered scarf. Even Billy Bridges sat in the stands to watch. Bridges rooted for the United States, but his father, sitting alongside him, couldn't help himself, letting out an occasional cheer for Norway. *iCan News* would report that there would "never be a louder game or maybe never even a better game" at the E Center than this gold medal one.[17]

The players were suiting up. Matt Coppens hung his head in prayer.

"They want to suck you in," said Middleton in his final speech. He warned that the Norwegians wanted to keep the Americans stuck in the corners. Players nodded. They weren't going to fall for it.

The rest of Middleton's rally was brief and brisk, much like himself. "They don't want to give up their gold medal." He pointed backwards at the wall behind him, in the direction of the rink. "We got no pressure on us. Let's go out and kick their ass."

But before Team USA could dive onto the ice, they received a phone call.

CHAPTER TWENTY-FOUR

Gold Medal Game—USA vs. Norway

March 15, 2002

If we played 'em ten times, they might win nine. But not this game.... Not tonight.... You were born to be hockey players—every one of you, and you were meant to be here tonight.
  —HERB BROOKS, 1980 USA HOCKEY HEAD COACH

"THIS IS MIKE ERUZIONE CALLING."

Assistant Coach Tom Moulton held a flip phone up on speaker in one hand. Astonished Team USA players, hearing the name, froze and looked up at it, hanging on each word. They smiled. In the background, slot machines chinked, and Eruzione said he was calling from an event in Las Vegas.

Mike "Rizzo" Eruzione is best known for being the captain of the "Miracle on Ice" 1980 U.S. hockey team. A left winger, #21, he scored the game-winning goal against all odds against the Soviets. After beating Finland in their final game two days later, the United States would take home the gold.

Tonight, Eruzione shared an intangible bond with the men about to try and repeat that miracle.

"Good luck tonight. Play hard. Win well. Last [Olympics] had two silver medals. I think we need gold. And I think you guys can do it."

U.S. and Norwegian players line up on opposing blue lines at the end of the game to hear the MVP announcements. Flis raises his stick. COURTESY OF SHIRLEY BENCH AND RICH DEGLOPPER

The players hooted and clapped.

"If you believe in yourself and believe in each other—and you guys have a lot of obstacles in your life to deal with—this is a great opportunity to show the world [what you're made of]."

Middleton said he'd also heard from Wayne Cashman (b. 1945), assistant coach of the Boston Bruins, and former Olympians Brian Rolston (b. 1973) and Billy Guerin (b. 1970) ahead of the game. "They all know what's going on here."

Just before 7:00 p.m., both teams were moments away from rowing onto the ice. Norway wore the home jersey, with Team USA in white. They'd originally dressed in their blue home jerseys but were told to switch at only fifteen minutes before the game. Hockey players are superstitious. Moulton was even carrying around two lucky coins in his pocket. But Middleton had shut down any mumbo-jumbo. He folded another piece of gum into his mouth.

"It doesn't f--ing matter, guys," someone said in an encouraging tone.

Middleton echoed that. "You beat Canada, best offensive game, I think, in white."

A minute to go before showtime.

"Nothing to save it for," said Middleton. "Nothing to save it for, guys. Blow it up tonight. Come out, be hot, and be ready. Be ready to f--ing take it over."

Now the players chimed in with their own cries.

"Not on this f--ing pond."

"Bury it," said Middleton, "bury it!" He was expertly working the players up into a crescendo.

"Like a war!" one said.

"We worked too long and too hard, guys!"

"This is our dream!"

They flooded onto the ice.

The crowd thundered overhead. Cameras flashed like diamonds among the stands. With a larger-than-life voice that echoed through the arena, the announcer beckoned Team USA onto the glow of the white ice. Immediately, American jerseys zoomed about like fighter jets distracting an enemy. Middleton slapped each player's back as they entered. Then, the announcer said, "Pleeeeeeaaase welcome . . . *Norway!*"

The fierce, bearish Norwegians fired into the rink as well. Reporters from CBC Sports joined A&E. The players looked around and realized they were in the arena of history.

Seconds before the puck drop, USA huddled by their net and raised all their sticks in unison.

Then, Lonnie Hannah and Stig Tore Svee met at center ice for the face-off. Chris Kit, the referee, leaned down and suspended the puck before their eyes.

He dropped it. And the game began.

The puck slipped right under Svee and wandered towards the boards. Joe Howard, all that energy finally exploding from within, careened for the puck in a *J* movement and carried it towards the offensive zone. Norway covered well, though, and bumped against his side the entire time.

He lost his command of the puck, and a Norwegian tipped and glided on his knees as he flung the puck away. In fact, Norway wanted to get rid of the puck in their zone so badly, the next player to collect it dumped it all the way to the other side of the rink.

At around 35 seconds in, Sylvester Flis tossed the puck from the neutral zone into the offensive zone corner. He was following their now tried-and-true strategy of "dump and run," handing Norway the puck but immediately barreling into the defense and scrambling their defensive corps. Matt Coppens charged from yards away into #14, Erik Sandbraathen, using his shoulder as a battering ram and keeping his head down. It was a violent hit. Howard arrived soon after.

But the whistle chirped, and the first penalties of the game went to Howard and Svee for slashing. They both got two minutes in the slammer. Howard, shaking his head, threw his stick against the wall.

At 1:35, Flis hurtled in from the right wing and carried the puck along the wall. Hannah rushed to set up the play with him but couldn't get there in time. Flis's backwards pass towards the center of the net missed.

For the next minute, Norway's passing aimed to play games with the Americans' heads. They zigzagged and backhanded the puck to each other.

Then, a red jersey tackled Kip St. Germaine before he could accept a pass from Jack Sanders, only a few feet away. Rolf Einar Pedersen hurtled into the ambush and intercepted the puck. He steamed forward, fired the shot, and scored the first goal of the game at 2:49. An American and a Norwegian, entwined in combat, crashed into the net as well and dislodged it.

This truly was looking like a warzone. And that was not the orderly performance Middleton needed.

Angry and eager to strike back, Flis and Hannah again tried to cooperate for a play. Flis was clapped on either side by two simultaneous hits. The red jerseys attacked and sped off in the same velocity so fast, it looked like they painted an X with Flis in the middle. With Flis's momentum collapsed, Hannah adopted the slow-moving puck and tried to force it past the goalie, Roger Johansen. It made it under Johansen's sled and stopped just inches away from the goal line. Johansen spun and covered it with his glove fast, the way one puts a bowl over a spider.

At 3:35, opportunity arose. Svee earned his second penalty of the game for interference. During this Paralympics, Team USA had converted 33% , or 6 of 18—compared to Norway's 15%, or 2 of 15—of penalties into power play goals. They were confident they could do so again.

For a third time, Flis and Hannah attempted to set up a play together, with Hannah arriving at center just as Flis flung the puck backwards, diagonally, to him. The shot was made—but saved.

Norway was doing a fantastic job of using its physicality to halt the pace of the game, just as pundits projected they would need to do when faced with the Americans' speed. The U.S. team play dissolved.

Middleton continued to chew his gum, but he leaned lower than ever on the wall now, his USA baseball cap low over his brow.

When Flis captured the puck next in the defensive zone, he fired it along the wall so that it made a horseshoe shape and accelerated up the opposite wing. Hannah chased it, only to be bombarded by Tommy Rovelstad. Together, they lost sight of the puck, heads jerking this way and that, until Hannah finally found it and dumped it towards the offensive zone.

The penalty clock ran out, Svee broke free of the sin bin, and no power play goal was made.

Amazingly, a power play opportunity arose again less than one minute later when Atle Haglund earned two minutes for raising his stick too high near another player. Team USA continued to struggle on its timing, however, and passes seemed to miss by a foot or so each time. Norway excelled at breaking up the American lines like pickaxes break up the earth. Even when the whistle blew on Rovelstad at 7:47 for interference, making the Norwegians *two* men down, or five-on-three, Team USA still did not score.

Worse, the next whistle admonished Chris Manns for charging. At 9:57, it was Norway's turn to go on the power play.

So far, the game had been low-scoring and high-penalty, making for overworked defensemen and a Team USA losing its confidence that the fates had aligned for them. The red jerseys were doing a stellar job at crowding the areas Flis and Howard preferred to set up plays in, placing their bodies right where the Americans needed the puck to be.

Team USA escaped the power play unscored against, but it looked like an opening for comeback would never appear.

Then, Flis soared up the ice carrying the puck and dodging an army of Norwegians. He tossed the puck to Howard and then allowed the Norwegian bodies to bury him in what resembled an act of martyrdom. Howard caught the puck and slapped it into the net.

Howard packed such force behind the shot that the puck hit the back of the net and instantly rebounded out. But it was good—the red lamp illuminated. The crowd screamed, and it was a tie game at 13:06.

The United States could not afford to lose this momentum. When Helge Bjørnstad next took the penalty box for interference at 13:52, still only in the first period, Team USA resolved to cash in this power play. Howard, without passing, carried the puck all the way from center ice. He swerved, screeched in front of the net, steadied the puck with the tip of his blade for just a moment, and fired. Score at 14:13! Johansen slammed the ice with his stick in anger. Team USA now led, 2–1, as the last seconds of the period ended.

In the locker room, the U.S. players mopped their faces with towels. Their sweating and panting mirrored their exhaustion at confronting the Norwegians for just one period. Middleton paced and spouted advice like incantations. Moulton knelt on the floor to look Sanders in the eye and mentor him. Sanders nodded. The break couldn't have felt shorter. But they were ready for more blood.

Team USA executed such a beautiful start to the second period, it almost looked scripted. Howard won the face-off, forcing the puck away from Norway and twisting 180 degrees to follow it. He passed to Flis, who launched for the offensive zone. Norwegian defense gradually pressured him towards the boards and he passed the puck across the middle of the ice—and inches from the sleds of two other red jerseys—onto the waiting stick of Coppens. Coppens fired so hard he lost one of his sticks, but the goal was good at just 12 seconds into the second period, and the crowd lost it. What the hell did they just see?

Norwegian heads spun. The play was flawless. 3–1, USA.

Not long after, Flis attempted to repeat the synchronous playmaking, but a little too much energy coursed through the players now. Howard lost control of the puck, and Norway regained possession. They campaigned into the American offensive zone and shot on Guerra, who made the save at 0:45.

Norway did not relent. Again they attacked Guerra, this time with Haglund literally wrestling the puck over the goal line at 1:04 of the second period, his body fumbling in front of Guerra with both of them inside the crease.

The score was now 3–2. Team USA was still in the lead, but Norway was catching up.

A minute passed, and the puck gained significant mileage back and forth in the rink. As Bjørnstad couriered the puck towards the offensive zone, Brian Ruhe skidded in front of him from behind, as if from nowhere. He tried to kidnap the puck, and the two spiraled against the boards in combat for possession. Ruhe lost a stick.

Flis and Coppens paired up to attempt a repeat of the play that had opened the second period, but this time, Norway was ready. Johansen saved the shot, the puck hitting his glove and flinging up into the air.

At 4:25 into the period, Rovelstad incurred a penalty for roughing, and Team USA prepared to prowl into their fourth power play opportunity of the game. However, the whistle convicted Dave Conklin for holding just twenty seconds later, at 4:45.

In chess, if one player is behind another in terms of points—as Norway was to the USA—trading equal pieces on the board is usually a bad idea. It clears the board and makes it easier for the player ahead to apply the advantage. A CBC announcer commented that just because numbers were even, with one player from each side in the box, didn't mean the game was equal. Team Norway relied on cluttering up the ice to stop the Americans from delivering on their lightning speed. This extra room would favor the United States.

But Ruhe's next pass hit the skates of the linesman. Norway broke away with it instead.

In order to reverse possession, Howard gained speed at a charging distance and slammed into Pedersen behind the net. Whether that should have been called by the referee could be debated. Flis recovered the relinquished puck and swooped in front of the net. His shot was deflected by

Johansen, but it sprang yards into the air—the fans, as if at a baseball game, could have caught it. In fact, even though there was no goal, Flis had to allow one of his charming head shakes and smiles as he cruised away.

At around 6:40 in the second period, Howard made almost a complete loop around the net, but Norwegians crowded the goal and denied any chance of a successful shot. Less than a minute later, Sandbraathen sent the puck soaring high with a long shot from close to the blue line. Guerra saved it easily.

The remainder of the second period stretched on. Howard balanced the puck on his stick like an egg in a spoon. He tossed it in the air and away from the defensive zone. Noticeably, the game had slowed down. Both teams were wary of making a costly mistake. Team USA found itself guarding the net more often than they had in the entire tournament. Guerra's voice, while unintelligible, echoed as he shouted at his teammates defending the puck near the crease. It seemed magic was starting to run out for the Americans. Middleton himself cost them a penalty at 13:45 of the second period for sending too many onto the ice. Norway entered a power play opportunity that would hold until the period ended. Conklin collided head-on with Rovelstad, both players jolting a few centimeters off the ice. Although Team USA managed to stave off a power play goal from Norway, their "untouchable" impetus from only one game before seemed to be fleeting. It looked like their Cinderella run—that magnetic underdog story reporters had gobbled up with their cameras—was coming to an end.

In the locker room after the second period, charged silence filled the air. No one spoke. They breathed hard and looked at one another. Howard lay on the floor next to his plastic legs. Coppens prayed. Again Middleton paced the room giving advice, but his words were fewer and his pauses longer. There was no energy for a victory rally. That would have to be proven on the ice and the ice alone.

"Remember the towers, boys," a teammate shouted to the players as they filed into the rink, referring to the collapse of the World Trade Center. "Remember the towers."

By the time the third period began, Flis had had no reprieve. He played on, inexhaustibly, under the banner of his words from before the game: "I can play 10 periods. It doesn't matter."[1] Manns, who was serving the penalty time for Middleton, started the period back in the box.

Less than a minute into the third period, Flis, who the announcer rightly called "dangerous," backhanded the puck in the direction of Coppens in what looked like it would be a gorgeous play, the kind that whiplashes the camera. When Coppens missed, the crowd audibly moaned.

The United States continued its struggle for possession. Coppens lost control carrying the puck—it lagged behind him, and when he turned to recover it, he tipped and spiraled like a plane with a blown-off wing. The Norwegians scooped it up and motored for the offensive zone. Flis whacked them hard as they approached. He bucked it out of Bjørnstad, but Svee caught it and shot. Guerra dove too early. Team Norway scored and the crowd gasped.

The board read 3–3. This just became a tie game once more.

The U.S. players were tiring, and the game seemed to be slipping away. Moulton stood with arms crossed, his youngest daughter, Cassie, sitting just behind him in the stands. The eleven-year-old looked at him, eyes wide with the innocent belief that her dad could solve anything. "What are we going to do?" the little voice asked.

"We're going to try to win," replied Moulton. And he turned back to the ice, knowing that facing her again with a loss would be the hardest thing in the world to do.

As the stakes rose in period three, so did tempers. A fight broke out between Henderson and Svee when Svee knocked into an unsuspecting Guerra. Later, Howard screamed in anger over conduct on the ice, raising his arm as if to berate the referee. Conklin did his best to halt the puck, he the iceberg and the puck a boat. He dished it over to an ally. But halting seemed to be exactly what was happening. When the period was more than half over and Ozzy Osbourne's "Crazy Train" echoed through the arena, players were shaking heads, panting hard, and sweating. Adrenaline and fury burned through them.

Haglund attempted one more goal on Guerra with just minutes to go until the end of what should have been the final period, if things had gone the way Team USA intended. Guerra saved it with his gorilla-like glove.

The clock was ticking down. With only one minute left to go, Bjørn-stad plowed up the left wing with the puck. Coppens cut through the ice diagonally and rammed into him, but Bjørnstad got rid of the puck at almost the same moment. Flis and Ruhe cooperated to bat it back to center ice each time the red jerseys made an advance.

The horn blasted with the score still locked at 3–3.

This battle for gold was heading into a ten-minute overtime. Sudden death.

Everything would come down to the goalies. Johansen had saved 16 of 19 shots, and Guerra boasted 11 of 14. The crowd was almost deafening—announcers had to shout to be heard. A *USA! USA! USA!* chant had begun. Onlookers shivered with goosebumps. At under half a minute into overtime, Howard fired a clear shot on the goal, but it went just a tad wide. The audience cried out. Speed was definitely picking up, however. Seconds later Coppens tried on the net again, and again Norway flicked it off.

Ruhe tried, miss. Coppens again! Miss!

The announcer commented that sometimes the way to win a game is not to finish first but to quit last. The Americans weren't quitting.

Referee Chris Kit seemed to be letting all hell break loose on the ice, allowing the hits and charges to accelerate on both sides. Near the three-minute mark, Pedersen squeezed past a defensive Flis and almost clinched a goal, but Flis hurled the puck down ice. Now Flis seemed to have a price on his head. Norway battered him hard, over and over, as he tried to maneuver towards the puck. Flis chased the puck into the boards, slamming and rebounding against them, but the red jerseys instantly covered him.

Moments later, a shot from Svee went wide. The Norwegians hollered at one another and regrouped, and soon Bjørnstad made another shot with too much altitude.

Half of overtime slipped away. Still no goal. The reflections of the players in the glass surrounding the rink flashed by with speed. Then Johan Siqveland, #12, crashed head-on into Coppens. The force was like a battering ram swinging into his stomach. Coppens fell to the ice.

He wasn't getting up.

The whistle blew on this calamity of an overtime at last. Coppens, writhing, also slammed the ice with his fist, as if angrier that he'd been compromised for the remainder of the game than because he was in agony.

Middleton walked calmly across the ice, followed by trainers. He leaned down, placing a hand on Coppens, and the others soon surrounded him. A towel was passed around, which usually served to clean up blood, but no spots of red appeared on it. The CBC announcer even suggested to viewers that Coppens might be exercising a little late-game "drama."

What he did not know was that Coppens lay immobile on the ice because, in his head, he heard the shattering of glass and the brakes of the car that had crashed into him years earlier. The colossal sled-on-sled hit ignited a flashback in his mind. Panic and anxiety arrested him, all the while the announcers bantered.

The crowd applauded as Coppens finally dragged himself to the bench.

When the game resumed, Conklin perched at the offensive zone faceoff, making eye contact through the cage of his helmet with his Norwegian rival. The whistle chirped, and Conklin shoved the puck over to Flis. Once again, it took the Flis Express down to offensive ice.

Flis, ever the conductor, arranged a beautiful setup down the right wing, passing the puck cleanly to Sanders, but Sanders slid away out of control.

Bjørnstad answered with a shot of his own. It went just a little high—Guerra raised his hand. Any lower into net area and it would have been out of Guerra's reach.

After several more seconds of pivoting around the puck and changing hands in the neutral zone, Flis and Howard teamed up for what they hoped would be a game-ending play with less than thirty seconds remaining in overtime. Flis sent the puck down the right wing and onto the stick of Howard. With the speed of a bullet, Howard curved and headed for the offensive center, his blades spitting up ice.

Then—*wham!*

Howard went flying into the air. He somersaulted and landed on his face. Rovelstad had just T-boned him, leaving him curled up on the ice, his stick spinning away. Howard's expression was twisted in pain. The crowd went silent.

Somehow, Howard dragged himself upright, and overtime ended with Howard shouting, his arms waving in the air, Rovelstad cursing in the penalty box (the ref called him for charging, not T-boning), and the score still 3–3.

Now the game would be settled once and for all in a shootout. Each team would be allowed to select five shooters, and whichever team scored the most at the end of the shootout would be awarded one goal to break the 3–3 tie and finish the game at 4–3.

Team USA chose Sylvester Flis, Joe Howard, Chris Manns, Kip St. Germaine, and Lonnie Hannah. Team Norway would send Helge Bjørnstad, Rolf Einar Pedersen, Roger Hansen, Stig Tore Svee, and Atle Haglund. Rovelstad, one of their better shooters, would be ineligible from the penalty box.

Guerra and Johansen took their places in the nets.

Flis would shoot first. The lead scorer made his way to center ice. Like a predatory snake, he wove towards the goal carrying the puck. Johansen edged far out to the border of the crease to meet him. When Flis shot, however, he was too close to Johansen. Johansen fell to his side and grabbed the puck just centimeters away from Flis's stick.

No goal.

At this point, "stopping the unstoppable" Sylvester Flis, as the announcers called it, ushered in the sound of giant structural walls collapsing for the United States. Their best scorer had just been silenced.

Next was Bjørnstad. He gained speed before meeting the puck in center ice, advanced on Guerra, and fired. Guerra, too early, dove to his right, while Bjørnstad shot instead to the left. The puck entered the net easily, with elbow room on either side of it.

1 to 0 for Team Norway.

Now it was time for Howard to answer for that body-flipping hit. He pounded the ice with his sticks like a bull, yet held his head high like a proud stallion. Johansen scooted forward once more to meet his opponent, but Howard deked around on his left and fired the puck far up into the net behind Johansen. The goal was good! Howard soaked in the applause as he confidently soared back to the bench. It was a mic-drop moment for him. Nothing else needing to be said. That was Howard's final word in this tournament laid out on the ice.

Pedersen shot next for the Norwegians. He surprised Guerra by switching to his undominant left hand at the last second, popping the puck into the net and leaving Guerra flopped over on his stomach.

In this shootout, Norway had now notched two goals for Team USA's one.

However, Norway was not the only team with a leftie shot. Middleton placed Manns, a natural leftie, in the middle of the lineup just to mess with Johansen. Manns took the ice next and balanced the puck on the paddle of his left stick as he carefully approached Johansen. As always, Johansen aggressively moved forward to the edge of the crease, but when Manns shot, the puck lifted high into the air and buried itself into a corner of the net over Johansen's shoulder. Goal! The crowd went wild as Manns returned to the player's bench, knowing he had done his job.

The two teams were now equal again. Next up for Norway was #18, Roger Hansen, a forward.

But Guerra had already allowed two goals on two shots so far. Middleton called out to Guerra from the bench to get his attention as the crowd hollered and Guerra's teammates sat very still. Middleton leaned over the boards and leveled a steady gaze on the young man.

"Are you going to stop one?" said Middleton.

Guerra nodded.

"Now would be a good time."

Back in the net, Guerra looked Hansen in the eye. The Norwegian advanced, and when he fired, Guerra made his first save of the shootout. The puck hit Guerra's bulky shoulder, and he shrugged and shook it off him so it would bounce in the opposite direction.

No gain for Norway, and two shooters each remaining for both sides. The teams were deadlocked at two goals apiece.

Kip St. Germaine took the ice. He advanced with what looked like caution, and then, so close he nearly collided with Johansen, he flicked the puck in a perfectly straight arc into the air and netted a goal. The move was so fast, just a blink, even the announcers exclaimed, "Oh-ho!"

Svee charged out of the bench next for the puck. Guerra readied himself. Svee fired, and Guerra caught the puck on his knees. He raised his arms as if to celebrate, momentarily thinking that this save gave Team USA the gold, then quickly smacked one back down as the puck tried to slide around his knees towards the net. But the save was good. Team USA was still up one.

Texan Lonnie Hannah would speak last for the United States offense. If he scored, Norway would not have enough chances to come back, and Team USA would take it all home. Johansen played mean again, though, lurching forward for Hannah, and Hannah skirted around him too wide. His shot missed.

Now the final shooter would be Atle Haglund. He twirled an entire 360 degrees in dramatic fashion as he skated onto the ice. If Haglund scored, the tally would be even again, and the two teams would head into an extended shootout until a winner was crowned.

The crowd roared. A pulsing energy reverberated through the entire arena. Haglund moved forward, Guerra braced himself, and then the shot fired as if in slow motion.

Guerra dove to his left. The puck glanced off the outside goalpost. Sprawled on the ice, Guerra stared in disbelief as the puck floated into the corner of the rink.

And the United States of America had just won gold.

ADAM PRETTY/STAFF/GETTY IMAGES SPORT VIA GETTY IMAGES

Final Score: 4–3
USA game MVP: Joe Howard
Fans in attendance: 8,317

CHAPTER TWENTY-FIVE

Lonnie Hannah, #1

Pos.	GP	G	A	PTS	PIM	"+/–"	GWG	GTG	PPG	SHG	S	SG%
F	5	1	4	5	20	6	0	0	0	0	7	14.29

On April 23, 2002, thirty-eight-year-old Lonnie Hannah waited in line to shake hands with the president. He gathered in the White House Rose Garden with his teammates and saw around him smiling faces against a backdrop of flowers and cameras. Team USA had won gold—the only American team to do so that year in hockey—and now one of the final rites would be a congratulations from George W. Bush.

Bush stood in a dark grey suit and red tie at the end of the receiving line. As cameras flashed, he offered his hand again and again to the approaching players. Ahead of Hannah were Pat Sapp and James Dunham, both from Texas. They told Bush as much. When Hannah finally grasped the president's hand, he introduced himself and stated his hometown in a friendly country accent: "Houston, Texas." The president knitted his brow and he laughed as if the information had finally become too much.

"There sure is a lotta Texas on an ice hockey team," he said.

Bush's surprise was not misplaced. Growing up, Lonnie Jackson Hannah II, born February 17, 1964, never watched the sport from his family's Houston apartment. In Texas during the late 1970s and early 1980s, hockey rarely was televised. The gallerias at Dallas and Houston— and even those were targeted more at figure skating—were the only ice rinks in the state until the 1990s, when the NHL Dallas Stars arrived from Minnesota. Only then did ice sports pick up interest in Texas. Hockey was, as Hannah described it, East Coast dominated, and athletes in Texas had other athletic prospects.

Football and roller-skating captivated Hannah's attention. He first stepped into roller skates at just sixteen months and was competing in leagues by age four, going on to win recognition in speed skating. Hannah's mother, Mary "Mary E" Warren, nurtured his talents by frequently pulling Hannah from school on Fridays to spend the weekend traveling to roller-skating tournaments across the country. They made it as far as Tampa and destinations in West Virginia and Alabama, totaling nearly sixteen hours behind the wheel in a single weekend, while Hannah's father and three older sisters remained home. Mary E would have her son back in school Monday morning.

The love of roller-skating persisted for Hannah until his twenties, when everything all changed.

After his parents' divorce in 1973, near the time he was in the fifth grade, aloe vera became the family business. Snapping an arm off the succulent cactus produces a gel-like natural salve which can be turned into lotions, liniments, soaps, and makeup. Hannah's stepfather founded Warren Laboratories (now called George's Aloe Vera) in Stafford, Texas, and produced all of these products. He employed Hannah and his sisters.

On Halloween in 1984, Hannah says he "got more trick than treat" when a home-built shelf holding nearly a thousand pounds of product collapsed on him. To say he "broke" three vertebrae would not be a strong enough expression. The bone was crushed almost to nonexistence—but Hannah recalled being grateful he had taken the blow rather than his sisters, who had been under the shelf just moments before. After all, those roller-skating ventures had trained his body into excellent condition, and he worried the weight of the shelf would have meant death for any of his other siblings.

The accident paralyzed Hannah. Surgery, therapy, and an arduous six-month recovery on morphine earned him only partial feeling and movement in his legs.

Roller-skating was out of the picture.

But Hannah was never one to be beaten. "Mom had her tubes tied, then had me anyway," he said, laughing. Even in the womb he was determined. Humor never escaped him in his pain—on the hospital bed, he beckoned his sister to come closer, *closer*, so he could whisper to her, and then shouted, "Boo!" He was promptly slapped.

An associate at Hannah's rehab ward introduced him to wheelchair tennis—which led to wheelchair basketball, which led to wheelchair skiing and hand cycling, which led to. . . . A whole new universe of sports for Lonnie Hannah.

By 1985, Hannah had traveled to Irvine, California, to compete (and win) in a beginning division of the disabled U.S. Open. He advanced to the intermediate division the following year, finishing in second place against England. By this time, Hannah had forged a name for himself in adaptive athletics. Quickie Wheelchairs, a manufacturer of power and manual wheelchairs, officially sponsored Hannah.[1]

Having obtained satisfying accomplishments in handicapped athletics, Hannah married his first wife, Lindsay Reads, and considered himself retired by 1994. He moved to Arlington, Texas, and in 1995 opened his own roller-skating rink called the Arlington Skatium—a comical homage to Arlington Stadium, home of the MLB Texas Rangers. Of course, being the first rink in the alphabetical phone book was a plus as well.

In 1999, sled hockey came to Texas. Credit to its arrival and success goes, like most things in life, to a determined mother. Christine Burns was the parent of ferocious ice hockey players and one darling daughter with a disability. A wealthy individual, Burns paid for three USA Hockey representatives to fly in and host the state's first-ever sled hockey exhibition. She also purchased ten sleds, reserving one for her daughter. Burns, of course, wanted her daughter to have the same opportunity to play the sport as her brothers had.

While the young Burns, ironically, did not fall in love with the sport, many others—including Hannah—did. Although he was busy as a new father (his son was born just the year before), Hannah loved sled hockey enough to "come out of retirement," joining a club team that would soon be known as the Dallas Sled Stars. It was here he met James Dunham, who one day would join the roster of the 2002 gold medal team alongside Hannah. Shortly after forming the team, the two of them traveled to Boston to compete in Hannah's first-ever game. The Boston tournament—called the Chowder Cup—was small, hosting one team each from Boston, New York, and Canada. Never knowing quite what to do with a hockey player from Texas, the tournament managers divvied up Hannah to the Boston team and Dunham to the New York team. Neither took home the victory, as Canada's superior experience with sled hockey showed once more.

Hannah followed up this small tournament with a larger one in Buffalo a few months later as he continued to refine his identity on the ice. By 2000, he was confident enough to seek a position on the U.S. team entering the world championship in Salt Lake City, but a personal conflict forced him to miss the tryouts in his area. Hannah called the coach and requested permission to travel to the team's second tryouts. He was denied. Considering that the United States would suffer an embarrassing last-place result in that championship, Hannah was not too devastated, in retrospect, not to have made the team.

He kept practicing.

While Hannah did not earn a reputation as a goal scorer, his specialty was lifting the quality of play for those around him. He could make passes, find open players, and lead in assists. His vision was excellent. Hannah was confident the United States team would have the goal-scoring roles spoken for, but they would need the right players to dish the puck to those people. That is where Lonnie Hannah shone.

When tryouts for the 2002 Paralympic team sounded, Hannah did not delay this time. He arrived with guns blazing (in case anyone forgot he's Texan) and met head coach Rick Middleton. Middleton, who already knew he'd have a headache in front of him because of the contention between the East Coast and Chicago players, was attracted to Hannah. The player had talent, yes, but especially appealing was his neutral, affable demeanor. Maybe the team needed this Texan to build a bridge between the East Coasters and the Chicagoans.

Hannah was among at least nine players alarmingly new to the sport who made the cut—and even more alarmingly among three Texans, including Dunham and Sapp.

Team USA did not enjoy months of training time. With fewer than ten practices before the Paralympics began, Hannah, despite not present-ing as a goal scorer, used this time to develop an almost unstoppable shot. His signature move married deception with pure physics: Hannah would feign left, swerve back to center, and then jerk his sled off the ice and shoot the puck underneath it. Chances usually were that the goalie would never even see the puck coming from such an unexpected direction. Even if the puck was spotted, however, Hannah's juke maneuver forced the goalie to mirror his body and position him off-center, invariably leaving open the net Hannah wanted.

Only two factors could thwart this shot. One was outskating the puck—going too fast in the sled and missing the sweet spot to whisk the puck from center circle and into goal. The second was losing balance in the sled. Balance, to Hannah, was everything. Without it, he said, it would be like trying to play hockey with skates three times too large.

Middleton studied Hannah's new move closely and named him assistant captain. He'd send Hannah headfirst into the games ahead, using him often for face-offs. As the team journeyed to Salt Lake City to begin the round robin showdown for gold, Hannah's family hit the merchandise stands and bought USA Hockey apparel head to toe. Mary E purchased a $1,000 suite and handfuls of tickets for relatives—but *only* for the gold medal game. It never crossed her mind that Hannah and his team would not reach the final match. That is not to say that Hannah's supporters ignored the other games taking place. After watching the bronze medal game between Canada and Sweden (Sweden would triumph), Mary E, still recovering from the suspense, called her son and said, "Whatever you do, do not go into a shootout."

But who obeys a mother's order?

A shootout in overtime is exactly where Team USA found itself after a 3–3 deadlock with Norway. Middleton was so sure of Hannah's signature shot, he selected him to go last in the lineup of four other teammates attempting to make goal.

When Hannah's turn finally arrived, he whacked his sticks into the ice to propel forward. That familiar chill of the rink rushed to his face and the crowd blurred around him. He cleared the first hurdle—not outskating the puck, instead sweeping it up at the right time—but immediately knew the second one would claim his victory. Something felt off in his sled. The center of gravity shifted slightly; the finely tuned balance that once felt like an extension of his body tampered with. This fumble of balance forced the first hurdle to reappear—by the time Hannah managed to lift his sled off the ground, the sweet spot to fire off the shot had passed. The shot went wide.

It was the only miss that move had ever reaped. Hannah could only skate away, speechless, wondering how the hell that happened. After the game, he learned that sometime between periods, an equipment official had inspected his sled and noticed it had been banged up in play so hard it no longer met regulation standards. Without alerting Hannah, the official adjusted the sled to satisfaction and Hannah strapped up during the next period none the wiser. "I'm not making excuses," Hannah said, "but I'm sure that's what happened."

While three of Hannah's teammates found net, and eventually one last save from Manny Guerra would ensure the win, Hannah still laments missing that shot.

Going home with Paralympic gold that year helped soothe any such regret, though. Hannah would take his medal not only to the Rose Garden, but to motivational public speaking events across the country thereafter. He served as an ambassador for Hartford Insurance, the first corporate sponsor of the Paralympics, and informally to his own USA team, keeping alive the relationships between players as the years went on. In 2006, Hannah moved to San Antonio and founded the San Antonio Rampage, a sled hockey team consisting exclusively of U.S. military veterans with disabilities from Brooke Army Medical Center. The team claimed a national championship victory, and five of its former players have gone on to play in subsequent Paralympics on the national team.

Growing up, Hannah never would have thought a boy from Texas could find such glory in such an out-of-state icy sport. The competitive spirit of Lonnie Hannah worked like that, though—whether it's pushing, pedaling, hitting, or sledding, somehow Hannah generated momentum and found the way forward.

CHAPTER TWENTY-SIX
Matt Coppens, #5

Pos.	GP	G	A	PTS	PIM	"+/–"	GWG	GTG	PPG	SHG	S	SG%
F	6	4	5	9	6	11	1	0	2	0	12	33.33

A FAVORITE PASTIME OF MATTHEW COPPENS (B. 1971) IS TO DRESS IN World War II gear, run out onto a reenactment field, and be the guy who gets blown up. He certainly has the physique for it. Coppens jokes that his double-amputee condition provides the perfect effect for stepping on a landmine during a performance and pretending to have his limbs blown off. He has an impressive collection of historical artifacts from the 1940s, including a garage full of period-accurate guns and vehicles. He often reenacts as a member of the 353rd Infantry, but his roles vary.

Coppens attended Crete-Monee High School in Crete, Illinois, and in his early twenties worked as an emergency services officer for Richton Park.[1] He also served as a firefighter for five years. On December 30, 1994, at around 9:20 p.m., and just six months into his service as a policeman, Coppens's unexpected next chapter would begin.[2]

Tasked with conducting traffic after a basketball tournament, Coppens leaned into the back of his trunk to grab safety cones. That's when an eighteen-year-old driver slammed into him from behind.

His right leg was immediately severed, and off came the left leg a day later. Nearly all ten of the doctors treating him expected he wouldn't make it.

Coppens played volleyball in the 2000 Summer Paralympics in Sydney and participated in other adaptive sports like softball. He began his career in sled hockey with the RIC Blackhawks. As an aggressive forward, Coppens deployed on the ice like a sharp barb ripping through a net of defensemen. He was adept at keeping the enemy always on alert.

Along with Brian Ruhe, Coppens used his story and achievements to speak to children at the Salt Lake Community College's Lifetime Activities Center during the 2002 Paralympics. The two demonstrated the sport and captured the imaginations of kids who now thought they could do just about anything.

Asked how he ever survived that night when his dreams of being a police officer were torn away with parts of his body, Coppens answers directly.

"You have to want to survive."[3]

CHAPTER TWENTY-SEVEN

Jack Sanders, #15

Pos.	GP	G	A	PTS	PIM	"+/–"	GWG	GTG	PPG	SHG	S	SG%
F	6	3	1	4	4	0	1	0	2	0	8	37.50

Born in 1958 in Galesburg, Illinois, Jack Sanders is a polio survivor. He dabbled in hand cycling and racing and was noticed by Dave
Conklin, who invited him to try sled hockey. Sanders soon excelled as
a player who "knew his role" and did it well, as teammate Brian Ruhe
recalls. At the time of tryouts for the 2002 team, Sanders worked full-
time as a circulation manager for a local newspaper and was one of the
oldest players at thirty-nine.[1] To train and keep up with the team, Sanders
drove twice a week to Chicago to hit the ice with the RIC Blackhawks.
It was a 250-mile round trip from his residence in Pekin, Illinois. That's
how much success meant to him. After the gold medal victory, Sanders
went on to give back to the rising generation of sled hockey players as a
coach for the Central Illinois Thunder.

CHAPTER TWENTY-EIGHT

Aftermath

Ultimately, it's up to you to decide whether you will become the person that you want to become.

—JORDIN TOOTOO, FIRST INUK NHL PLAYER[1]

"UNREAL."[2]

Sylvester Flis's one word said it all.

When the puck ricocheted off the goalpost and the crowd exploded, Rick Middleton sprinted onto the ice. His usual reserved poker face broke into a large grin as he jumped onto the pile of ecstatic players near the net. Joe Howard draped the U.S. flag over his shoulders and spread it out like eagle's wings. He screamed out the ecstasy and the hurt, the joy and the anger deep within. Looping around the rink, Howard evoked the image of a similarly flag-draped Mike Eruzione from 1980. "The Star-Spangled Banner" playing brought tears to eyes as the flag that was raised in the rubble of Ground Zero still waved in everyone's minds.

"It's gold. I don't know what to think. I didn't know what it would feel like. Now I know."[3] Kip St. Germaine.

"Unbelievable."[4] Joe Howard.

"It's almost like you leave one world and go to another."[5] Jack Sanders.

"Did we just win gold?"[6] Patrick Byrne.

Yeah. They did.

On March 19, 2002, four days after the victory, Senator Orrin Hatch (R-UT; 1934–2022) spoke on the senate floor. "Today," he said, "I rise, as

219

a Senator from the great State of Utah, to call attention to and express support for the Salt Lake 2002 Paralympic Games."[7] He went on to divvy out praise, as politicians do, but the well-intentioned words seemed a few days late.

Team USA had already made headlines.

USA Hockey, Olympic Beat, American Hockey, and even *USA Today* ran articles on the climactic final game and its historic gold.[8] Finally, the world was seeing what Rick Middleton saw from the start: "I don't see the sleds out there anymore. I just see hockey."[9]

As the Paralympic flag lowered in Medals Plaza, surrounded by U.S. servicemen, the Games were being hailed as the best in Paralympic history.[10] The March 16, 2002, closing ceremonies included fireworks, flags, and Patti LaBelle on stage.[11] Governor Mike Leavitt and Mitt Romney, CEO of the Salt Lake Organizing Committee (SLOC), poured out their emotions, specifically noting Team USA's sled hockey win.[12] The original plan to shut off the lights illuminating the giant murals of athletes with disabilities stretched across buildings was canceled.[13] The lights stayed. International Paralympic Committee president Sir Philip Craven, upon the close of the Paralympics, said, "The Games will end tonight, but the spirit will travel on."[14]

He had no way of knowing just how prophetic those words would be for sled hockey in the United States.

Ahead for the sport was official USA Hockey sponsorship—the dream of so many early sled hockey pioneers come true—and the funding necessary to save it from extinction. It turned out that no amount of diplomacy was going to get USA Hockey's commitment faster than a gold medal. Their sponsorship—which advocates had been after for more than a decade—became official by 2006, only four years later. It seemed they first wanted another medal in the 2006 Torino games, just to be sure. They got it.

On April 23, 2002, President George W. Bush addressed both Olympians and Paralympians on the South Lawn of the White House. Manny Guerra was on his left, the medal around his neck. In a moment of tone-deaf irony, Bush began his speech to an audience of wheelchair-users with, "Thank you all. Please be seated."[15] The plain yet good-natured address went on to extend presidential congratulations to the pool of talented athletes of varying physical challenges around him. A few who were present remember the congregation pausing once to look up at a large Boeing 707, a little too close, tilting in to land at Reagan National Airport. The relief when it passed held the bittersweet reminder of what this moment truly represented for the grieving nation in need of faith. Eyes returned from the sky and fell on the American heroes persevering before them. Bush concluded his remarks by carefully hedging around the impact of 9/11 without saying the date: "We've always supported our athletes here in America. But this year we looked at them with even more pride and even greater hope. . . . It was an important time for America, and you didn't let us down."[16]

Guerra, representing the Paralympics, and Tristan Gale (b. 1980), a skeleton racer representing the Olympics, presented Bush with a ceremonial jacket.[17] A White House tour followed, and then the U.S. sled hockey team dined in the evening with U.S. senator and former presidential candidate Bob Dole (1923–2021), who stood from his seat and humorously toasted them with, "I got the silver in '96."[18]

Middleton won USA Hockey's Coach of the Year for facilitating what *Hockey Magazine* called a "Miracle on Ice."[19] New Hampshire Legends of Hockey enshrined him in its Hall of Fame in 2014.[20] His exceptional achievement with the 2002 Paralympic team featured prominently in his qualifying details on both accounts. Middleton would call this experience the proudest of his career. Additionally, the entire team was nominated for a place in the United States Hockey Hall of Fame.[21] Although unsuccessful (so far) in this pursuit, the team also won the USA Hockey Bob Johnson Award and the 2002 Olympic Spirit Award.[22] Then, in May of 2022, only months before the release of this book, the 2002 team received official word that they would be inducted into the United States Olympic and Paralympic Committee's (USOPC) Hall of Fame.

Hall of Famers at last.

On June 24, 2022, I sat in the audience with my father as NBC Sports' Mike Tirico honored the likes of Michael Phelps, Michelle Kwan, and other Hall of Famers in Colorado Springs. A canary sun set behind the dry Rocky Mountains ahead of us. Halfway through, Tirico leaned on the podium and said, "You folks are talented and all . . . but you're not as fun as the sled hockey guys." To that the players cheered and whistled. They rolled up on stage.

Along with accolades came expansion. When John Schatzlein tallied the participants of sled hockey in 1994, his total number of prospective players attending clinics was 159, with four standing teams.

By 2014, that number shot to nearly 1,200 players on fifty-eight teams nationwide.[23]

For the 2002 national team tryouts, thirty men showed up. For the 2022 Paralympics in Beijing, that number was as high as eighty-five.

Ask anyone involved in sled hockey today and they will identify the 2002 team as the reason. Dan Brennan (b. 1963) of USA Hockey, now the national governing body for sled hockey, said, "I don't let a camp go by where I don't talk about that 2002 group." He says the early pioneers of the sport and that first gold medal inspired the attitudes of equality in the Olympic-Paralympic relationship. "It's not what you see when you work with people with disabilities, it's what you don't see . . . many misjudged why people played sled hockey. It's not to be a story. It's to be normal."

That desire to feel "normal" touches those with disabilities, young and old. Players from the 2002 team used their newfound celebrity for good in this regard. Many, such as Pat Sapp, attended events for children with disabilities, laying the gold medal around their necks and watching smiles of amazement dazzle their faces. Because of the 2002 team, kids

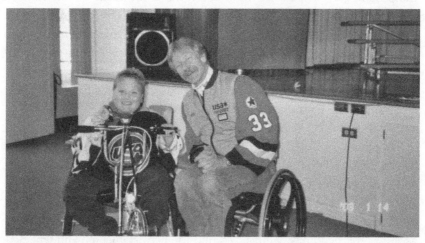

Patt Sapp and a child with a disability, who is wearing Sapp's gold medal. COURTESY OF PAT SAPP

who may have just been starting to realize how different they look from others soon believed they could win anything, too.

In 2015, Washington, DC, speechwriter and author Bruce Valley began research to write a book about this story. Valley sent out an update that the book was underway in late August of that year, and in the body of his email intoned that "for a book about a sports event now years in the past to be commercially successful, it must get readers personally and emotionally involved."[24] He asked the players to recount all the "despair and euphoria, love and anger, even fury" of this journey.[25] Valley succeeded in interviewing most of the players (at least one more than I was able to), extracting that emotion he sought, and he employed a tremendous amount of digital fact-finding, complete with printed articles and circled names and dates. Sadly, Valley's wife fell ill and he relinquished the project. He passed his notes along with his blessing to the succeeding author—me. His efforts were integral to keeping the flame of this story alight. Further, a feature film project tentatively titled *Tough Sledding* based off these inspiring historical events is also in the works and was part of the pitch I received before signing on. These examples demonstrate how the 2002 story is bleeding into a new generation and catching the interest of storytellers almost a quarter century later.

Readers may survey the stellar success of the 2002 team and wonder why neither Rick Middleton nor Tom Moulton proceeded on the coaching staff in subsequent years. Trails of letters and emails provide evidence that the brewing dissent leading up to the games finally caught up to the pair. Middleton sent a fax to Jeff Jones on March 29, 2002, inquiring about the $10,000 bonus promised to the head coach (Middleton) and the $5,000 bonus promised to the assistant coach (Moulton) if the team won gold.[26] Jeff Jones himself responded by email on April 12. "Unfortunately," wrote Jones, "USSHA's Board of Directors is now faced with a very difficult situation. We were completely unaware of that contract [Middleton's Fee for Services Letter of Agreement, signed by Rich DeGlopper] existed [*sic*] before the Games . . . we do not anticipate being able to pay [these] bonuses for quite some time, if at all."[27] Jones, who was president of the United States Sled Hockey Association at the time, assured Middleton that USSHA had attempted to contact DeGlopper with regard to where that bonus money would come from, to no avail. "It appears that in Mr. DeGlopper's enthusiasm to secure your services and determine an adequate fee for those services last August, he failed to identify a sufficient source of income to fulfill this obligation."[28] Jones requested Middleton forgo the bonus and write it off on his taxes.

Indeed, Jones's high-ranking position at USSHA, on top of this indiscretion, hastened Middleton's departure. USSHA tentatively sent Middleton camp and budget proposals for the upcoming seasons but exercised uncertain allegiances, replying suspiciously slowly—and sometimes never at all—to Middleton's emails. Finally having enough of it, Middleton wrote to Joe Walsh at the United States Olympic Committee, referring to the hypocrisy of the U.S. Paralympic mission statement's emphasis on recruiting world class coaches. "You have already started to fail in what you state your mission is," wrote Middleton, "before you've even got started!"[29] He made sure to put "Head Coach/2002 Gold Medal Champion" under his title when signing off on the email.

Understandably, the patterns of disrespect befuddled Middleton and Moulton. Equally as confusing was Jones's April 3, 2002, email to the players, which, after laying out plans for ice time and the future of the team, stated, "Unfortunately, Team USA had little if any true leadership."[30]

Had he not seen the headlines?

Or did he think anyone could have led such a talented team to victory?

Jones continued to alienate Middleton, leaving him off invitation lists for team events.[31] Middleton and Moulton, finally fed up—their packed bags heavy with paraphernalia lauding their accomplishments—walked away.

But Jeff Jones never became head coach of Team USA. He disappeared from the Rehabilitation Institute of Chicago under mysterious circumstances.

The Rehabilitation Institute of Chicago became the Shirley Ryan AbilityLab in March of 2017. The RIC Blackhawks have been renamed the Shirley Ryan AbilityLab Blackhawks. Derek Daniels is now the director of adaptive sports and the head coach of the ever-growing sled hockey program. "The program roster is double what it was in 2002," said Daniels.[32] The team today welcomes women and has five military veterans currently on their roster.[33] One is Travis Dodson, a USMC corporal injured in Iraq. As well as being a Blackhawk, he competes on the national team, and won gold at the 2018 Paralympics in Pyeongchang. Daniels described the annual five-day sled hockey camp the AbilityLab hosts for veterans each summer: "The entire program is free of charge to veterans with a disability, including travel to and from our Chicago clinic."[34]

After conflicts in the Middle East following September 11, 2001, sled hockey has offered wounded servicemen and servicewomen a lifeline of renewed hope. Military veterans with disabilities, as evidenced above, find an environment of equality and optimism in the sport. Josh Sweeney, USMC, stepped on an improvised explosive device in Afghanistan in October of 2009.[35] The blast tore off both his legs from above the knee. Now, he's a gold medalist on Team USA. Sled hockey, he says, "provides me with just a little bit of closure. I'm still the same person I was before."[36] Except thanks to the sport, he now feels he is in the best shape of his life.

James Dunham, defenseman from the 2002 team, recalls volunteering to assist wounded veterans transitioning into sled hockey. "They were signing up with sand still in their hair," said Dunham, referring to how many injured servicemen and servicewomen discovered sled hockey while still recovering in the hospital. He describes one soldier who sat in a chair and just stared at the rink—and maybe a few thousand yards beyond it, too—with a dazed expression. Scar tissue covered his arms. Dunham approached him and said, "Hey. We need you on the ice." Soon, that soldier found himself in a sled, on a team. New life animated him; he looked like a different person. "He needed to be needed," says Dunham. Today, the U.S. sled hockey team includes more Purple Heart recipients than its pioneers in the early years ever could have imagined.

Again, the 2002 victory, and its ability to secure official sponsorship from USA Hockey and therefore sustainable funding, made this possible.

Another compelling change since the 2002 Games is the cultural response to the Paralympics and adaptive athleticism in recent years.

Social attention to athletes with disabilities has taken a turn for the better. The athletes are often positioned as "superhumans" with dramatic backgrounds; advertisements for the 2012 London Paralympics showed images of athletes in wheelchairs or with prosthetics, in sports attire, staring defiantly into the camera akin to a group of X-Men.[37] Although the risk remains that athletes with disabilities will be pigeonholed as icons of inspiration, the presentation is at least similar to that of lionized able-bodied athletes on billboards. The 2002 sled hockey team certainly had no such fanfare leading up to the Salt Lake Paralympics.

Attracting the positive interest of the public bodes well for Paralympic funding. But athletes with disabilities do not want to be seen as beneficiaries of a charity. The Paralympics and the Special Olympics, an entity more closely focused on intellectual disabilities and personal fulfillment rather than intense competition, still struggle to ensure the public does not confuse one for the other.[38] In fact, Romney caught heat in 2002 for putting the Paralympics on a list of "charitable causes," along with environmental and cultural programs, to which the public could donate money.[39] With an attitude of reproach towards this faux pas, Visa, Chevy, and Bank of America extended their 2002 Olympic financial support to include the Paralympics. "We don't see it as a charity," said George Perry, vice president of event marketing for Visa. "I've skied with a couple of these athletes. They're phenomenal." When the 2002 team competed, the Paralympics indeed suffered several injustices compared to its able-bodied counterpart. For one, every disabled athlete winning a gold medal received $2,500—able-bodied athletes received $25,000 per gold medal. The Paralympics made up just 4% of the USOC budget, and state-of-the-art Olympic training facilities would place Paralympic athletes eighth in line on their schedule.[40] National governing bodies complained about allowing the Paralympics to come under the USOC umbrella, fearful they'd suck away money.

Dan Brennan remembers looking out of his USA Hockey headquarters window in Colorado Springs to the building across the street. Called the World Arena, it housed three ice rinks and hosted Paralympian sled hockey players in late 2001. One day, he walked across to watch them train and noticed the players had no team apparel. He was one of the first to petition USA Hockey to equip them with proper jerseys. In fact, he grabbed a handful of jerseys with his own two hands right from the headquarters and walked them over. In 2002, Brennan remembers that Paralympians had less than $30 a day budgeted to them for all three meals. Four years later, at the Games in Torino, Italy, he was surprised to receive a "standing ovation" (irony noted) from the athletes with disabilities when he bought them simple meals of roast beef, potatoes, and vegetables.

Now, in 2022, a lot has changed. Since 2018, U.S. Paralympians receive $37,500 per gold medal—the same as Olympic gold medalists.[41] Paralympians no longer wait from eighth place on the schedule to train at world-class facilities.[42] Countries are more apt to lend support to their Paralympic programs; in fact, an interesting study from McGill University demonstrated that countries with a Paralympic team have higher psychological and physical well-being (when correlated with data on life expectancy and national happiness) than those that don't.[43] Respect for the Paralympics, indeed, may correlate to a more honest and more humble look we are taking at our own imperfections against unreasonable body standards. Cultural scientist Karin Harrasser wrote, "The whole idea of a purity of sports is based on the fiction of an equal-ity of all bodies, the myth that every body can be virtually perfected by training."[44] They cannot—but what is universally "perfected" anyway? Some native Inuit hockey players view not the flawlessness of the body, but *impairment and injury*, on the ice as status-boosters, as marks of the most intrepid teammates.[45]

"I think you guys deserve to be treated like U.S.A. Olympians," Middleton wrote of the team in an early email. "It's a lot easier to be physically tough than mentally tough."[46]

And nothing about the 2002 team's legacy said "easy."

Hockey is not only a sport, but an identity. University of Ottawa professor Michael A. Robidoux goes as far as calling ice hockey one of Canada's strongest postconfederation national and masculine identities, and I would argue that in the United States, a country which actually has more registered players than does Canada as of 2021 (albeit coming from a larger population), it is not far behind.[47] Dynamic individuals involved in U.S. sled hockey worked to expand that identity to include sled hockey. Thanks to their efforts, professional players in able-bodied leagues took greater notice of their physically challenged counterparts. Yes, it's a lot colder down there in a sled. It's also, in many ways, harder. At the qualifier tournament for the 2002 Paralympics, the 2000 IPC World Championships, NHL defenseman John W. Gibson (1959–2020) and professional left winger Mike Degurse (b. 1974) made an appearance to try out hockey in a sled. They wobbled and bumped around on the ice, far less graceful than they were used to, and left with a new respect for these members of the ice hockey family. "We get to walk away," they commented. "They don't."[48] This, along with the diplomatic networking in the NHL—Patrick Byrne with the Chicago Blackhawks and Pat Sapp with the Dallas Stars—fostered relationships and awareness between organizations.

But there is still much work to do. Canadian Paralympians, for example, still receive no money per gold medal, compared to about $20,000 CAD awarded to their Olympic gold medalists. The strides made by the 2002 cohort do not negate the journey still ahead for the United States or the international Paralympic teams of today—or for disability advocates in general.

The latest Paralympics in Beijing came to a close around the time of this project's completion. On March 12, 2022, the United States sled hockey team seemed to ring this book in with one of the world's most recent gold medals and a 5–0 shutout against Canada. On the all-time record displayed on national TV, the names of Joe Howard and Sylvester Flis still stood. Their legacy echoes in the roaring crowds of today, twenty years later.

"Averted vision" in astronomy is the suggested method for viewing cool or distant stars. When one looks just to the side of the star rather than directly at it, the star's hidden light pops out better against the blackness of the sky. Understanding the true radiance of this story requires looking not directly at it, but around it at everything else—the stories of the players, the impact on youth, the post-9/11 American dream it proved still had a pulse, to name a few. As this story comes to a close, it cannot be left unsaid that the zero-to-hero legacy left by the 2002 team does not end with this book, nor does this book capture everything it entailed. Sometimes, the legacy itself is a living entity, changing, growing, and shedding more light on the lived reality of today.

The legacy goes on.

DONALD MIRALLE/STAFF/GETTY IMAGES SPORT VIA GETTY IMAGES

CONCLUSION

Some, however, call the Paralympic athletes the only true Olympians. For, unlike most able-bodied athletes, they demonstrate the very heart and soul of amateur sports, compete for the love of sport, and are untainted by commercialism. There is something undeniably stirring in seeing people compete for the sheer joy of competition. This is the case for Paralympic athletes, who have overcome their disabilities to compete, and who often work full-time jobs around their training and yet have little or no hope of turning their passion into a career. When we realize what these athletes have accomplished, despite missing limbs or the ability to walk, we cannot help but be inspired.

—BRUCE VALLEY, FORMER NAVAL OFFICER,
WASHINGTON, DC, SPEECHWRITER, AND SPORTS AUTHOR

BEFORE THERE WAS GOLD, THERE WERE CHOICES.

None of the 2002 U.S. sled hockey players were choosing gold in the beginning. None knew that their choices would lead there.

No; before all of this, the only choice they made was life.

It is easy to boil down the story just told and produce many sports commonplaces: "Don't give up" or "Attitude is everything," perhaps. Sure, those could apply here—as they could with stories of discipline from able-bodied athletes. But what really happened in this story, and what set it apart, was the shared choice of life. Fifteen men, at some point in their lives, due to accident or genetics, found themselves deep in the gutter of physical and emotional anguish, on their backs, looking up at the sky—and they chose to stay down here where the fight was still waging. Their fateful meeting on the roster of Rick Middleton could be regarded as a council of spiritual and athletic titans.

I use the word *spiritual* not to assume that every player engaged in faith in a religious sense to become what they are today. Rather, I think none would argue that something inside of them went beyond the limitations of their bodies, met the refiner's fire of their choices to proceed through pain, and produced the performance of champions history will remember them for.

John Schatzlein started it all with the straightforward words: "Choose to care."[1]

Laurie Howlett chose to answer the call of his heart to make toys for the children with disabilities he saw playing and laughing. They would turn into cutting-edge sleds.

Manny Guerra made the choice to stop outside the door of Schatzlein's office and watch sled hockey on a small overhead television screen. He made the choice to fix what did not work for him—and his goalie equipment improvisations are the standard today.

Joe Howard made the choice—one could argue—not to abandon his body for good when he saw it on the gurney from above. He made the choice to remove his prosthetics when in the sled, putting something above his pride and his speed above all.

Kip St. Germaine—to his own surprise—made the choice to try sled hockey while dressed in his business suit.

Jack Sanders made the choice to travel 250 miles twice a week to train.

Trainer Jim Olson chose to go against the norms of his field and focus his therapy on the performance of athletes with disabilities *as well* as injury prevention. His methodology, at the time, was radical.

Patrick Byrne and Pat Sapp made the choice to be bold and ask their NHL teams—the Chicago Blackhawks and Dallas Stars, respectively—for startup money when the fledgling sport was searching for footing in the United States.

And Sly Flis? He made the choice to play—play with spina bifida or not, play as an American or not, play with all the Blackhawks in the lineup or not—play at all costs.

Rick Middleton made choices as well. His most impactful choices, in contrast to those of his players, were his less personal ones: particularly those connected to creating a simple strategy for the team. By selecting his roster on execution rather than allegiance, by rearranging the position of Joe Howard and forcing him off center stage and into the ecosystem of his team, by implementing the "dump and run" tactic, and by using cool, calm repetition, he evoked the strongest performances possible.

He did not leave all challenges conquered, however. Where Middleton succeeded in marshaling unity long enough to triumph in the final game, he failed in healing rifts that would extend decades. Ultimately, two teammates never connected with us on this project. Anger is not the primary emotion I encountered regarding this tension, though—sadness was. Heads shook, sighs wilted shoulders, and old sorrow touched eyes. The emotional fallout of what happened—the story *of* the story—became bigger than the happenings themselves. In other words, this project was not only about the story, but about me being told the story.

Some insisted Middleton could have done more, that these lasting scars could have been prevented. Others felt he had done well what his job required and that interpersonal remedies were not his responsibility. Many recognized his coaching as the best they had ever experienced. Times arose where I encountered both sides telling me contradicting information, and rather than pursue unobtainable certainty, I just had to leave both interpretations on the page for the reader to decide.

Every lively and dynamic sports team experiences friction. In some capacity, that friction can drive performance as disgruntled athletes resolve to outdo one another and take emotions out in a physical manner. Team USA was no exception in 2002, and this head-bumping may have been one of the "perfect storm" ingredients that helped them win it all. The players, who themselves had faced horrors and social rejection due to their disabilities, carried with them the baggage of cause to distrust the world and also to aggressively prove themselves. This instilled in them an understandable self-interest, a survivalist take-no-prisoners drive, and that, too, for all its faults, could be considered an ingredient to the victory.

The wounds from the chasm between Blackhawk and East Coaster, however, would never be entirely mended by gold.

On a wider level, the impact of the 2002 victory goes beyond individual strife and achievement. That rise to gold set the precedent for Team USA's pattern of medaling at every Paralympics since, and induced the explosion of sled hockey clubs throughout the nation. The number of aspiring athletes with disabilities touched by this team—boys and girls at last seeing champions in people who look like them—is uncountable.

So too is the 2002 team intertwined in the story of September 11, 2001, and post-9/11 America, as yet one more layer from the endless rippling—told and untold—of that terrible day. This victory shares space in the trauma of that chapter of the nation's history, but offers reasons to celebrate in the present-day reality, in a 2020s United States deeply polarized and plagued—literally—by COVID-19. This triumph, if the nation is willing, has the potential to occupy a page in the scrapbook of American victories before it, right alongside the 1980 "Miracle on Ice" game and the moon landing—images meant to be conjured up in *this* moment for comfort and inspiration about who we are as a people.

Anthropologist and historian Michel-Rolph Trouillot (1949–2012) wrote, "The past does not exist independently from the present. Indeed, the past is only past because there is a present, just as I can point to something *over there* only because I am *here*. But nothing is inherently over there or here."[2] This gold medal victory does not live in 2002. It is now, today, affecting every sled hockey program in the world, affecting me as the author who has inhabited this epoch for more than a year, and, hopefully, affecting you.

"Hockey is a brotherhood," Josh Wirt told me, "whether you're able-bodied or not."

Through my small but meaningful role, I am a member of this team myself now.

I am proud to be a part of that brotherhood.

Before there was gold, there were choices.

We hope this book gives you the courage to make yours.

Acknowledgments

Overall, I am grateful to have been a part of this worthy endeavor.

Thank you to Mom (Megan). She and Kilty Mahoney introduced me to this project and, as always, Mom supported me throughout, laying out little snacks for me to find as the deadline approached. Thank you to Dad (Larry, who I cherish being next to when we cheer for the Islanders and Rangers, or a lacrosse team, or football, or any team I learn to love because it means being closer to him) and to my amazing sister, Kelley—an excellent athlete, and teammate to everyone. You are the most important parts of my life and have always believed I can achieve beyond the limitations of my disability—including winning anything made of gold.

Thank you to my agent, Jessica Sinsheimer. I am your biggest fan.

To Rowman & Littlefield, especially Christen Karniski, acquisitions editor; Erinn Slanina, associate acquisitions editor; Nicole Carty, production editor; Susan Hershberg, publicity manager; Veronica Dove, marketing manager; Jamie Prahasky, marketing assistant; Amanda Wilson, (a very patient) cover designer; and Meghann French, copyeditor, I extend my profound gratitude. You provided this story a platform with grace and professionalism.

Probably the greatest debt I owe is to Gary Brandt. Gary was the project manager for this story long before I came on board. He facilitated the meetings with the players and relevant figures. He ticked off my to-do list to make my life easier. And he was this book's first editor, correcting fine details with his experience in hockey. All this aside, he's just the kindest soul you'll ever collaborate with. Hit him up if you want to come as close as possible to working with Mr. Rogers.

Tom Moulton and Rick Middleton—you took a chance on me. You trusted me with your baby, this story. I am honored; I love you; I hope I did it justice. (By the way, Rick, I adore your liberal use of exclamation points! You make me smile! Tom, you know I'm still disappointed that your finger guns photo didn't make the cover, but it sure as heck made my desk, in a frame).

Also important to this book coming together were Rich DeGlopper, Pat Sapp, Helen and Erica Schatzlein, Peter Noonan, and Kay Robertson. They provided contacts, heaps of materials for me to study, and their generous time. Kay, I cherish the adorable Otto the Otter you gave me, and Rich, your valentine. Thanks to you all so much.

Jeff Uyeno, I am really glad you made that call.

Billy Bridges, thank you for being awesome and helpful throughout. I now bestow upon you your nickname: Deathmetal. You know why! Hope you love it. If you don't, I don't know what to tell you. We're making it stick.

I was not the first author to engage with this project. Bruce Valley was supposed to write this book. Unfortunately, family health tragedies prevented this from happening. Mr. Valley freely circulated his preparatory notes, which gave me an immense head start. I share this triumph with you, Mr. Valley.

My appreciation, as always, to my writing groups: the Writers of Chantilly, the Hourlings, Varsity, and the Scribes of Eldion. Marty Wilsey, thanks for opening your home to our writing retreat! We had too much fun. Nick Bruner, we downed some beers over this one. Honestly, when are you going to tell your wife about me?

Thank you to my family—aunts, uncles, cousins, grandparents, and animals. Rudy, welcome to our wolf pack!

Thank you to my dear friends, especially Cat and Travis Caldwell, Max Markon, Kelsey Schoeman, Georgia Kashnig, Christopher Gurley, Josephine Kim, and John H. Matthews, for celebrating the book's completion with me.

To my dear students, Stuart Ondricek and Tayla Tran, I give my thanks. The latter, Tayla, contributed as a diligent notetaker for one interview. I am honored to be teacher to these beautiful, rising world-changers.

Hefty thanks to the historians and ethnographers who have coached me in the discipline, including Wes Fleming and James Sullivan (Northern Virginia Community College), Rich Barnett and Penny Von Eschen (University of Virginia), and Annalisa Butticci (Georgetown University).

Thanks to the instructors at Windham Ski Mountain who took me down those slopes.

Thank you to the 2009–2010 Westfield girls' varsity lacrosse team, who honored me as their team manager with the Bulldog Spirit Award and made me feel like a part of the sports family.

Honestly, thank you to the Centreville, Virginia, Marriot SpringHill Suites, Room 116. I completed a large chunk of this book holed up in that room. Thanks also to Lisa Gibbon Laing for scanning materials for me in a gorgeous, organized fashion, which saved me time.

I want to express my gratitude to Kiffin Steurer. Somehow, I left out his name in the acknowledgments of my very first published novel, which thanked the affiliates of the literary world who helped me when I was green and vulnerable. Kiffin, who was an editor at Penguin, read my first-ever manuscript and provided constructive but warm feedback to nurture me at an extremely high level. Now, he gets his very own paragraph in my second traditional publication. Thank you.

Thank you to Elliot Segal (a major hockey fan) from *Elliot in the Morning* for the times you've invited me on your show and made me feel like a somebody. You are awesome. And I won't tell anyone what you said off-air if you do the same for me.

If you contributed to this team, this victory, or this book and I failed to include your name or efforts adequately, please accept my heartfelt apology. You matter.

These acknowledgments remember the life of Evelyn Judith O'Shea (1934–2021), my precious grandmother, who loved sports. They also memorialize my great uncle, Roger Amole (1939–2020), whose last words, among others, asked if I was taken care of. I am, Unc.

Finally, Matt. You will be saved for last every time. If Mom and Dad had never bought you those Hershey Bears tickets—and you didn't have to take me along—this book would never have happened.

Once again, you're the reason.

You are always the reason.

SCM

NOTES

CHAPTER 1. LAKE OF LEGEND: SLED HOCKEY'S HISTORY, RULES, AND EQUIPMENT

1. Barry Popik, "When Hell Freezes Over, I'll Play Hockey There, Too," *The Big Apple* [blog], June 12, 2015, https://www.barrypopik.com/index.php/new_york_city /entry/when_hell_freezes_over_ill_play_hockey.

2. Helen Burchell, "Handy Bandy Guide . . ." Local History, BBC, February 21, 2006, https://www.bbc.co.uk/cambridgeshire/content/articles/2006/02/15/bandy_sport _feature.shtml.

3. Joscelyn Moes, "Why Do They Call It . . . Hockey?" WFMZ.com, October 10, 2019, https://www.wfmz.com/news/why-do-they-call-it-hockey/article_00a66ec2 -335b-56fd-b488-24a0d0567b3f.html.

4. I only found one English book that provided even slightly more information than the standard tagline passed from news article to news article. Amusingly, the book was *A Guide to Gambling*, by Nicolae Sfetcu.

5. Rolf Johansson, "Jag var med och startade idrottsgrenen kälkhockey, vintern 1963–1964 (I was one of the founders of the sport of sledge hockey, winter 1963–1964)." Excerpt from *The Wheelchair Phantom* by Rolf Johansson (N.p., n.d).

6. Johansson, "Jag var med och startade idrottsgrenen kälkhockey, vintern 1963–1964."

7. Johansson, "Jag var med och startade idrottsgrenen kälkhockey, vintern 1963–1964."

8. The teams at the Nackas rink competing in the 1969 mini-tournament were Nacka (likely Rolf's team), BT, LKB, IFAH (possibly Idrottsföreningen För Alla Handikappade, a disabled sports association), and Hugin.

9. Rolf Johansson, "Kälkhockyhistoria (The Story of Sled Hockey)." May 4, 2019.

10. Johansson, "Jag var med och startade idrottsgrenen kälkhockey, vintern 1963–1964."

11. Johansson, "Jag var med och startade idrottsgrenen kälkhockey, vintern 1963–1964."

12. "Para" means "alongside of," which indicates the Paralympics being *alongside* of the Olympics. With this in mind, some argue that true side-by-side equality would require the Paralympics and the Olympics to occur simultaneously, sharing the same media coverage, time, and space.

13. "Paralympics History," International Paralympic Committee, https://www.para
lympic.org/ipc/history#:~:text=Ludwig%20Guttmann%20opened%20a%20spial,and%20
then%20to%20competitive%20sport.&text=On%2029%20July%201948%2C%20
the,London%201948%20Olympic%20Games%2C%20Dr.

14. "Paralympics History."

15. "Paralympics History."

16. Walter Attenai, photograph, Associated Press.

17. Johansson, "Kälkhockyhistoria."

18. Ian Brittain, *From Stoke Mandeville to Sochi: A History of the Summer and Winter
Paralympic Games* (Champaign, IL: Common Ground, 2014).

19. Johansson, "Jag var med och startade idrottsgrenen kälkhockey, vintern 1963–
1964."

20. Howard Liss, *Goal! Hockey's Stanley Cup Playoffs* (New York: Delacorte Press,
1970).

21. Daniel S. Mason, "The International Hockey League and the Professionalization
of Ice Hockey, 1904–1907." *Journal of Sport History* 25, no. 1 (1998): 1–17, http://www
.jstor.org/stable/43606915.

22. Johansson, "Jag var med och startade idrottsgrenen kälkhockey, vintern 1963–
1964."

23. John Schatzlein, "RE: History/Present Status ASHA," email to sled hockey
leaders, November 28, 1995.

24. Oslo Sports Federation for the Disabled, "USA Sledge Hockey," February 22,
1993.

25. To the best of my summation, the full roster was as follows: Dave Conklin #20,
Joe Baird #22, Manuel Guerra #1, Dan Henderson #15, Dave Johnson #14, Mike Kult
#27, Charles Lindsey #16, Tom McNally #21, Chad Olson #17, John Schatzlein #3,
Mark Schmitt #18, Mike Wilson #9. This comes from a 1993 document, so names on
the 1990 team may have been slightly different; however, note that three players, Conklin, Guerra, and Henderson, would make it to the 2002 gold medal game.

26. John Schatzlein, "Proposal," n.d.; author copy.

27. Brian J. Williams to John Schatzlein, letter, October 7, 1993.

28. Well, "The puck has just begun to glide" would have been better.

29. Williams, letter to Schatzlein.

30. Jan Wilson to John Schatzlein, letter, October 21, 1993.

31. Mike G. Morreale, "Dave Ogrean Has Been Huge Force for USA Hockey."
NHL.com, June 8, 2017, https://www.nhl.com/news/ogrean-has-been-big-force-for-usa
-hockey/c-289833474; Jan Wilson to John Schatzlein, letter, January 12, 1994.

32. American Sled Hockey Association, "U.S. Sledge Hockey Progress Report:
October 23, 1993–June 7, 1994," presented to USA Hockey, Inc., June 7, 1994.

33. Johansson, "Kälkhockyhistoria."

34. 0–11 to Norway, 1–11 to Sweden, 0–5 to Canada, 1–5 to Estonia. The United
States won one game against Japan, 3–0.

35. USA Hockey, *2019–20 Official Rules of Sled Hockey*, https://cdn2.sportngin.com
/attachments/document/0103/3572/19-20_Sled_Hockey_Playing_Rules.pdf#_ga=2
.208907345.2125198105.1637082370-1468821994.1637082364.

36. USA Hockey, "USA Hockey Sled Hockey Officiating Video," YouTube, April 7, 2016, https://www.youtube.com/watch?v=3AYe9-TDTHE&feature=emb_logo.

37. USA Hockey, "Officiating Sled Hockey," https://www.usahockey.com/sledreferees.

38. Referees must also take care not to get taken out from behind by fast-moving sleds traveling below their knees. I was told that in 2002, Team USA had beer cases stacked up in the referee room after the gold medal game. Apparently, the referees had to buy a case of beer for the other refs if they got taken out by a player's sled during the play.

39. Rich DeGlopper, "RE: History Help!" email to Shea C. Megale, January 27, 2022.

40. Laurie Howlett, "uniqueinventions@nexicom.net sent you Shea 2022.pdf via WeTransfer," email to Shea C. Megale, January 25, 2022.

CHAPTER 3. NAGANO

1. "Ice Sledge Hockey," 1998 Winter Paralympic Games Team Media, n.d.

2. Caroline Williams, Dave Schaefer, and Karen Rountree, "Gold Rush: Following the Successful Olympics in Nagano, Japan, Athletes with Disabilities Had Their Shot at Grabbing the Glory." *Sports 'N Spokes* 24, no. 3 (May 1998), 16.

3. A power play in hockey is a numerical player advantage enjoyed by a team when an opposing player is in the penalty box due to a rule violation. It can last two, five, or ten minutes depending on the penalty. Hockey statisticians keep track of how many power plays are converted into goals.

4. Brenda Bushnell, "Shutouts at Aqua Wing." *Paralympics Nagano* 98, no. 8, March 11, 1998, 8.

5. Williams, Schaefer, and Rountree, "Gold Rush."

6. Advertisement, *Paralympics Nagano* 98, no. 8, March 11, 1998.

7. Ian Brittain, *From Stoke Mandeville to Sochi: A History of the Summer and Winter Paralympic Games* (Champaign, IL: Common Ground, 2014), 320.

8. Mary Bach Fleming, "New Sled Hockey Team Hopes to Ice a Medal," n.d.

9. Fleming, "New Sled Hockey Team Hopes to Ice a Medal."

10. Fleming, "New Sled Hockey Team Hopes to Ice a Medal."

CHAPTER 4. JOE HOWARD, #23: "MOMO"

1. "Nu Börjar Jakten På Nya Guld (Now the Hunt for New Gold Begins)." *Sport Bladet*, March 11, 2006, https://www.aftonbladet.se/sportbladet/a/a2loEa/nu-borjar -jakten-pa-nya-guld.

2. "Terry O'Reilly Career Profile," Hockey Draft Central, http://www.hockeydraft central.com/1971/71014.html.

CHAPTER 5. GATHERING THE TEAM

1. A little more needs to be said about this event. While the second IPC World Championship games were a total unsuccess for Team USA, they exemplify a marked increase in public enthusiasm for adaptive athletics. Nearly thirty thousand local students attended the games throughout the week. One thirteen-year-old, Nich Farr, asked the athletes with disabilities for their autographs. "Michael Jordan used to be

what I thought was a hero," he said. "Now that I've seen these guys play, I know what a real hero is." His change of perspective, for sure, was worth more than the 2D plastic trophies the IPC gave to the winners.

2. Susan Fahncke, "The Time of My Life," *Sled Hockey*. September 25, 2000.

3. Mike Zhe, "Middleton to Be Enshrined in New Hampshire Legends of Hockey HOF," *Seacoast Online*, October 5, 2014.

4. "Guidelines for Evaluation," United States Sled Hockey Association, June 20, 2001, author copy.

5. Patricia Shepherd, "Selection Criteria," United States Sled Hockey Association, June 20, 2001, author copy.

6. Bob O'Connor, "Individual Player Report," United States Sled Hockey Association, n.d.

CHAPTER 6. SYLVESTER FLIS, #4: "SLY"

1. An Act for the Relief of Sylvester Flis, S. 1172, 105th Cong., 2nd sess., *Congressional Record* 144, pt. 1.

2. An Act for the Relief of Sylvester Flis.

3. Another "rooster," this time not attacking him! The irony is noted.

CHAPTER 7. TRAINING CHAMPIONS

1. Rick Middleton, "Montreal Tournament," email to the 2002 U.S. sled hockey team members., 12:08 p.m., September 11, 2001.

2. Jeff Jones, "The envelope please," email to Dave Conklin, Manny Guerra, Kip St. Germaine, Joe Howard, Sylvester Flis, and Mike Doyle, August 8, 2001.

3. Jones, email.

4. Rick Middleton, email to the 2002 U.S. sled hockey team members, August 21, 2001.

5. Jeff Jones, "Call the roll?" email to Rick Middleton, 11:56 a.m., August 23, 2001.

6. "I Formation Penalty Kill Forecheck," Ice Hockey Systems, https://www.icehockeysystems.com/hockey-systems/i-formation-penalty-kill-forecheck.

CHAPTER 8. PATRICK BYRNE, #14

1. C. Bernard Ruffin, *Padre Pio: The True Story*, 3rd ed. (Huntington, IN: Our Sunday Visitor, 2018).

2. Colm Fitzpatrick, "A Saint of Our Time," *Irish Catholic*, March 21, 2018, https://www.irishcatholic.com/a-saint-of-our-time/.

3. Jay Shefsky, "Sled Hockey." WTTW News, September 19, 2013, https://news.wttw.com/2013/09/19/sled-hockey.

4. "Greediest Owners in Sports," ESPN, https://www.espn.com/page2/s/list/owners/greediest.html.

CHAPTER 9. ARRIVING IN SALT LAKE CITY

1. Carla O'Connell, "U.S. Ice Sledge Hockey Team to Face Japan in Opening of 2002 Paralympic Winter Games," *USA Daily*, n.d.

2. Sheila Brosz and Pat Sapp, "Olympic Sled Hockey Comes to Dallas," *Stargazer: The Official Newsletter of the Dallas Stars Booster Club* 3, no. 3 (2002): 4.

3. O'Connell, "U.S. Ice Sledge Hockey Team to Face Japan."

4. Estonia had joined Great Britain and Germany petitioning the IPC to allow the latter two to play as well. They argued that the original announcement for the Games, published in a newsletter in 2000, had indicated eight countries would be invited, and that the IPC only announced *after* the fact that in order to qualify, teams would had to have played in the 2000 World Championships in Salt Lake City. Great Britain and Germany had not competed there but asserted that they would have had they known it would be a requirement. The petition amassed at least forty-four signatures from the three teams, but ultimately did not succeed. ("Petition for the Ice Sledge Hockey," to IPC-Robert D. Steward, Carol Mushett, Francois Terranova, David Gravenberg, Thor Kleppe; SLOC-Xavier Gonzales, Jack Benedict; NPCs of countries playing ice sledge hockey, national sledge hockey teams of United States, Canada, Japan, Norway, Sweden, Czech, 1:22 p.m. October 15, 2001.)

5. Angela Scholze, ed., *U.S. Paralympic Team Delegation Handbook: XIII Paralympic Winter Games—Salt Lake City, Utah* (N.p.: Fittje Brothers, 2002); author copy.

6. Matt Canham, ed., *Paralympic Record* 10 (March 10, 2002); author copy.

7. Brian Ruhe, "More concerns" email to Rick Middleton, 6:47 p.m. October 12, 2001.

8. Never Dull Productions, "TV Sports Projects," http://www.neverdullproductions.com/tv-sports-projects-.html.

9. Members of The Church of Jesus Christ of Latter-day Saints, commonly known as Mormons, are not explicitly prohibited from specific foods and drinks, but are advised against "hot beverages" in the "Word of Wisdom," a section from *The Doctrine and Covenants*, which their prophets have clarified to only mean hot tea and coffee.

10. "Paralympic Games Could Be Most Watched in History. 28 Countries Gain Access to Air Live and Prerecorded Games," Paralympic News Service, March 6, 2002.

11. ARD, or *Arbeitsgemeinschaft der öffentlich-rechtlichen Rundfunkanstalten der Bundesrepublik Deutschland* (in English, "Working group of public broadcasters of the Federal Republic of Germany") worked in tandem with ZDF, or *Zweites Deutsches Fernsehen* (in English, "Second German Television").

12. "Paralympic Games Could Be Most Watched in History."

13. Scott Hettrick, "A&E Going for Gold: Cabler in Sporting Mood with Paralympic Games," *Daily Variety*, March 6, 2002.

14. Megan N. Houston, Johanna M. Hoch, Bonnie L. Van Lunen, and Matthew C. Hoch, "The Development of Summary Components for the Disablement in the Physically Active Scale in Collegiate Athletes," *Quality of Life Research* 24, no. 11 (2015): 2657–62, http://www.jstor.org/stable/44849368.

15. Scholze, *U.S. Paralympic Team Delegation Handbook.*

16. P. David Howe, "The Tail Is Wagging the Dog: Body Culture, Classification and the Paralympic Movement," *Ethnography* 9, no. 4 (2008): 499–517, http://www.jstor.org/stable/24047912.

17. Eric Adelson, "Let 'Em Play," ESPN, April 21, 2008, https://www.espn.com/espn mag/story?id=3357051.

18. Adelson, "Let 'Em Play."

19. "Salt Lake Paralympic Games," *Republican and Evening Herald*, February 5, 2002.

20. Cindy Mulkern, "Salt Lake City Venues Ready for Two 'Games.'" *Amusement Business*, July 30, 2001.

21. Scholze, *U.S. Paralympic Team Delegation Handbook.*

22. Amy Donaldson, "Paralympics Were a Learning Experience for Leavitt," *Deseret News*, March 17, 2002.

23. Scholze, *U.S. Paralympic Team Delegation Handbook.*

24. The emblem of the winter games changes every four years at the new Paralympics. The 2002 version consisted of a large red dot hovering over two broad, wavy strokes of green and blue. In the bottom left corner was the triad of green, red, and blue "agitos," or apostrophe-looking symbols, the logo of the Paralympics. This does not change from games to games (save restyling). The large red sphere at the top of the 2002 logo represented the globe and the thick strokes represented fluid motion, alluding to the expansion of physical capacity to the realms of mind and spirit.

25. Mulkern, "Salt Lake City Venues Ready for Two 'Games.'"

26. Inside the busses, amputee players used the ceiling grips like monkey bars to travel up and down the rows of seats. Middleton rode with them.

CHAPTER 11. GAME ONE—USA VS. JAPAN: MARCH 8, 2002

1. Weihenmayer had, in fact, been passed the torch himself hours earlier. Gordon B. Hinckley (1910–2008), prophet, seer, and revelator as well as president of The Church of Jesus Christ of Latter-day Saints, had gathered with members of the Quorum of the Twelve Apostles to make ceremony of the torch. The spiritual leader said to the athletes with disabilities, "Claim the pennant! Be happy, be happy. We're all with you." Julie Dockstader Heaps, "Paralympic Winter Games a Triumph of Spirit: First Presidency Again Passes Torch," *Church News*, week ending March 16, 2002.

2. Erik Weihenmayer, "Pretty sure it was SEIGO who was my second dog—a big hundred pounder," Facebook, January 19, 2022, https://www.facebook.com/erik.weihen mayer/posts/460344982139559?comment_id=462838621890195&reply_comment_id =463147321859325&notif_id=1642614130402150&notif_t=comment_mention&ref =notif.

3. Ian Brittain, *From Stoke Mandeville to Sochi: A History of the Summer and Winter Paralympic Games* (Champaign, IL: Common Ground, 2014).

4. Lisa Riley Roche, "2002 Paralympics; Return of the Fire," *Deseret News*, March 8, 2002, https://www.deseret.com/2002/3/8/19642009/2002-paralympics-return-of-the -fire.

5. Ryan Warren, "Sledge Hockey." *Sports 'N Spokes* 28, no. 3 (May 2002), 49.

6. "Athletes Glide, Slide to Victory," *Deseret News*, March 9, 2002.

7. Salt Lake Paralympics 2002, "Flash Quotes," news release, n.d.

8. Salt Lake Paralympics 2002, "Flash Quotes."

9. Salt Lake Paralympics 2002, "Flash Quotes."

10. Salt Lake Paralympics 2002, "Flash Quotes."

11. Salt Lake Paralympics 2002, "Flash Quotes."

12. Salt Lake Paralympics 2002, "Flash Quotes."

13. "二宮清純の視点 (The 2nd 'Encounter with Ice Sledge Hockey')." 障害者スポーツをスポーツとしてとらえるサイト"挑戦者たち, Challengers TV, April 16, 2010, https://www.challengers.tv/seijun/2010/04/305.html.

CHAPTER 13. GAME TWO—USA VS. CANADA: MARCH 9, 2002

1. Howard Liss, *Goal! Hockey's Stanley Cup Playoffs* (New York: Delacorte, 1970), 1.

2. "Billy Bridges | Ice Sledge Hockey | Canada," Sochi 2014, Paralympic Winter Games, 2014. http://sochi2014.arch.articul.ru/www.sochi2014.com/en/paralympic /athlete-billy-bridges.htm.

3. Sal Barry, "Helmet Holdouts: The Last Players Not to Wear Helmets in the NHL," *Hockey News*, May 16, 2019, https://thehockeynews.com/all-access/helmet -holdouts-the-last-players-to-wear-helmets-in-the-nhl.

4. Salt Lake Paralympics 2002, "Flash Quotes," news release, n.d.

5. "Hockey Hall Displays Salt Lake Loonie," CBC News, March 9, 2002, https:// www.cbc.ca/sports/hockey/hockey-hall-displays-salt-lake-loonie-1.317667.

6. *Deseret News*, Saturday, March 9, 2002.

7. Salt Lake Paralympics 2002, "Flash Quotes."

8. "Canada Tops Sweden in Sledge Hockey," Associated Press, March 13, 1998, https://ap.news.com/article/49bb1251dac27c106bfe113e8f057956.

9. "Todd Nicholson—Para Ice Hockey: Paralympic Athlete Profile," International Paralympic Committee, https://www.paralympic.org/todd-nicholson.

10. Salt Lake Paralympics 2002, "Flash Quotes."

11. A&E, "Salt Lake 2002: Paralympic Winter Games," hosted by Harry Smith and Joan Lunden, TV miniseries, March 2002.

CHAPTER 14. JOSH WIRT, #19

1. NHL, "Memories: Mullen Becomes First American to Score 500," YouTube, 2017, https://www.youtube.com/watch?v=196hsi3YrbA.

2. Dave Sell, "Lemieux Scores in Noisy Return," *Washington Post*, March 3, 1993, https://www.washingtonpost.com/archive/sports/1993/03/03/lemieux-scores-in -noisy-return/f460a8c3-aca3-4dea-862d-149087759263/.

3. Saul L. Miller, *Hockey Tough* (Champaign, IL: Human Kinetics, 2016), 109.

CHAPTER 15. GAME THREE—USA VS. NORWAY: MARCH 11, 2002

1. PictureQuotes, http://www.picturequotes.com/hockey-is-figure-skating-in-a-war -zone-quote-718535.

2. Salt Lake Paralympics 2002, "Flash Quotes," news release, n.d.

3. Salt Lake Paralympics 2002, "Flash Quotes."

4. Salt Lake Paralympics 2002, "Flash Quotes."

5. Salt Lake Paralympics 2002, "Flash Quotes."

6. Salt Lake Paralympics 2002, "Flash Quotes."

CHAPTER 17. KIP ST. GERMAINE, #12
1. Peter Quartuccio, "An Icon and a Gentleman." *Sports 'N Spokes* 37, no. 1 (January 2011): 28–32.
2. Quartuccio, "An Icon and a Gentleman."
3. Quartuccio, "An Icon and a Gentleman."

CHAPTER 18. GAME FOUR—USA VS. SWEDEN: MARCH 12, 2002
1. Salt Lake Paralympics 2002, "Flash Quotes," news release, n.d.
2. "Björn Ferber," Elite Hockey Prospects, https://www.eliteprospects.com/staff/7558/bjorn-ferber.
3. Salt Lake Paralympics 2002, "Flash Quotes."
4. Salt Lake Paralympics 2002, "Flash Quotes."
5. "Klart: NY Ungdomsansvarig till Hammarby Hockey (READY: New Youth Manager for Hammarby Hockey)," Hammarby Hockey, https://www.hammarbyhockey.se/klart-ny-ungdomsansvarig-till-hammarby-hockey/.
6. "Dedjo Engmark—Para Ice Hockey: Paralympic Athlete Profile," International Paralympic Committee, https://www.paralympic.org/dedjo-engmark.
7. ESPN, Twitter post, May 12, 2014, 7:40 p.m. https://twitter.com/espn/status/465999890221244416.
8. Hannah would, in fact, come away from the Games as the second most-penalized player, behind only Estonian Maksim Vedernikov.
9. A&E, "Salt Lake 2002: Paralympic Winter Games," hosted by Harry Smith and Joan Lunden, TV miniseries, March 2002.
10. A *natural* hat trick would be when one player scores thrice in a row without a player from either team scoring in between.

CHAPTER 20. GAME FIVE—USA VS. ESTONIA: MARCH 14, 2002
1. Dennis Romboy, "Sled Hockey as Violent as Stand-up Counterpart," *Deseret News*, March 14, 2002, https://www.deseret.com/2002/3/14/20634137/sled-hockey-as-violent-as-stand-up-counterpart.
2. Romboy, "Sled Hockey as Violent as Stand-up Counterpart."
3. Salt Lake Paralympics 2002, "Flash Quotes," news release, n.d.
4. Salt Lake Paralympics 2002, "Flash Quotes."
5. Ryan Warren, "Sledge Hockey," *Sports 'N Spokes* 28, no. 3 (May 2002): 51.

CHAPTER 22. PAT SAPP, #33: "LT. DAN."
1. Paralyzed Veterans of America, "Tom Wheaton," https://pva.org/about-us/leadership/tom-wheaton/.

CHAPTER 23. THE STORM BEFORE THE STORM
1. The quote ends magnificently with: "It cuts deep into me, and I'd rather not talk about it. It's very personal with me. Ask me about broads or booze, anything else."
2. Salt Lake Paralympics 2002, "Flash Quotes," news release, n.d.

3. Salt Lake Paralympics 2002, "Flash Quotes."

4. Salt Lake Paralympics 2002, "Flash Quotes."

5. Salt Lake Paralympics 2002, "Flash Quotes."

6. Kay Robertson, email likely to Bruce Valley, May 2, 2017.

7. Jeff Jones, "Change in time, time to change" email to RIC Blackhawks players, 11:31 a.m., April 3, 2002.

8. "Ryan Whitney and I Now Have Something in Common," *The Sidney Crosby Show* [blog], August 17, 2008, http://sidcrosby.blogspot.com/2008/08/ryan-whitney-and-i-now-have-something.html.

9. *Paralympic Record,* issue 15, 2002.

10. Salt Lake Paralympics 2002. "Flash Quotes." News Release. March 14, 2002.

11. *Paralympic Record,* 10 (2002).

12. Christy Karras, "U.S. Sled Hockey Team in Hunt for Gold," *New York Times*, March 15, 2002.

13. Brett Prettyman, "Estonia No Match for U.S.," *Salt Lake Tribune*, March 15, 2002.

14. Salt Lake Paralympics 2002, "Flash Quotes," news release, March 14, 2002.

15. Salt Lake Paralympics 2002, "Flash Quotes," news release, March 15, 2002.

16. "Official Game Report," Salt Lake Organizing Committee for the Paralympic Winter Games of 2002, game no. 18, n.d.

17. Tom Henderson, "Overtime, Sudden Death, Shootout—Then Sledge Hockey Goes for U.S.," *iCan News*, March 16, 2002.

CHAPTER 24. GOLD MEDAL GAME—USA VS. NORWAY: MARCH 15, 2002

1. Salt Lake Paralympics 2002, "Flash Quotes," news release, n.d.

CHAPTER 25. LONNIE HANNAH, #1

1. The author would like to note having also operated a Quickie power wheelchair many years ago, lovingly nicknamed "Zippy-by-Quickie."

CHAPTER 26. MATT COPPENS, #5

1. Scott Merkin, "U.S. Paralympians Thinking Hockey Glory Too," *Chicago Tribune*, March 5, 2002, https://www.chicagotribune.com/news/ct-xpm-2002-03-05-0203060052-story.html.

2. Ashley E. Broughton, "The Will to Win, Even on Ice: Chicago Men Rebound from Accidents and Reach the Paralympics," *Salt Lake Tribune*, sec. B, March 15, 2002.

3. Broughton, "The Will to Win."

CHAPTER 27. JACK SANDERS, #15

1. Jack Sanders, "Re: 2002 Olympic Sled Team Book," email to Bruce Valley, 11:10 a.m., November 9, 2015.

CHAPTER 28. AFTERMATH

1. "Jordin Tootoo Discusses His Time in NHL and Losing His Brother to Suicide | Hometown Hockey," Sportsnet, March 3, 2019, https://www.youtube.com/watch?v=81ucr8-AdDc.

2. Salt Lake Paralympics 2002, "Flash Quotes," news release, n.d.

3. Salt Lake Paralympics 2002, "Flash Quotes."

4. Salt Lake Paralympics 2002, "Flash Quotes."

5. "Sled Hockey Skates on Inclusiveness, Fun," WAND, March 2, 2018, https://www.wandtv.com/news/sled-hockey-skates-on-inclusiveness-fun/article_230edb69-60f5-536a-8b4a-805564f24434.html.

6. Salt Lake Paralympics 2002, "Flash Quotes."

7. Salt Lake 2002 Paralympic Winter Games, S. 2069, *Congressional Record* 184, pt. 32.

8. Dickson Darnell, "U.S. Ice Sledge Hockey Team Wins Gold," *USA Hockey*, March 20, 2002; United States Olympic Committee, *Olympic Beat*, April 2002; Harry Thompson, "Reversal of Fortune: U.S. Sled Hockey Team Goes from Worst to First with Dramatic Gold-Medal Victory," *American Hockey*, April/May 2002; Steve Goldberg, "Surprising USA in Hockey Final," *USA Today*, March 15, 2002. "Goal'd!" was the clever headline of another article, which happened to be my favorite: Dennis Romboy, "Goal-d!: Team USA Wins 1st Medal," *Deseret News*, March 16, 2002.

9. Tom Henderson, "U.S. Sled Hockey Coach Adds Experience to the Equation," *iCan News*, February 27, 2002.

10. Linda Fantin, "Paralympics Get 'Best Ever' Label," *Salt Lake Tribune*, March 17, 2002.

11. Mike Gorrell, "Romney Choked up as 2002 Winter Games Come to an End," *Salt Lake Tribune*, March 17, 2002.

12. Gorrell, "Romney Choked Up."

13. Lisa Riley Roche, "Goodbye to the Games," *Deseret News*, March 17, 2002.

14. Roche, "Goodbye to the Games."

15. Office of the Press Secretary, "Remarks by the President to the Olympians and Paralympians," news release, April 23, 2002.

16. Office of the Press Secretary, "Remarks by the President."

17. Charlie Snyder, "White House Visit: President Bush Greets the 2002 U.S. Olympic, Paralympic Teams," usolympicteam.com, April 23, 2002.

18. "Blotter," *Sports Illustrated*, n.d.

19. "A Miracle on Ice: Sled Hockey Team Wins Gold, Rick Middleton Named USA Hockey Coach of the Year," *Hockey Magazine*, New England Edition 2, no. 8 (October 2002), 23.

20. Mike Zhe, "Middleton to Be Enshrined in New Hampshire Legends of Hockey HOF," *Seacoast Online*, October 5, 2014.

21. United States Hockey Hall of Fame, "2016 Nomination Form."

22. United States Hockey Hall of Fame, "2016 Nomination Form."

23. Roche, "Goodbye to the Games."

24. Bruce Valley, "2002 Olympic Sled Team Book," email to Shea C. Megale, 1:22 p.m., August 30, 2015.

25. Valley, "2002 Olympic Sled Team Book."

26. Rick Middleton, Fax #3129081051, fax to Jeff Jones, March 29, 2002.

27. Jeff Jones, "FYI," email to Rick Middleton, April 12, 2002.

28. Jones, "FYI."

29. Rick Middleton, email to Joe Walsh, n.d.

30. Jeff Jones, "Change in time, time to change," email to RIC Blackhawks players, 11:31 a.m., April 3, 2002.

31. Rick Middleton, letter to Jeff [no last name, but certainly not Jones, who is spoken about in third person in the body of the letter], November 11, 2002.

32. Derek Daniels, "Olympic Interview Questions Derek Daniels," interview with author, January 25, 2022.

33. The national sled hockey team has eight military veterans on it, and also welcomes women as of 2014. As late as 2006, two women bravely showed up to try out and were turned away on the basis of gender—they were Erica Mitchell (defense) and Hope Bevilhymer (goalie), who both now play on the development team.

34. Daniels, "Olympic Interview Questions Derek Daniels."

35. Nicole Kwan, "Paralyzed Marine Turns to Growing Sport of Sled Hockey for Rehabilitation, Community," Fox News, December 22, 2015. https://www.foxnews.com/health/paralyzed-marine-turns-to-growing-sport-of-sled-hockey-for-rehabilitation-community.

36. Kwan, "Paralyzed Marine."

37. Karin Harrasser, "Superhumans-Parahumans: Disability and Hightech in Competitive Sports," 171–200, in *Culture—Theory—Disability: Encounters between Disability Studies and Cultural Studies*, ed. Anne Waldschmidt, Berressem Hanjo, and Ingwersen Moritz, by Vaja Eleana and Tarapata Olga (Bielefeld: Transcript Verlag, 2017), http://www.jstor.org/stable/j.ctv1xxs3r.13.

38. Variants of the Special Olympics, with their own rules for qualification, developed as well, one such being the Rainbow Games, in which I won several trophies for "fastest wheelchair."

39. Linda Fantin, "Once-Neglected U.S. Paralympians Finally Getting USOC Support," *Salt Lake Tribune*, May 28, 2002, https://www.sltrib2002.com/Main/Story.asp?VOL=03102002&NUM=718112&OPT2=OLY.

40. Fantin, "Once-Neglected U.S. Paralympians."

41. Liz Roscher, "Paralympians Are Now Paid the Same as Olympians for Winning Medals," Yahoo!Sports, https://sports.yahoo.com/paralympians-are-now-paid-the-same-as-olympians-for-winning-medals-231622163.html.

42. Fantin, "Once-Neglected U.S. Paralumpians."

43. Michelle Downie and Richard Koestner, "Why Faster, Higher, Stronger Isn't Necessarily Better: The Relations of Paralympian and Women's Soccer Teams' Performance to National Well-Being," *Social Indicators Research* 88, no. 2 (2008): 273–80, http://www.jstor.org/stable/27734700.

44. Harrasser, "Superhumans-Parahumans."

45. Peter Collings and Richard G. Condon, "Blood on the Ice: Status, Self-Esteem, and Ritual Injury among Inuit Hockey Players," *Human Organization* 55, no. 3 (1996): 253–62, http://www.jstor.org/stable/44126857.

46. Rick Middleton, "Re: more concerns," email to U.S. national team players, 2001.

47. Michael A. Robidoux, "Imagining a Canadian Identity through Sport: A Historical Interpretation of Lacrosse and Hockey," *Journal of American Folklore* 115, no. 456 (2002): 209–25, doi:10.2307/4129220; "IIHF Season Summary," International Ice Hockey Federation, 2020–2021.

48. Shawn Windsor, "Hockey with a Difference," *Huntsville Times*, September 10, 2000.

CONCLUSION

1. Jane McClure, "Schatzlein, Mundl Remembered for Contributing to Community," Access Press, July 23, 2019, https://accesspress.org/schatzlein-mundl-remembered-for-contributing-to-community/.

2. Michel-Rolph Trouillot, *Silencing the Past: Power and the Production of History* (Boston: Beacon Press, 2004), 15.

Bibliography

"A Miracle on Ice: Sled Hockey Team Wins Gold, Rick Middleton Named USA Hockey Coach of the Year." *Hockey Magazine*, New England Edition 2, no. 8 (October 2002).

A&E. "Salt Lake 2002: Paralympic Winter Games." Hosted by Harry Smith and Joan Lunden. TV miniseries, March 2002.

Advertisement. *Paralympics Nagano* 98, no. 8 (March 11, 1998).

Adelson, Eric. "Let 'Em Play." ESPN, April 21, 2008. Accessed December 6, 2021. https://www.espn.com/espnmag/story?id=3357051.

American Sled Hockey Association. "U.S. Sledge Hockey Progress Report: October 23, 1993–June 7, 1994." Presented to USA Hockey, June 7, 1994.

An Act for the Relief of Sylvester Flis, S. 1172, 105th Cong., 2nd sess., *Congressional Record* 144, pt. 1.

Associated Press. "Canada Tops Sweden in Sledge Hockey." March 13, 1998. Accessed January 6, 2022. https://apnews.com/article/49bb1251dac27c106bfe113e8f057956.

"Athletes Glide, Slide to Victory." *Deseret News*. March 9, 2002.

Barry, Sal. "Helmet Holdouts: The Last Players Not to Wear Helmets in the NHL." *Hockey News*, May 16, 2019. Accessed December 6, 2021. https://thehockeynews.com/all-access/helmet-holdouts-the-last-players-to-wear-helmets-in-the-nhl.

"Billy Bridges, Ice Sledge Hockey, Canada." Sochi 2014 Paralympic Winter Games, 2014. Accessed December 6, 2021. http://sochi2014.arch.articul.ru/www.sochi 2014.com/en/paralympic/athlete-billy-bridges.htm.

"Björn Ferber." Elite Hockey Prospects. Accessed January 6, 2022. https://www.elite prospects.com/staff/7558/bjorn-ferber.

"Blotter." *Sports Illustrated*. N.d.

Brittain, Ian. *From Stoke Mandeville to Sochi: A History of the Summer and Winter Paralympic Games*. Champaign, IL: Common Ground, 2014.

Brosz, Sheila, and Pat Sapp. "Olympic Sled Hockey Comes to Dallas." *Stargazer: The Official Newsletter of the Dallas Stars Booster Club* 3, no. 3 (January 2002): 4.

Broughton, Ashley E. "The Will to Win, Even on Ice: Chicago Men Rebound from Accidents and Reach the Paralympics." *Salt Lake Tribune*, March 15, 2002, section B.

Burchell, Helen. "Handy Bandy Guide . . ." BBC, February 21, 2006. Accessed January 6, 2022. https://www.bbc.co.uk/cambridgeshire/content/articles/2006/02/15/bandy_sport_feature.shtml.

Bushnell, Brenda. "Shutouts at Aqua Wing." *Paralympics Nagano* 98, no. 8 (March 11, 1998).

Canham, Matt. *Paralympic Record* 10 (March 10, 2002). Author Copy.

———. *Paralympic Record* 15 (March 15, 2002). Author copy.

Collings, Peter, and Richard G. Condon. "Blood on the Ice: Status, Self-Esteem, and Ritual Injury among Inuit Hockey Players." *Human Organization* 55, no. 3 (1996): 253–62. Accessed May 18, 2021. http://www.jstor.org/stable/44126857.

Darnell, Dickson. "U.S. Ice Sledge Hockey Team Wins Gold." *USA Hockey*, March 20, 2002.

"Dedjo Engmark—Para Ice Hockey: Paralympic Athlete Profile." International Paralympic Committee. Accessed January 7, 2022. https://www.paralympic .org/dedjo-engmark.

Deseret News, Saturday, March 9, 2002.

Dockstader Heaps, Julie. "Paralympic Winter Games a Triumph of Spirit: First Presidency Again Passes Torch." *Church News*, March 16, 2002.

Downie, Michelle, and Richard Koestner. "Why Faster, Higher, Stronger Isn't Necessarily Better: The Relations of Paralympian and Women's Soccer Teams' Performance to National Well-Being." *Social Indicators Research* 88, no. 2 (2008): 273–80. Accessed May 18, 2021. http://www.jstor.org/stable/27734700.

Fahncke, Susan. "The Time of My Life." *Sled Hockey*, September 25, 2000. http://www .sledhockey.org.

Fantin, Linda. "Once-Neglected U.S. Paralympians Finally Getting USOC Support." *Salt Lake Tribune*. May 28, 2002. Accessed May 18, 2021. https://www.sltrib2002 .com/Main/Story.asp?VOL=03102002&NUM=718112&OPT2=OLY.

Fantin, Linda. "Paralympics Get 'Best Ever' Label." *Salt Lake Tribune*, March 17, 2002.

Fleming, Mary Bach. "New Sled Hockey Team Hopes to Ice a Medal." N.p., n.d.

Goldberg, Steve. "Surprising USA in Hockey Final." *USA Today*, March 15, 2002.

Gorrell, Mike. "Romney Choked Up as 2002 Winter Games Come to an End." *Salt Lake Tribune*, March 17, 2002.

"Greediest Owners in Sports." ESPN. Accessed January 6, 2022. https://www.espn.com /page2/s/list/owners/greediest.html.

"Guidelines for Evaluation." United States Sled Hockey Association. June 20, 2001. Author copy.

Harrasser, Karin. "Superhumans-Parahumans: Disability and Hightech in Competitive Sports." In *Culture—Theory—Disability: Encounters between Disability Studies and Cultural Studies*, edited by Anne Waldschmidt, Berressem Hanjo, and Ingwersen Moritz, by Vaja Eleana and Tarapata Olga, 171–200. Bielefeld: Transcript Verlag, 2017. Accessed May 18, 2021. http://www.jstor.org/stable/j.ctv1xxs3r.13.

Henderson, Tom. "Overtime, Sudden Death, Shootout—Then Sledge Hockey Goes for U.S." *iCan News*, March 16, 2002.

———. "U.S. Sled Hockey Coach Adds Experience to the Equation." *iCan News*. February 27, 2002.

Hettrick, Scott. "A&E Going for Gold: Cabler in Sporting Mood with Paralympic Games." *Daily Variety*, March 6, 2002.

"Hockey Hall Displays Salt Lake Loonie | CBC Sports." CBC News, March 9, 2002. https://www.cbc.ca/sports/hockey/hockey-hall-displays-salt-lake-loonie-1.317667.

Houston, Megan N., Johanna M. Hoch, Bonnie L. Van Lunen, and Matthew C. Hoch. "The Development of Summary Components for the Disablement in the Physically Active Scale in Collegiate Athletes." *Quality of Life Research* 24, no. 11 (2015): 2657–62. Accessed May 18, 2021. http://www.jstor.org/stable/44849368.

Howe, P. David. "The Tail Is Wagging the Dog: Body Culture, Classification and the Paralympic Movement." *Ethnography* 9, no. 4 (2008): 499–517. Accessed May 18, 2021. http://www.jstor.org/stable/24047912.

"I Formation Penalty Kill Forecheck." Ice Hockey Systems, Inc. https://www.icehockeysystems.com/hockey-systems/i-formation-penalty-kill-forecheck.

"Ice Sledge Hockey." 1998 Winter Paralympic Games Team Media. N.d.

"IIHF Season Summary." International Ice Hockey Federation. 2020–2021.

Johansson, Rolf. "Jag var med och startade idrottsgrenen kälkhockey, vintern 1963–1964 (I Was One of the Founders of the Sport of Sledge Hockey, Winter 1963–1964)." Excerpt from *The Wheelchair Phantom* by Rolf Johansson. N.p., n.d.

Johansson, Rolf. "Kälkhockyhistoria." May 4, 2019.

"Jordin Tootoo Discusses His Time in NHL and Losing His Brother to Suicide." Sportnet, March 3, 2019. https://www.youtube.com/watch?v=81ucr8-AdDc.

Karras, Christy. "U.S. Sled Hockey Team in Hunt for Gold." *New York Times*, March 15, 2002.

"Klart: NY Ungdomsansvarig till Hammarby Hockey (READY: New Youth Manager for Hammarby Hockey)." Hammarby Hockey. Accessed January 8, 2022. https://www.hammarbyhockey.se/klart-ny-ungdomsansvarig-till-hammarby-hockey/.

Kwan, Nicole. "Paralyzed Marine Turns to Growing Sport of Sled Hockey for Rehabilitation, Community." Fox News, December 22, 2015. https://www.foxnews.com/health/paralyzed-marine-turns-to-growing-sport-of-sled-hockey-for-rehabilitation-community.

Liss, Howard. *Goal! Hockey's Stanley Cup Playoffs.* New York: Delacorte, 1970.

Mason, Daniel S. "The International Hockey League and the Professionalization of Ice Hockey, 1904–1907." *Journal of Sport History* 25, no. 1 (1998): 1–17. Accessed May 18, 2021. http://www.jstor.org/stable/43606915.

McClure, Jane. "Schatzlein, Mundl Remembered for Contributing to Community." Access Press, July 23, 2019. https://accesspress.org/schatzlein-mundl-remembered-for-contributing-to-community/.

Merkin, Scott. "U.S. Paralympians Thinking Hockey Glory Too." *Chicago Tribune*, March 5, 2002. https://www.chicagotribune.com/news/ct-xpm-2002-03-05-0203060052-story.html.

Miller, Saul L. *Hockey Tough.* Champaign, IL: Human Kinetics, 2016.

Moes, Joscelyn. "Why Do They Call It . . . Hockey?" WFMZ, October 10, 2019. https://www.wfmz.com/news/why-do-they-call-it-hockey/article_00a66ec2-335b-56fd-b488-24a0d0567b3f.html.

Morreale, Mike G. "Dave Ogrean Has Been Huge Force for USA Hockey." NHL, June 8, 2017. https://www.nhl.com/news/ogrean-has-been-big-force-for-usa-hockey/c-289833474.

Mulkern, Cindy. "Salt Lake City Venues Ready for Two 'Games.'" *Amusement Business*, July 30, 2001.

Never Dull Productions. "TV Sports Projects." Accessed December 6, 2021. http://www.neverdullproductions.com/tv-sports-projects-.html.

NHL. "Memories: Mullen Becomes First American to Score 500." YouTube, 2017. https://www.youtube.com/watch?v=196hsi3YrbA.

"Nu Börjar Jakten På Nya Guld (Now the Hunt for New Gold Begins)." *Sport Bladet,* March 11, 2006. https://www.aftonbladet.se/sportbladet/a/a2loEa/nu-borjar-jak ten-pa-nya-guld.

O'Connell, Carla. "U.S. Ice Sledge Hockey Team to Face Japan in Opening of 2002 Paralympic Winter Games." *USA Daily,* N.d.

O'Connor, Bob. "Individual Player Report." United States Sled Hockey Association. N.d.

Office of the Press Secretary. "Remarks by the President to the Olympians and Paralympians." April 23, 2002.

"Official Game Report." Game No. 18. Salt Lake Organizing Committee for the Paralympic Winter Games of 2002. N.d.

Olympic Beat. United States Olympic Committee News. April 2002.

Oslo Sports Federation for the Disabled. "USA Sledge Hockey." February 22, 1993.

"Paralympic Games Could Be Most Watched in History. 28 Countries Gain Access to Air Live and Prerecorded Games." Paralympic News Service, March 6, 2002.

"Paralympics History." International Paralympic Committee. Accessed January 27, 2022. https://www.paralympic.org/ipc/history#:~:text=Ludwig%20Guttmann%20 opened%20a%20spinal,and%20then%20to%20competitive%20sport.&text =On%2029%20July%201948%2C%20the,London%201948%20Olympic%20 Games%2C%20Dr.

Paralyzed Veterans of America. "Tom Wheaton." Accessed March 11, 2022. https://pva .org/about-us/leadership/tom-wheaton/.

"Petition for the Ice Sledge Hockey." To IPC-Robert D. Steward, Carol Mushett, Francois Terranova, David Gravenberg, Thor Kleppe; SLOC-Xavier Gonzales, Jack Benedict; NPCs of countries playing ice sledge hockey, national sledge hockey teams of United States, Canada, Japan, Norway, Sweden, Czech. October 15, 2001.

PictureQuotes. Accessed March 11, 2022. http://www.picturequotes.com/hockey-is-fig ure-skating-in-a-war-zone-quote-718535.

Popik, Barry. "When Hell Freezes Over, I'll Play Hockey There, Too." *The Big Apple* [blog], June 12, 2015. Accessed March 11, 2022. https://www.barrypopik.com /index.php/new_york_city/entry/when_hell_freezes_over_ill_play_hockey.

Prettyman, Brett. "Estonia No Match for U.S." *Salt Lake Tribune,* March 15, 2002.

Quartuccio, Peter. "An Icon and a Gentleman." *Sports 'N Spokes* 37, no. 1 (January 2011): 28–32.

Robidoux, Michael A. "Imagining a Canadian Identity through Sport: A Historical Interpretation of Lacrosse and Hockey." *Journal of American Folklore* 115, no. 456 (2002): 209–25. Accessed May 18, 2021. doi:10.2307/4129220.

Roche, Lisa Riley. "2002 Paralympics; Return of the Fire." *Deseret News,* March 8, 2002. https://www.deseret.com/2002/3/8/19642009/2002-paralympics-return-of-the-fire.

Romboy, Dennis. "Goal-d!: Team USA Wins 1st Medal." *Deseret News,* March 16, 2002.

Romboy, Dennis. "Sled Hockey as Violent as Stand-up Counterpart." *Deseret News,* March 14, 2002. https://www.deseret.com/2002/3/14/20634137/sled-hockey -as-violent-as-stand-up-counterpart.

Roscher, Liz. "Paralympians Are Now Paid the Same as Olympians for Winning Medals." Yahoo! Sports. Accessed January 30, 2022. https://sports.yahoo.com/para lympians-are-now-paid-the-same-as-olympians-for-winning-medals-231622163 .html.

Ruffin, C. Bernard. *Padre Pio: The True Story.* Third Edition. Huntington, IN: Our Sunday Visitor, 2018.

"Ryan Whitney and I Now Have Something in Common." *The Sidney Crosby Show* [blog], August 17, 2008. Accessed May 4, 2022. http://sidcrosby.blogspot.com /2008/08/ryan-whitney-and-i-now-have-something.html.

"Salt Lake Paralympic Games." *Republican & Evening Herald,* February 5, 2002.

Salt Lake Paralympics 2002. "Flash Quotes." News Release, n.d.

———. "Flash Quotes." News Release, March 14, 2002.

———. "Flash Quotes." News Release, March 15, 2002.

Salt Lake 2002 Paralympic Winter Games, S. 2069, *Congressional Record* 184, pt. 32.

Schatzlein, John. "Proposal." N.d. Author copy.

Scholze, Angela. *U.S. Paralympic Team Delegation Handbook: XIII Paralympic Winter Games—Salt Lake City, Utah.* N.p.: Fittje Brothers, 2002. Author copy.

Sell, Dave. "Lemieux Scores in Noisy Return." *Washington Post,* March 3, 1993. https:// www.washingtonpost.com/archive/sports/1993/03/03/lemieux-scores-in-noisy -return/f460a8c3-aca3-4dea-862d-149087759263/.

Shefsky, Jay. "Sled Hockey." WTTW News, September 19, 2013. https://news.wttw .com/2013/09/19/sled-hockey.

Shepherd, Patricia. "Selection Criteria." United States Sled Hockey Association. June 20, 2001. Author copy.

"Sled Hockey Skates on Inclusiveness, Fun." WAND, March 2, 2018. https://www .wandtv.com/news/sled-hockey-skates-on-inclusiveness-fun/article_230edb69 -60f5-536a-8b4a-805564f24434.html.

Snyder, Charlie. "White House Visit: President Bush Greets the 2002 U.S. Olympic, Paralympic Teams." White House, April 23, 2022. https://georgewbush-white house.archives.gov/news/releases/2002/04/20020423-8.html.

"Terry O'Reilly Career Profile." Hockey Draft Central. Accessed March 6, 2022. http:// www.hockeydraftcentral.com/1971/71014.html.

Thompson, Harry. "Reversal of Fortune: U.S. Sled Hockey Team Goes from Worst to First with Dramatic Gold-Medal Victory." *American Hockey,* April/May 2002.

"Todd Nicholson—Para Ice Hockey: Paralympic Athlete Profile." International Paralympic Committee. Accessed December 26, 2021. https://www.paralympic .org/todd-nicholson.

Trouillot, Michel-Rolph. *Silencing the Past: Power and the Production of History.* Boston: Beacon Press, 2004.

USA Hockey. "USA Hockey Sled Hockey Officiating Video." YouTube. April 7, 2016. https://www.youtube.com/watch?v=3AYe9-TDTHE&t=1s.

Warren, Ryan. "Sledge Hockey." *Sports 'N Spokes* 28, no. 3 (May 2002).

Williams, Caroline, Dave Schaefer, and Karen Rountree. "Gold Rush: Following the Successful Olympics in Nagano, Japan, Athletes with Disabilities Had Their Shot at Grabbing the Glory." *Sports 'N Spokes* 24, no. 3 (May 1998).

Windsor, Shawn. "Hockey with a Difference." *Huntsville Times*, September 10, 2000.

Zhe, Mike. "Middleton to Be Enshrined in New Hampshire Legends of Hockey HOF." *Seacoast Online*, October 5, 2014.

"2016 Nomination Form." United States Hockey Hall of Fame. 2016.

2019–20 Official Rules of Sled Hockey. USA Hockey. Accessed December 3, 2021. https://cdn2.sportngin.com/attachments/document/0103/3572/19-20_Sled _Hockey_Playing_Rules.pdf#_ga=2.208907345.2125198105.1637082370 -1468821994.1637082364.

"二宮清純の視点 ('The 2nd 'Encounter with Ice Sledge Hockey')." 障害者スポーツをスポーツとしてとらえるサイト "挑戦者たち." Challengers TV, April 16, 2010. https://www.challengers.tv/seijun/2010/04/305.html.

EMAILS

DeGlopper, Rich. "RE: History Help!" Email to Shea C. Megale, January 27, 2022.

Howlett, Laurie. "uniqueinventions@nexicom.net sent you Shea 2022.pdf via WeTransfer." Email to Shea C. Megale, January 25, 2022.

Jones, Jeff. "Call the roll?" Email to Rick Middleton, 11:56 a.m., August 23, 2001.

———. "Change in time, time to change." Email to RIC Blackhawks players, 11:31 a.m., April 3, 2002.

———. "The envelope please." Email to Dave Conklin, Manny Guerra, Kip St. Germaine, Joe Howard, Sylvester Flis, and Mike Doyle, August 8, 2001.

———. "FYI." Email to Rick Middleton, April 12, 2002.

Middleton, Rick. Email to Joe Walsh, n.d.

———. Email to the 2002 U.S. sled hockey team members, August 21, 2001.

———. "Montreal Tournament." Email to the 2002 U.S. sled hockey team members, 12:08 p.m., September 11, 2001.

———. "National Team." Email, n.d.

———. "Re: More Concerns." Email to U.S. national team players, 2001.

Robertson, Kay. "Re: Sled Book Questions." Email likely to Bruce Valley, May 2, 2017.

Ruhe, Brian. "More Concerns." Email to Rick Middleton, 6:47 p.m., October 12, 2001.

Sanders, Jack. "Re: 2002 Olympic Sled Team Book." Email to Bruce Valley, 11:10 a.m. November 9, 2015.

Schatzlein, John. "RE: History/Present Status ASHA." Email to Sled Hockey Leaders, November 28, 1995.

Valley, Bruce. "2002 Olympic Sled Team Book." Email to book interviewees, 1:22 p.m., August 30, 2015.

FACEBOOK POSTS

Weihenmayer, Erik. 2022. "Pretty sure it was SEIGO who was my second dog—a big hundred pounder." Facebook post, January 19, 2022. https://www.facebook.com

/erik.weihenmayer/posts/460344982139559?comment_id=462838621890195
&reply_comment_id=463147321859325&notif_id=1642614130402150&notif
_t=comment_mention&ref=notif.

Faxes
Rick Middleton. Fax #3129081051. Fax to Jeff Jones, March 29, 2002.

Letters
Middleton, Rick. Letter to Jeff [no last name, but certainly not Jones, who is spoken
about in third person in the body of the letter], November 11, 2002.
Williams, Brian J. Letter to John Schatzlein, October 7, 1993.
Wilson, Jan. Letter to John Schatzlein, January 12, 1994.

Tweets
ESPN. Twitter post. May 12, 2014. 7:40 p.m. https://twitter.com/espn/status/465999
890221244416.

INDEX

About the Author

S. C. Megale—or Shea—is an American and the author of *Hockey's Hidden Gods* (2022), *American Boy* (2019), and *This Is Not a Love Scene* (2019). Megale was born with a permanent form of muscular dystrophy but rushes for life and all its joys with the help of a Labrador retriever service dog, Pierre II, and an army of family and friends. Diving the Great Barrier Reef, meeting the pope, officiating weddings, sneaking onto Hollywood red carpets (okay, perhaps by invitation), and studying at the University of Virginia (*cum laude*) and Georgetown University are less notches under Megale's belt than they are grand adventures to connect with other human beings and, if possible, ease their sufferings along the way. For more information, please visit www.scmegale.com.

CPSIA information can be obtained
at www.ICGtesting.com
Printed in the USA
LVHW111107301122
734190LV00001B/19